KOSOVA EXPRESS

JAMES PETTIFER

Kosova Express

A Journey in Wartime

HURST & COMPANY, LONDON

First published in the United Kingdom by
C. Hurst & Co. (Publishers) Ltd
38 King Street, London WC2E 8JZ
© James Pettifer, 2005
All rights reserved.
Printed in India

A catalogue record for this book is available
from the British Library.

ISBNs
1–85065–744–0 *casebound*
1–85065–749–1 *paperback*

To Miranda Vickers

Lavdi e deshemoreve te kombit

Contents

Preface

This book is about Kosova in the ten years or so before the start of the NATO bombing campaign in the spring of 1999. It also concerns the coverage of the Kosova war in the media, and in *The Times* of London in particular, for which I wrote news reports and analysis from the Balkans over several years. The history of the evolution of reporting and perceptions of Kosova in Britain is important, both in political and in media terms: Kosova graduated from being an obscure province of communist Yugoslavia in 1989 to international prominence in March 1999 and the focus of NATO's first war. I therefore hope the book will be useful to contemporary historians and students of the mass media, as well as to those interested in the wars in ex-Yugoslavia. The problems of writing about Kosova apply to many other places in the world in a media climate where independent foreign reporting is often liable to manipulation by governments and their 'spin' machines. In Kosova they were used ruthlessly for many years by both the British and Yugoslav governments, and the issue is of general interest to all those seeking to protect freedom of speech and reporting.

These difficulties with the authorities are not new for journalists. The distinguished Balkan correspondent Reginald Wyon wrote in 1903: 'The writer who continually predicts a war is generally accused of striving to bring it about, and many indignant epithets are hurled at his unlucky head.' He was referring to the Ilinden rising in Macedonia against the Ottoman Empire in that year, but many of the same obscurantist forces were still at work in the 1990s trying to limit knowledge of the events in Yugoslavia, particularly under the Conservative government in Britain in the mid-1990s. Governments nowadays have the benefit of an immensely powerful telecommunications interception apparatus to augment their media 'management'. The controversies with the Blair government over media 'spin' and the Iraq war issue took place after most of this book was drafted, but the general pattern of events bears out the points I make. Some aspects of the 'spin' culture are certainly not new, but others are, and some have a history in Foreign Office culture dating back to the Greek Civil War and even earlier. They in turn took their cue from the Second World War propaganda experience. Some new techniques were pioneered and perfected during the recent Balkan wars along the lines I have attempted to indicate, mostly those using communications intercept technology.

Without the encouragement and tolerance of the Foreign Desk and other colleagues at *The Times*, later at the *Sunday Times*, and earlier, between 1989 and 1992, at *The Independent*, this book could not have been written. I also remember gratefully other newspapers and journals such as the *Wall Street Journal, The Scotsman, The Economist* and *The World Today*, which took my copy on occasions and paid for it so that I was able to spend time in the region. Albanian and Serbian newspapers, *Koha Ditore, Epoka e Re, Nasa Borba, Zeri I Popullit* and *Koha Jone*, and in Athens *Eleftherotypia* and *Ta Nea*, have offered similar support. In the electronic media CNN, Bloomberg, CNBC and, on occasion, the BBC have been kind enough to invite me to appear as a commentator on events. If I express critical views of any colleagues, I hope that I have made clear the difficult and increasingly complex climate in which all foreign correspondents and Foreign Desk work takes place.

I have dedicated the book to Miranda Vickers, who has been an example to all our generation for her uncompromising and dedicated work in both the open and underground struggles for democracy and freedom in Albania and Kosova.

I thank Bob Churcher, Julia Pettifer, Averil Cameron and Ed Joseph for their comments on parts of the draft text. In Prishtina I owe thanks to General Agim Ceku, Arsin Sinani, Veton Surroi, Valon Murati, Ramush Haradinaj, Robert and Ada Curis, Louis Sell, Blendi Kraja, Bexhet Baliu, Alush Gashi, Gazi Maliqi and Laura Kryeziu. I owe the deepest thanks to Hashim Thaci for his stalwart support and encouragement over the years in the midst of his many pressing responsibilities in the military and political spheres. I am also grateful to Dr Ibrahim Rugova for the time he gave me in interviews and discussions, particularly in the early 1990s.

In Germany and Albania I am indebted to Ambassador Gert Ahrends, an example of the most admirable traditions of German diplomacy in the Balkans, and Dr Konrad Clewing and colleagues at the Südost-Europa Institut, Munich.

I have recently worked at the Conflict Studies Research Centre within the Defence Academy in England, where Charles Dick, Anne Aldis and colleagues have been particularly helpful. In Prishtina and Skopje after 1999 the offices of the International Crisis Group have been a source of good debate, much coffee and invaluable practical assistance. In the United States I owe thanks to Antonia Young, Gani Perolli, Cindy Jebb and colleagues at West Point, Vehbi Bajrami and the late Zijadin Qira, an inspiring and heroic figure in the Albanian-American diaspora.

There are many controversial areas where future research is bound to lead to the modification of our understanding of this history. I have had the benefit of reading some of the numerous memoirs of the period published in Prishtina over the last three years, and have learned a great deal from the work of two friends in particular, *War for Kosova* by Rustem Mustafa (Captain Remi) and *A Narrative about War and Freedom* by Ramush Haradinaj. I have been privileged to discuss the wartime experience with them. The rapid flow of other participants' memoirs and local historical studies of the KLA and Kosova in the 1996–9 period augurs well for the future historiography of this subject.

My deepest gratitude goes to my editor Christopher Hurst of Hurst & Co., and everyone in that firm, for making the process of bringing this book to birth as painless for its parent as possible.

I hope in future to write a companion volume focussing on the military development of the Kosova Liberation Army and its successor organisation, the Kosova Protection Corps. Some aspects of the specifically Tirana and Albanian dimensions of events have been covered in another book, written with Miranda Vickers, that will appear shortly.[1]

My main sources are newspapers, eyewitness accounts and my own notebooks, interviews and contemporary records. All responsibility for fact and opinion is mine.

May 2004   JAMES PETTIFER
Bath/Prishtina

---

[1] *The Albanian Question*, London: I. B. Tauris, 2005.

Some Important Dates in Kosova History

Language and Terminology

There have always been two main languages in use in Kosova: Albanian, the language of the 95% majority, and Serbian, with smaller minorities speaking other languages such as Turkish, Croatian and Rom. Other Slavic minorities such as the Gorani, Torbesh and Bosniacs use their own dialects. Some of these are closer to Macedonian, others to Serbian. Albanian is spoken in the northern Gheg dialect, but generally written using the standard Albanian literary language, which is based on the southern Tosk dialect. Kosova Albanian also retains some Turkish words, particularly in rural areas and small towns in eastern Kosova.

I have used the verbal forms most common in daily usage as I encountered them. Most Kosova place names have an Albanian and Serbian form, i.e. Vucitrin/Vushtri. In this book I mainly use the Albanian majority community language conventions, terminology and spelling—i.e. Kosova, not Kosovo, although the latter Serbian form continues to be more common in some sections of the international community. In some cases, though, I have not been entirely consistent, since language usage varies from place to place, thus the book keeps the Serbian form Podujeve rather than Albanian Besian, but uses the Albanian form Peje rather than the Serbian Pec. In both cases this is the adoption of the most common current usage practised by the international community in Kosova, and represents too a personal view on common usage in the Albanian majority community. Thus Serbian Urosevac has been generally displaced by Albanian Ferizaj, but Besian has yet to displace Podujeve fully. The UN Humanitarian Information Office in Prishtina publishes a very useful Atlas of Kosovo/Kosova, which reflects current usage.

Street names are changing yet again in Kosova, for the third time in fifteen years, but the process is not complete and many towns do not yet have official street name maps. I have generally used street names applicable at the time of the events described in the book,

between 1989 and 1999. Many streets, particularly in Prishtina sub-
urbs and in most villages and small communities, do not have names.
Equally, most communities have main streets newly renamed after
the Kosova Liberation Army and its founders, the Jashari family in
particular. In Serbia itself there has been a return to pre-communist
or royalist Yugoslav street names in some places, but this process is
far from complete.

Abbreviations and Acronyms

BBC	British Broadcasting Corporation
CARE	International humanitarian INGO
CIA	Central Intelligence Agency
CNN	Cable News Network
CSCE	Conference on Security and Cooperation in Europe
EU	European Union
FCO	Foreign and Commonwealth Office
FARK	'National Army of Kosova'
FRY	Federal Republic of Yugoslavia
FYROM	Former Yugoslav Republic of Macedonia
GCHQ	Government Communications Centre in Britain
IC	The 'International Community'
IDP	Internally displaced person
INGO	International non-Governmental Organisation
IRA	Irish Republican Army
JNA	Yugoslav Peoples Army
KLA	Kosova Liberation Army (*also* UCK)
KVM	Kosovo Verification Mission
LDK	Kosova Democratic League
LKCK	National League for the Liberation of Kosova
LPK	Kosova Peoples Movement
MI6	British secret intelligence service (*also* SIS)
MUP	Serbian Interior Ministry Police
NATO	North Atlantic Treaty Organisation
NSC	National Security Council (USA)
OSCE	Organisation for Security and Cooperation in Europe
SAJ	Serbian anti-terrorist units
SPS	Socialist Party of Serbia
UCK	Ushtria Climitare e Kosoves (the KLA)

UDBA	Serbian Secret Police
UNHCR	United Nations High Commission for Refugees
UNPROFOR	UN border control force in FYROM, 1993–8
USAF	United States Air Force
VOA	Voice of America
VJ	Yugoslav Army (the JNA before 1996)

Albania, Kosova and Western Macedonia

xvii

1. A Wartime Journey

The old Kosovatrans buses—white, with a blue stripe along the side—are resting in Prizren now, rusting quietly behind the bus station. They have been humbled by age and time on blown and cracked tyres, so that they are on their knees with the wheel arches resting on the weedy ground. They have broken windows, and are seemingly redundant. Yet they move memory, if nothing else about them moves any longer. They took the Way across Milošević's Kosova, an endlessly testing journey. Some took fire in the war, there are bullet holes in the poor-quality sheet steel that ran off the Skopje steelworks line forty years ago to make them. But they saw great events, and carried people through bad times, and survived. Kosova life can be very tough and to survive is an achievement.

'The Way' is a term the Sufi mystics use to promote their concept of life in the Kosova *tekkes*. The *tekkes* are the shrines of the dissident sects who were so important in Albanian and Kosova history. But the Way is a metaphor for all human life. We all took it after Trepce in 1989, until 27 March 1999—Christians, Muslims, atheists, women, men, children, dogs, cats, agnostics, reporters, diplomats, soldiers, cattle, sheep, political leaders, farmers, mineworkers, everybody. It was very hard. This book remembers that time and those like Fehmi Agani and others whose names I never knew who did not survive.

17 November 2001: Gjakova, Kosova

Gjakova is a town in the heart of western mountain Kosova, with a number of Ottoman stone bridges looping over the rushing river Drin. They have crumbling magnificent arches over which the Pasha once rode, his metal horseshoes scraping the grey stone. In the centre of town there is a large *tekke*—the shrine, club and prayer room of the Dervish Sufi order. The great Ottoman market and

1

some other *tekkes* were destroyed by the Serbs in the war, but this Sufi shrine survived. On election day in 2001, ten years after I first visited Gjakova, I went to see the Sheh, and to drink coffee and smoke a cigarette with him.

Across the drifts of grey tobacco smoke under the carved wood ceiling of the *tekke* of Sheh Masur, a tall young man with a black moustache sat cross-legged on a well-washed stretched white sheepskin. He is the Sheh, a twenty-first century Kosova dervish. In his *tekke*, Kosova is warm, Kosova is sheepskin, the best bed underlay in the world. Sheep are Tradition but, like us, they take the Way, the narrow tracks through the oak scrub, the search for good grass, green spring bite.

'Our religion is that of the Path, the Way', he said, dropping a little Marlboro ash upon his thin grey cheap nylon worker's sweater, 'but you know that, you are an educated man'

He could have been a car mechanic or a plumber taking a break from manual work, but he is the inheritor of five generations of Sufism, the dissident mystics of Islam. The *tekke* was founded by his great-great-grandfather Sheh Masur in 1855 after he came from study under Sufi masters in Istanbul. He is good-looking in a fierce Gjakova way, with chiselled features, a hawk-like nose and deep-set eyes.

Outside in the busy street, in bright November sun, a cold north wind blows down from Montenegro into the political campaigning, the dust blowing through the massive carved *tekke* double doors leading from the Ottoman courtyard into the street.

'We know what we can see of the candidates. We can see Ramush there. I like him. But what is inside?'

He was asking one of the basic philosophical questions of the Sufi mystics, in the tradition of his sect.

Above the supermarket there is a poster of Ramush Haradinaj— tough and magnetic, every general's dream brigade commander with a happy open face and jet-black close-cropped hair. He was once commander of the Kosova Liberation Army for the whole wild Dukagjin region. He held off the Serbs from Kosare against overwhelming odds and two of his brothers were left broken and dead. Ramush is a local man, from a few miles up the road, and will be well supported. On another poster 100 yards away is Hashim

Thaci, leader of the Democratic Party of Kosova and once political spokesman of the Kosova Liberation Army.

On the mountain in 1998 only the external mattered: the Serbs' T-62 tanks, light artillery pieces, special force troops in blue overalls and flak jackets. Ramush Hardinaj's brothers died so that the young Sheh could choose whether to vote. Hashim Thaci could have lived an easy life as a Kosova exile in Zurich.

The Sheh is not planning to vote for either of them, or Ibrahim Rugova, another party leader. It is his privilege.

'We can see what is on the outside of the leadership. But what is inside them?'

The Sufis are concerned with the mystery of the inner life. The light and sun from the street, a short walk away from Gjakova's glorious Ottoman old town, filters into the chiaroscuro half-light in the *tekke* coffee room. Prayer meetings were held upstairs at night under communism; the communists could not stop them but Tito's hatchet-men stopped the dervishes dancing. Tito was admired in the West but here he was a tyrant. To him spirituality meant nothing, all that mattered was cold, material, external, production figures, technocrats, dry statisticians. His men in Gjakova tried to demolish the *tekke* by building a road through it, but they failed: it was a historic monument, and there were many Gjakova people in the leadership of the communist party in Kosova.

The communist road would not have been the Way, not a path up to Peje and its great market and mosques, or the hard path at Kosare and Drenice, the way of sacrifice for Kosova. Sacrifice and blood, blood among the great oak and beech forest of north-west Kosova, north by north-west, blood, *gjak*—the crispest and clearest of all Albanian words.

In the *tekke* there are many magnificent nineteenth-century wood-panelled rooms, but the finest and most evocative is the chamber where the dervishes dance. On the walls below the wooden gallery that runs round the room below the ceiling hang venerable musical instruments, the drums, like Irish bodrans, and the huge flat metal cymbals. On this election morning the *tekke* is very quiet, and the Sheh explains to me that the musical instruments are used only occasionally, when there is a reason for celebration. What that might be is a mystery. I can see what is visible—the musical instruments themselves—but the invisible, the knowledge of them is hidden.

But the election should be a cause for celebration: in the last ten years or so, everyone concerned with Kosova has been through a great deal for the right to vote, some have given everything they have for the love of the country with the Great Plain and the forests and the mountains and their horses and birds and flowers. Beyond the posters of Hashim Thaci and Ramush Haradinaj there are many shadows, shadows of the brave and determined who are no longer here and will not be able to enjoy the luxury of the vote for which they gave everything they had.

Journalism and writing about Kosova is a journey—into a complex reality, a part of the world where great historical forces, religions and peoples collide, Simon Winchester's 'fracture zone'. Even in its most mundane aspects, journalism involves philosophy and can embody the eighteenth-century tradition of philosophical inquiry into life while travelling. In my experience in Kosova, this condensed itself into one single issue, the nature of modern peace and war, the difficulty of knowing where one condition begins and the other ends. We are, at the time of writing, involved in a war against terrorism, against the evil forces of destruction which that embodies. But for most of the time and for most people that war makes no difference to their lives. In Kosova 'normal' life carried on, often a few miles from village massacres, poisoned wells and the rotting corpses of farm animals. Was that peace or war? It was not a static question. I preferred reading the Kosova landscape as we went along: every hill, shed and dwarf oak tree intensified my sense of affinity, engaged with my longing, and had a history I must try to understand.

Western Kosova, 8 January 1999

North of Prizren the road runs like a dark thread through the grey mist of a cold Kosova winter afternoon. Kosova has a mythical poetic quality in the rural landscape at any time of year, but most of all in the coldest months. The cloying January air hangs in the dripping trees; the beeches are half frozen. The nearest fire is in a hearth five miles away. Perhaps the devil was hiding somewhere near this place where the battle of 1389 was fought when the Ottoman Turks

confronted the Christians of the Balkans. He could also have been
watching an old blue and white Kosovatrans bus in the gloom.
The twenty-three passengers and one foreign journalist on board
were travelling through a twentieth-century war. Six centuries on
from that mythic battle a new battle was in progress, to free Kosova
from the government of Slobodan Milošević and the Socialist Party
of Serbia. Ten years before—it seemed like yesterday—I had filed my
first Kosova story. All over Kosova the war was no longer a myth, but
living, violent history. It was spreading, as in a story by the master
Albanian novelist Ismail Kadare, through the beech woods, along the
town streets, in muddy alleyways by the great carved doors of farmhouses belonging to Kosova Albanian families. After a single shot
rings out in the distance, the blood from new wounds was running
warm for a second over frozen green moss, then an Albanian child or
a Serbian policeman lies dead. The Kosova Liberation Army soldiers
are unseen, they are breaking hard bread and harder cheese, sleeping
at night hidden under plastic sheeting deep in the oak scrub and
beech woods. This is a war of quiet endurance, the winners would
be those who could endure the most. They were often spare and
thin when it all began at Drenice in central Kosova, and now they
would be thinner.

Where was the war? Could journalists find it? Some days it was
nowhere. Back in the Media Centre at the Grand Hotel in Prishtina,
Kurt Schork of Reuters mused into his coffee on the great care and
planning needed to find the action. The best journalist of the
Bosnian war was scholarly in his approach to Kosova, his glasses
misting with steam from the cup. He had written the story of the
dying lovers on the Sarajevo bridge, the greatest story of that war.
What would he write here? The heart of the war was in Drenice.
Where was Drenice? There, in central Kosova, the war was everywhere, in holes in the ground with the little animals and mice, with
the birds cowering in the frozen trees, in the water of the icy streams,
wrapped around the minarets far south in the Ottoman town of
Prizren. In Kosova, as the journalist Veton Surroi has written, peace
is war, and war is peace. Or is it?

The winter might have been as cold as this when the imperial
Roman army came here, the legions marching to quell miners' un-
rest in northern Vicianum, modern Vushtri, 2,000 years ago. The
Romans dug the great Trepce mine at Mitrovica in northern

Kosova for heavy grey metal to make sarcophagi, the oblong metal caskets in which the Roman élite encased themselves for eternity. Kosova had opened for business. Slaves had two lead shackles around each ankle, weighted by the metal they were mining, and they were broken like sticks from a tree in the Llap hills. If he was lucky, a man lasted two or three years underground; once down the mine, he never saw the light again, and lived a living death. The Emperor worked his Trepce slaves to death but Slobodan Milošević drove them into exile after the failure of their great strikes in 1988 and 1989. Two thousand years later the same rich ore was still being mined and the Serbian SAJ anti-terrorist units in blue overalls were sent into the Trepce mines, and there was again blood on the lead ore—just as British miners used to say there was blood on the coal. The Belgrade government became the new Caesar.

Our bus was winding slowly northwards from Prizren, the most important town in south-west Kosova. The Kosovatrans buses at the heart of this story are big, dirty, dented and paint-scratched, and shake convulsively when their great diesel engines spring to life, belching black smoke. They are nevertheless great vehicles. They are like veins transporting life through the body of Kosova, motion in a society locked in its Titoist communist past. The engine is at the heart of a bus, with its bulbous black air-cleaner bolted on to the top of the engine. Below it are the thick rubber belts linking the cam drives, wide black strips spinning madly. The newspaper was interested in a story about the western Kosova towns and the war. Gjakova was always a tough militant town, much more so than Prizren, and west of it were the wild hills around Junik and the frontier with Albania.

I needed to go to Gjakova—it was like the Texas blues song 'I got to get to Galveston by Saturday night'. The Serbs had lost control of those hills over a year earlier, despite their brutal shelling of the rebels and the farmhouses in the 1998 First Offensive period after Kosova had exploded into war. In the spring of 1998 little Junik had been crowded with refugees, driven from their large old farmhouses near the main road which ran across oak and beech woods and open arable fields.

I had never been to Junik before, and back in England before coming out to Kosova I stared at a map and the sound of the pretty word echoed in my head and I wondered how its people were coping, and what unreported horrors were happening there. Now it was still inaccessible; the Serbs held the lower main road, nobody knew what the military situation was there, and in this cruel winter unless you were a bird that enjoyed flying through hailstorms there was no way of finding out. On the map of Kosova back in England Junik had seemed so lonely and lost in the hills, as if anything could happen there. But a story from Gjakova would be possible, and not unduly dangerous. *The Times*'s foreign desk was a tolerant place then, and left you to get on with it: there was no agenda. Action, James—tell us about the action. There was always the crusty raw warm Brisbane voice of Des Houghton down the phone line (some people said Rupert Murdoch brought bad things to *The Times*, but Des was one very good one).

Yet this was a war where sometimes the action was hard to find. As Martin Bell has recently written, war reporting is usually about the victims—the refugees, the dead, the routine story from the hospital ward. Balkan wars have few front lines—Sarajevo was the exception, not the rule. But in the Kosova conflict foreign desks were still thinking of Bosnia, Vietnam or even earlier, or Soviet-style wars. Foreign desk staff can be marvellous, but like generals, they can wish to refight the last war. Kosova was different, elusive, but this was difficult to convey to people who had not been there. Most of all, we thought, the war was in the villages, not in most of the towns, and most of all not in Prishtina, the capital, 60 miles west across the plain which dominated our lives and where the cognoscenti sat and talked over coffee and ice cream as if they were an English or American university town. That was quite wrong, but I did not discover it until much later in the conflict. The war was in Prishtina, in fact it was being run partly from there, but I did not know it in January 1999.

Then, without warning, there was action in the fog. The bus slowed and I found I had made a clenched fist on top of the bus seat. The diesel fumes from the floor rose and half choked us. The windows were misted over, the woman next to me, forty, with an attractive red jacket, tangled black curls, was still marking an examination paper. They were learning French in her Gjakova school, it seemed. Then the driver really hit the brakes hard. She was thrown forward, then against me, a soft female bounce. '*Me fal*' ('Excuse me' in Albanian). Her eyes were black coals.

The long snout of the Yugoslav machine-gun raked us. Mounted on top of a small blue armoured personnel carrier, the MUP, the feared Serbian Ministry of the Interior police, had come out of a small wood at the roadside and blocked the main road. The curly-haired driver rubbed the pocket of his old leather jacket nervously. This is how you die in Kosova. You travel on one of Mr Milošević's roads and something bad happens to you, sometimes something very bad. Often nobody finds about it for some time, the little beech and oak trees hide the dead body.

Something very bad was a tall man in blue camouflage overalls and a nose; perhaps he had a face but you could not see it under the black wool of his balaklava helmet. He was the psychopath's dream, the killer without responsibility. I thought of Hegel, Phenomenology, Terror, a dusty red book on shelves in my home in England, so far away. I had worshipped Hegel when I was young but that was a long time ago. Perhaps it was time to look into it again. Amid terror history was changing here. History had to be put into newsprint. Back in Wapping the huge trucks would be unrolling the even larger rolls of newsprint—how was the Terror to find its way on to them?

The foreign correspondent communicates the news, using a small machine. My mobile phone and link with Wapping and the world, the little Nokia brick, rested in my anorak pocket. This was a mobile phone war in Kosova, maybe the first; the roaming agreements that British companies had signed meant that copy could be directly filed to London from a Kosova wood. This was a revolution and democratised coverage of the war. Mobiles were little used in Bosnia, the technology was not quite ready, and reception was poor in the Bosnian mountains. On the Kosova plain it was much more reliable. The mobile phone democratised reporting, lessening the advantage of people working for rich TV networks with their bulky and expensive satellite phones. The KLA also used them in the woods in the absence of proper military radios. It was something the Belgrade military planners never understood, the kind of post-modern force the KLA had become.

Milošević's army was collapsing under the weight of bureaucrats in the Defence Ministry, books about doctrine, ill-remembered texts from Soviet war schools, heavy armour that was useless except for shelling defenceless villagers. The Albanians had none of these things, only themselves, their guns and their Nokias. The Serbs were top-heavy, over-commanded and over-organised, while the Albanians were dynamic, chaotic and under-organised. In those days it seemed as if neither side could win, and someone from *The Times* or the *Wall Street Journal* might be coming to cover the conflict in a thousand years time.

There was a very long aching silence. The bus-driver drew on his cigarette and blew grey smoke over the plastic flowers on the dashboard and the pictures of seaside Ulcinje in Montenegro and a Dortmund football scarf. These were the timeless relics for the Kosovatrans pilgrim, of a driver with memories of learning to drive a bus as a *Gastarbeiter* in Germany, then still better days in the 1980s when he could·afford a seaside holiday with his family. They shook on the dashboard to the rhythm of the bus engine, both moving and still, like Kosova, eternal and dynamic, from the alpha of peace to the omega of war. The plastic flowers would travel to the end of the road, not to an Adriatic beach but to the battered concrete of Gjakova bus station.

Nothing happened. The MUP policeman held the gun barrel closer and closer to his windscreen. The bus door hung open, the freezing cold air swept into the bus. They were coming in to lift somebody. The little old lady behind the driver sat very still. She was a veteran of many years living under the terror, and knew that the authorities liked stillness in Albanians, it showed respect. Movement could spring into rebellion. We knew the Killing Fields were not far away, in the woods; in the poor villages of the Drenice uplands there had been a turkey-shoot going on for over a year, with murders, rapes and disappearances, while the 'international community' sat with Slobodan Milošević and talked. If the Terror was spreading to the roads, there would be total war in Kosova; always, since Ottoman times, Balkan governments had been concerned above all to control the roads. If Emperor John Palaeologus or Sultan Ahmet or Comrade Tito, Milošević's teacher, lost control of the roads, he had lost control of the people. Our bus was old but necessary and inoffensive, trundling north with towering Mount Pashtrik lost in the fog to the west and the Drenice forests to the east. It was a little rock in that stormy sea, we hoped to stay above the waves, but they were rising around us.

The balaclava man waved an arm, the driver opened the door to the full, and he and a colleague mounted. We sat low, they were very tall, the taller man moved down the bus, staring at faces, not bothering to check passports. They did not need to, they knew who they were looking for, young Albanian men of military age. Two were lifted like thin young fish from the sea, one boy with lank black hair, the other with a torn brown jacket, country boys who had come into Prizren for something and were busing back to their villages. They had grown up with nothing and had nothing to lose. In Belgrade they were worried that more and more young men were joining the KLA. The Serbs knew Mount Pashtrik was lost, the KLA had performed miracles there on the steep bare slopes. The boys went off with the MUP men, one proud and arrogant, the torn brown jacket was more or less dragged off. God knows what pain awaited them, a good kicking in Gjakova MUP barracks at the best, maybe worse. The friend of a London Albanian contact had died in the cells there, his kidneys had blown after so many heavy boots and kilos of Serb weight on his lower back. They jumped on him until he died. Blood, *gjak*, there would be blood on the concrete floor. Gjakova in the early 1990s was the Dodge City of Kosova, a byword for violence and repression. They told the family he had resisted arrest while he tried to escape. The two lads followed the police off the bus with bent heads looking at their feet. In a land with no law, there was nobody to help them. They knew they would face the Serbian state on their own, in a lonely dirty freezing cold cell. They might live, or they might die. We would never find out.

The Foreign Desk would want to know what I had seen, would want a report with action and colour of which there was no shortage. A single electricity pylon stood against the sky, bullrushes fringed the edge of huge fields. Kosova is a mirror into which God looks down, seeing us all making our Way. There is an infinite pattern of colour seen out of the bus window, the dull brown of weed stalks beside the road, green fields fading to pale blue, the hard grey and white clouds heavy with snow against the mountains. But the terror was invisible.

The Serbs had taken their hostages. The tall man returned to the armoured car, and waved for the bus to proceed. His eyes had disappeared into his balaclava, he was without a face again. The bus driver grasped the old steering wheel, white knuckles clenched, while the Serbs played with us. He inched forward, the armoured car moved out and the gun swung again to a few inches from the window. The driver took them on, and inched towards them, even waved an arm, they pulled back, the blue armoured car broke a branch off a beech tree. It fell, very dead, into a pool of muddy water. There was a splash. The edge of the road glistened white and wet, the boundary between life and death. The boys being driven up the road towards Gjakova will be shitting in their pants now if they have any imagination, the muscles in their stomachs will be knotted and they know there will be no-one to help them. The schoolteacher on my left played with the clasp on her handbag.

'You are from America? Germany?'

'No, England.'

'Ah.'

'Yes.'

'We have a lot of trouble with the police here.'

Feeling the blood beginning to circulate properly in my feet again, that was a great understatement, but even in wartime, when at last the international community has woken to the fact that there is a real war here, there is room for understatement.

She made a very sensible and balanced English sentence. But she is middle-class Gjakova, there is a gulf between families like hers and the coal-face deadly struggle in the villages which rely on the KLA. Tito created a class society in Kosovo—for so many years the sad illusions of the peaceful way to liberation survived in the decent homely flats of middle-class Gjakova with their long sheepskin-covered sofas along the walls. In the villages this was a fantasy. And the war in the villages spread over all of Kosova.

We trundled slowly on up the road, the bus blowing out black fumes from its half-burnt cheap diesel. It was as if nothing had happened. In the London clubs someone might be asking an acquaintance if there was anything new from Kosova in today's *Times*. How could this make tomorrow's paper? What *was* the story? This was the dilemma for so many years. How could this slow, measured and usually invisible terror be brought home to people? Would one's story mean anything? How do newspaper stories gain meaning? Do the modern media destroy meaning in a foreign story, however good it is? Or, however good, would it satisfy those, like John Major over Bosnia, who maintained that the media exaggerated everything? Faced with the terrorist machine and these perennial philosophical and practical problems, you are very English: Kosova is 'the Other'. The fear on the road soon turned into a terrible loneliness and a desire to drink.

In the wet trees and clinging mist the jackdaws and hooded crows watched us as we approached the ancient, brave, irrepressible town of Gjakova, where a hundred years ago there was so little respect for the oppressor's law that the Sultan gave up and his soldiers abandoned the town. But Slobodan Milošević and the Serbs had not. The radar scanner revolved slowly on the roof of the army barracks at the edge of the town. As the Bible says, there are those who hold the keys of death and Hades.

March 1991
After the Trepce strikes, Mister Arkan comes to Kosova

Eight years before taking that Gjakova road in 1999 I was standing in Prishtina street market in the spring mud. Then and since it could have been in any city in postcommunist eastern Europe, with people in cheap anoraks studying piles of cheap trainers, a slightly shapeless and profoundly working-class community with little money trying to enter a different world. Yet, because it was the capital of Kosova, it was different: there was an armoured car between the market and the football ground, parked behind the stalls. Prishtina life has always had the drama and intensity of war, the adrenalin of a wartime city, even in peacetime. Earlier that year, on 2 March 1991, *Politika*, the Belgrade party newspaper of the Socialist Party of Serbia and mouthpiece of Slobodan Milošević in Kosova, announced that 'Enverism' had ended in Kosova, but that 'echoes of the latest riots in Albania can also be heard in Kosova and Metohija'. The writer, Milivoje Mihajlović, was referring to the mass movement of the people in Tirana in 1990 and 1991 against the Albanian one-party state, and communism, clearly a disturbing prospect for Milošević and the communist leadership in Belgrade. Tens of thousands of people had bravely confronted the one-party state in Tirana, as they had that spring in Belgrade. 'Enverism', named after the recently

dead Albanian communist leader Enver Hoxha, was a Serbian code-
word for any sort of militant activity by the 90 per cent Albanian
majority in Kosova to try to improve their lot. He went on to say
that 'many in Prishtina' envisage a 'separatist uprising' in Kosova
later in March.

Fear gripped the Serbian political establishment as much as the
Albanians in daily life, although the causes were different. Fear had
been the dominant feature of Kosova life generally for many years.
This was the time when darkness was falling over the entire region,
but we were all slow to recognise it. In 1991 the term 'ethnic cleansing' appeared, supposedly coined by a Russian military observer in
Croatia, and was first used in the London *Times* on 9 July. News of
what was happening in northern Yugoslavia soon reached Kosova,
and everybody, in Kosova and outside it, waited to see what would
unfold around us in Prishtina. That terror on the road two months
before NATO began bombing in March 1999 was very routine
eight years before, and for years before that. In the running metaphor, fear lived in the trees, the wells, the maize fields, the streets, the
memories of men and women and children like moisture in a damp
cellar. The rose bushes were frightened of the garden wall they
rested on, the dogs were afraid of the cats, the plums in July shook
uneasily from their branches. Old notebooks in my safe at home
smell of damp anxiety, which returns from that distant past imprisoned in my 1991 notes. Journalism is often about the experience of
fragmentation, the collection of single elements to make a mosaic
we call the story, single strokes to make a rough picture that means
something for a time. The following was said to me by a recently
wounded man in 1991, his sub-conscious running as raw as the fresh
blood on his arm:

'I am Fatmir Uka, from Ternovo, twenty-three years old. They
shot me with a dum-dum bullet. That was when the police came.
They fired into every house in the village, and said we had arms. We
didn't, the Albanians were the most unarmed people in Yugoslavia. I
was refused permission to go to hospital. They beat people up in
front of their wives and children. They smashed everything. Even
the pickles. Our grandmother had made them. Even the pickle jars,
they smashed those, broke the furniture, people were beaten up in
front of their wives and children. We know violence is often used to

extract confessions. But they were not interested in confessions. We are not a minority. We are the second biggest language in Yugoslavia. 'Milošević? Milošević has no ideology, no ideology except a Greater Serbia. Tito fed on the weak. Milošević eats them. Prison conditions? Mitrovice is dreadful, there are girls as young as seventeen in there. They do not let the Red Cross in to see them. Five police beat up a ten-year-old girl, she was mentally handicapped. She gave them a V sign. Two men were shot dead in Pollate. The police up there, high in the Llap valley, they said they had arms. Nothing, just a few hunting rifles. We have no one now in the police to help us, fifteen hundred Albanians have left the police. Our only hope is the Western democratic world.

'But the Serbs have stolen all our money, what can we do? We try to be sensible with our demands here. It is a difficult struggle. They are a formidable enemy, they have modern surveillance equipment. Twelve months ago all hunting rifle permits were revoked. Now only the Serbs are heavily armed. It was like 1956. Tito against us. That was very violent. My father went to Montenegro to get a rifle. But it was too late, we had no organisation. In 1981 there were demonstrations, we have always struggled. The Serbs are running a risk, we have always struggled, our patience is running out.

'In prison it is terrible. There is no change of clothes. You cannot see your lawyer alone. If you are ill, it is terrible, the prison director is in charge of treatment, you have to be treated in bad conditions in prison. The Serbs want to use Kosovo as an example for the other republics, to show what they can do, how they can frighten people. So they rob returning workers from Germany of their money. A doctor is sacked for "breaking the Hippocratic oath" by writing his prescriptions in Albanian. A man had a cassette of Albanian songs in his car. The police found it, he had forty days in prison. They are very clever. They have a list of families they don't like. They summon them to bring their arms to the police, but they don't have any. So they raid and burn the house and break people's bones. But time is on our side. We will endure. We will win. Kosova will be independent and free.'

Endurance was the key quality Kosovar Albanians needed in those early years of the 1990s. The heroic days of the mass strikes at Trepce mine in northern Kosova in 1988 and 1989 were over. It was not a very pacifist Dr Ibrahim Rugova who was around then, but a man standing on the violent picket lines with the miners, something both his current detractors and admirers seem to have forgotten. The leader of the Kosova Albanians through all these years was plunged into the violent chaos of Slobodan Milošević's rise to power. His party, the Kosova Democratic League, was born out of the struggle to resist Milošević and preserve the autonomy of Kosova that had developed under late Titoist communism. It reached towards independence. As Titoism disintegrated after the leader's death in 1980, the people of the different republics sought to recapture the national rights that communism had taken away. At the same time Rugova's political approach, with its emphasis on pacifist opposition to the Belgrade regime, was seen by some Kosovars as ineffective and misguided. The other Yugoslav republics were moving away from Belgrade because they had armies that could fight, but Kosova had nothing.

Some young people began to see the lack of progress as a political problem, a reflection of the LDK political leadership. Rugova was having regular arguments with a totally unknown young man from rural Drenice in central Kosova, from an obscure village called Broje. The name of this tall, thin young man was Hashim Thaci, who was then president of Prishtina University's student union, and a secret member of the banned League for the Liberation of Kosova organisation. Years later in 1999 he would become the political spokesman of the Kosova Liberation Army. Rugova was the Sorbonne-educated superintèllectual, a prominent literary critic who had studied under Roland Barthes, and he found the clever, forceful and good-looking young man a thorn in his flesh. In the heavily communist political culture of Titoist Kosova, an academic was next to God, a figure of extraordinary authority, and one with a PhD from Paris was virtually divine. A clever country boy like Thaci should count himself privileged to sit at Rugova's feet and learn from him. In the highly patriarchal society the intellectual leader's word was the same as that of the village headman or a communist official. A mutual antipathy was founded that has been central to Kosova politics ever since. In reality Ibrahim Rugova was as much of a country boy as Hashim Thaci, or even more: he came from a small village near Istog in the north-west hills, not Prishtina, and he does not speak French particularly well. Thaci speaks fluent German, and was to study history at Zurich university. Rugova was already a myth, Thaci was not. Their conceptions of political leadership were to be very different. But in the meantime the organised working class would be taking the lead against Belgrade, for the first and last time since the Second World War, and the great mines and smelting plants would come to a standstill.

Trepce then resembled something out of a Popular Front film made in the 1930s. The miners occupied the vast mine, the largest, oldest and richest base metal mine in eastern Europe, and slept and ate far underground for weeks. They were inheritors of a great tradition: the mixture of lead, zinc and silver it produced had decorated the clothes of Roman and Byzantine emperors, and fascinated the Ottoman Turks. Intricate filigree work, with silver woven as fine as hair, was a mark of Trepce. The nineteenth-century imperial powers such as the Habsburgs and the French coveted the great mine, in the 1930s it was developed by the British for the Yugoslav monarchy, and it then became so important to Hitler's war machine that it was put under direct German government control. The complex of mines in and around Mitrovica was an industrial behemoth, with shafts thousands of feet deep and galleries several miles long and always threatened by millions of gallons of water that had to be pumped to the surface. The chimneys of the Zvecan ore reduction and smelting plant deep in the Ibar river valley to the north were some of the highest in Europe. A mile away on a high rock the Byzantine and Ottoman castle of Zvecan stands towering above it all.

Trepce miners were the aristocracy among the Kosova workers, and felt able to confront the regime in Belgrade, which at the beginning of the Greater Serbia project wished to Serbianise the labour force and bring all the wealth of Trepce into Serbian hands. When hundreds of their fellows were sacked from their jobs, the Albanian workers went on indefinite strike in protest. Belgrade was alarmed, since strikes were uncommon in Titoist Yugoslavia, and decidedly unwelcome in the Greater Serbia that Slobodan Milošević was starting to build. The police occupied the minehead, laid dynamite at the top of the shafts, and moved in for the duration. The Trepce workers' union had to be broken to secure Kosova for Greater Serbia. Milošević and the Serbs had stripped Kosova of all the elements of statehood on 23 March 1989, despite the wish of the overwhelming majority of inhabitants to protect the 1974 constitution with its Kosova autonomy provisions. Most wanted, like Croatia and Slovenia, to leave Yugoslavia and become an independent state. Hundreds of thousands of people took to the streets all over Kosova and twenty-eight Albanians were killed and over 300 wounded in clashes with the heavy Serbian forces. Among the dead were three children, Jajrim Badallaj, Afrim Bytyqi and Shukrie Obertinca. Trepce, as ever, was at the forefront of the struggle for democracy. The Serbs had already started to move then, long before the final act in March 1989. The strident headlines of the small underground newspapers say it all, the tough words from *Zeri I Kosoves, Rrofte Kushtetuta e vitet 1974, Rrofte Autonomia, Rrofte klasa punetore* and *Rrfote Kosova Republike.* Up with 1974 Kosova autonomy, Up with the working class, Onward the Kosova Republic.

In that revolutionary year 1989, with the end of the Berlin Wall, the bloody collapse of the Ceauşescu regime in Romania and the opening up of all of Central Eastern Europe, why did the West not do more to help the Trepce miners and the democratic movement in Kosova, which was dying under communism? What did the world do, other than Belgrade embassies sending military observers to watch the repression? The diplomats in Belgrade did not see it as a struggle against a one-party state, their beloved Tito had not been long dead, his legacy was in danger, the Serbs must be kept on top. The archhardline communist state of Albania was red; Albanians were 'Muslim', while Serbs were 'Christian'. The British Foreign Office and Tory Yugophiles thought Yugoslavia was 'ours': pale pink and getting paler by the day. It was the British, along with the French, who had brought Yugoslavia into being with the Treaty of Versailles after the First World War, and British backing for Tito and his Partisans was crucial to their victory over the royalists in the Yugoslav Resistance after 1942. Many British political and military élite figures believed that Slobodan Milošević, as Tito's successor, was a progressive force, who would move Yugoslavia further towards Europe in an evolutionary way, without violence. If Western governments had done anything to support the Trepce workers, they would have been seen as endorsing revolutionary syndicalism throughout Yugoslavia—or so it seemed to them, with unpredictable consequences for Titoism. Even more dangerous, the Trepce strikes were already spreading. In the Socialist Republic of Macedonia, to the south of Kosova, Skopje, the capital, was seeing the largest anti-government demonstrations since the Second World War. The miners of Stan Trug, Hajvalia, Kishnica and Galeshi were on hunger strike for eight days down the shafts. The Albanian people were moving, but the world wanted them to stay still and forgotten.

An important part of the problem was that the Kosova movement was quintessentially working-class: there were few privileged and well-educated intellectual leaders like Václav Havel in Prague who could be an alternative national leader and open dialogue with Western intellectuals and diplomats. Ibrahim Rugova at this stage was almost unknown outside Kosova. The Trepce movement was a mass strike that Lenin or Trotsky would immediately have recognised, quite different from middle-class German students taking hammers to the Berlin Wall. The Trepce workers and technical staff were being slowly crushed by the power of the Yugoslav state machine. The Albanians had no army to resist the tanks going into the towns. It took weeks for the miners to be defeated, like a consumptive trying to suck in the last oxygen in the air with failing lungs, or the French miners in Emile Zola's novel *Germinal*. Kosova was a powder-keg, with thousands of Yugoslav army and police units moved into every town, and T-62 tanks in town squares. The West did nothing but watch.

Particularly in London with its close historic links to Belgrade, officials were conscious of the US Central Intelligence Agency reports forecasting the break-up of Yugoslavia and war, and were quietly pleased that at least in Kosova it had been forestalled. This book is in small part an exploration of anti-Americanism in the Balkans, of which an early example was the consistent attempts by European governments to prove the CIA's forecasts wrong. They perhaps had little idea of the price the Albanian people were paying every day for their conservatism. With this background it is not surprising that the United States has an unchallenged place in the hearts and minds of Kosovar Albanians today.

Once the strike was beaten, in 1990, the Serbs took their revenge, and 3,388 miners were condemned to gaol sentences. Many fled abroad, most to Germany and Switzerland, and laid the foundations of the continuously tough and creative opposition to Yugoslavia in the Albanian diaspora there. A few young men began preparations to form a Kosova Liberation Army, but the time was not propitious. After 1990 the Serb state was very powerful in Kosova, and the Albanians were demoralised. After destroying Kosova politically, the Serbs were moving to destroy it economically. There were protests in Hamburg, Geneva and Zurich as the Albanian diaspora was being born as a political force. But it was small and weak, and like a child it had much to learn.

The Serb state was also very ruthless with political opponents. In the middle of it all, on 25 June 1990, its secret police murdered Enver Hadrin in Brussels as a warning. An architect from Peje, Hadrin worked for the Belgian committee to defend Kosova rights, and was a member of the same underground organisation as Hashim Thaci. State terrorism from Belgrade spread to mainland Europe, but Europe remained silent. In the political underground the dangerous odyssey of Thaci and his colleagues was beginning. They were forming links with radical student leaders from the 1980s protests in Prishtina, many of whom, like Hydajet Hyseni and Bajram Kosumi, had spent years in Tito's gaols. It seemed a mad dream—to make a political force that could support an Albanian people's army to drive the Serbian army and police out of Kosova and bring democracy. To do this needed the political and organisational skills of the French Resistance or the pre-revolutionary Bolsheviks, the comrades known only by a false name, the rendezvous in the back room of a bar announced by an anonomous call made from a Zurich telephone kiosk by someone you never met. For Thaci it meant entering Kosova on foot several times a year across the lethally dangerous mined border with Albania, meeting a recruit in a hay barn or sheep fold, giving instructions on how to work as a 'sleeper'—a secret member of the movement in the period of preparation of the Kosova Liberation Army. Recruits were expected to work quietly for movement in their own profession, whether as teacher, doctor, farmer or worker. Telephones were never used, meetings were always face to face. Thaci is a young man with charisma that was later to fascinate Madeline Albright and others in the Bill Clinton circle, but in those days he was often a shadow between buildings, or waiting in the trees at the edge of a village for a dangerous and uncertain meeting, or a young man behind dark glasses in a café in

Prishtina watching for police informers. His nickname in the movement was Snake, a tribute to his capacity to disappear into the most
determined anonymity. Such underground political movements
breed profound internal personal loyalties, as the international community's officials in Kosova discovered after June 1999.

But in the dark depths of Milošević's Yugoslavia in the early 1990s
those days were far away. To build an army that could take on the
might of the Serb state machine, with its panoply of organisations,
open and covert, must have seemed a dangerous and impossible fantasy to many Kosovars, who needed the comforting faith in diplomacy and foreign help put forward by Rugova and his Kosova
Democratic League. These allowed you to stand in the street with a
good conscience, and avoid the difficult commitment of the activists
in the nascent KLA.

In any society there are only so many heroes, those who are prepared to risk their lives for freedom, with the commitment of
Ramush Haradinaj with his clandestine survey of the Kosova-
Albanian border in 1996, or activists slipping into Kosova at night
for a meeting, walking through driving rain in darkness for miles to
avoid the police. It was a lonely struggle, and few felt strong and
brave enough to take part. In the political vacuum Serbian ambitions
in Kosova prospered in 1990. By September 1991 *Politika* in Belgrade was reporting that 'the situation in Kosovo and Metohija has
changed significantly', and that although the last year had been
characterised by the 'continued and increased actions of Albanian
'nationalist separatists', ever more weapons being smuggled, and the
special militia units were 'simply doing their job professionally', there
was an improvement in 'security', so that 'who-ever visits this part of
Serbia's territory knows that, until a few years ago, it was not recom-
mended to visit some communes and villages, which were controlled by the most aggressive Albanian separatists. Most is changed
now.' In the absence of a Kosova Albanian military force, Milošević
and Belgrade were winning during these years.

Slobodan Milošević was then Tito's successor and the West's partner,
it was said, against Russian influence in the Balkans. This principle
had been the whole basis of British-Yugoslav policy for many years,

and in practice meant turning a blind eye to almost any degree of violations of human rights and legality by the Serb-dominated Belgrade government. In March that year there had been a large demonstration in Brussels against the Serbs, which Enver Hadrin helped organise. There were rumours as to who within the Yugoslav state security mafia was responsible for his murder. Some thought that one Arkan, then little known, was responsible. Who was Arkan? Nobody really knew. In Kosova it was said that his mother came from Lkosova, which was true. His real name was Zeljko Raznjatović and he was supposed to work for Milošević's secret police as well as for himself: this was an early mystery for Kosovars, both Serb and Albanian. He was wanted by Interpol for bank robbery and a variety of crimes, and was rumoured in Prishtina to have escaped from gaol. Only time would tell. Meanwhile Belgrade built its new monuments, the message of which was easy to understand. South of Trepce, on what the novelist Kadare has called the Cursed Plain, stands the lonely column of stone and four steel markers built on the beautiful empty heathland of Kosova Polje to mark the 600th anniversary of the 1389 battle. The tomb of the Ottoman Sultan Murat who fell in the battle is a mile away. Over a million Serbs went there to hear Milošević. His message and that of the monument was that Kosova was Serb land and would always remain so.

A DIGRESSION

A few personal words from Slobodan Milošević
'The Kosova heroism has been inspiring our creativity for six centuries, and has fed our pride. It does not allow us to forget that at one time we were a great, brave and proud army, one of the few that remained undefeated when it was losing.
    'Now, six centuries later, we are being engaged again in battles and are facing battles. They are not armed battles, though such things cannot yet be excluded. But, regardless of what kind of battles they are, they cannot be won without resolve, bravery and sacrifice, without the noble qualities that were present here in the field of Kosovo in the past.' (from a speech delivered in Kosovo on the 600th anniversary of the Battle of Kosovo Polje, 1989)

I had to go up to Cetinje, and it was wet as only Montenegro can be in the Balkans. I walked across Prishtina to the bus station between the tall threatening blocks of flats and rubbish-strewn parks and crushed broken bottle glass under my feet. Lumps of concrete were falling off the new shopping centre, a dead cat covered in flies hung out of a garbage can. Bits of paper collected in the fresh deep tank tracks in the mud by the bus station. Most normal societies do not need the city bus station to be protected by tanks and armoured cars against the people who use the buses. But the authorities knew how important buses and bus stations are in Kosova. Kosovatrans buses are where people meet, where it is possible to talk without danger of a room being bugged, buses mean a whiff of freedom. The Belgrade regime was in a daily war against the people, but outside Kosova, as long as the tanks were not firing rounds into the bus queues and leaving piles of bleeding flesh, nobody cared and Kosova was seen as being at peace. For a foreign correspondent there was no story: 'Tank at bus station' was not a viable headline. The bus pulled out into the road, and in a few minutes we were on the plain. A cow with brown and white spots strode across a vast ploughed expanse, and twenty paces behind it a man in a brown suit and white *pliss* (a conical white felt hat traditionally worn by senior males in a Kosovar Albanian family) plodded along with a walking stick—as much Kosova as the soil from which he sprung. It was one of those days when winter can suddenly creep up out of nowhere like Death coming into a room full of healthy people.

On the bus I was jammed behind a Serb woman with a baby and her young man with a beautiful sculptured face, a beaky nose and jet-black hair—he could have been Prince Lazar come back from 1389. The reed-beds at the edge of Lake Shkodra were a deep emerald, and one of the passengers on this bus was, of all people, the English transworld yacht explorer Rosie Swale—buses bring you into contact with the unexpected. Rosie had been wandering around Shkodra and the north with a rucksack for a month for the *Daily Mail*, writing up the end of communism in Albania, but she felt that she had walked into a war and people told her that Kosova was a much more dangerous place. I told her that it was, but the people were not as poor as in Albania.

But there was little for her to see clearly here. North of the border the rain and fog was winning, it seemed as though the whole of

Montenegro had come to a halt. Lonely conscripts said good-bye to their families at Podgoritsa, nervously smoking as they were carried off on the train to the Croatian front. A little group of black-haired Montenegrin girls sang old Partisan songs on the platform as they went. The war train was the only thing that seemed to be moving. These were the early days of the Yugoslav war. In the tradition of these matters, I thought it would be over in two or three months, and that I would then return to the study of ancient monuments. Fourteen years later the people still have their guns. The empty and derelict houses of the dead in the northern Balkans are monuments themselves now, with young birch trees poking up between the walls.

The cruel winter, February 1992

The bus travels through the snow, the great frozen wasteland of Kosova in January, the farms lost and frozen solid. The vast and ugly new church of Christ the Saviour in Prishtina had been consecrated during that month early in the war, but the weather was so bad that the four Orthodox bishops could not be exposed to the elements and instead performed the consecration in the bizarre modernist pile of the university library, three hundred metres away. The library, according to *Politika*, was 'a hub of Muslim fundamentalism', and the reader was meant to feel that the bishops were brave to go there. A group of Serbian toughs had made a sacrifice of their own to celebrate the consecration: they killed several pigs in front of a Prishtina mosque a mile away down Tito Street, sliced their warm flesh into bacon and dumped it on the mosque steps as an insult to the Albanian Muslims inside.

In a state supposedly at peace and under the rule of law, the law was very difficult to find. Kosova was not a normal society. Prishtina seethed with violence, open and suppressed. Even Arkan only ventured into the street outside the Grand Hotel surrounded by his heavily armed retinue, and he travelled around in a high-wheelbase Toyota four-wheel-drive with blacked-out windows. He was fit and active, aged forty, with a freshly shaven pinkish face, and cheerful good looks. He might have been the up-and-coming young sales director of a multinational company (actually he owned an ice cream parlour and a baker's shop), with drive and energy and the ability to motivate others. Milošević used him to present a better image of the future to the Kosova Serbs. Some of the road signs are plastered (illegally) with his election posters, saying he is Zeljko Raznjatović, 'a Serb guerrilla leader from Slavonija and Bosnia' (as if there was still anybody who did not know it). When his minions drink a toast, they say '*Ziveli za Serbje*' ('Onward Serbia'), the war cry of the developing Croatian and Bosnian wars. Arkan did not look particularly Serbian but he wore a paramilitary uniform. His election mascot was a child's stuffed tiger, he is a showman as well. But in Croatia his paramilitary group was called 'The Tigers', and their arrival meant mayhem and bloodshed. Out campaigning in Prishtina, he met an Albanian shopkeeper, cowering and blinking in his shop doorway and said 'Are you paying taxes? You should, because this is a state governed by law.'

Albanians tried not to pay state taxes, as a form of political protest but more commonly because they had no money. In fact Kosova had little or no law then, but was top-heavy with police. Community policing in Kosova was having a sub-machine-gun pointed at your head while the policemen checked your driver's licence. The fields had no law other than the progress of the seasons. Out in the country the snow is not so deep, maybe nine inches covering the dead maize stalks, the cow dung, the brown soil, the little pools of dirty water and reeds at the edge of the fields. Until modern land drainage started in the twentieth century, the plain had been an impassable quagmire in the winter months and a mosquito-breeding marsh in the summer. The authorities, the police are at the edge of the field, they are imposing and professional and heavily armed. The two MUP men are like something dropped from a Homeric sky, we watch them from the bus, they have blue camoflague uniforms, flak jackets, black boots reaching half way up the calf, and Hecklers, that most dreamy and desirable gun in the Yugoslav small arms hierarchy. They see themselves as being near the edge of civilisation: to the east is the Muslim world, to the west and north is Christendom, and the Serbs guard the border—that was the myth they wished foreign journalists to believe.

The Albanian man who sits next to me on the bus is reading a strange little newspaper, *Bujku*, printed on coarse paper, and points at the policemen. 'The Serbs believe they are protecting us from Islam,' he says, and laughs bitterly. He has read my thoughts. 'Without Islam we Albanians would have been assimilated and lost. What religion are you?' I tell him I am a Protestant, an inefficient member of the Church of England, and a member of the last generation to have been brought up with our heritage of the King James Bible and the 1662 Book of Common Prayer unsullied before the clerical vandals moved in. He looks mystified. The conversation stops. It is easier for us both to look back at the police. The bus gives you quite a privileged position. Staring at the authorities in the street is unwise—they might dislike it. Here, on the plain, the police are in a great mythical open expanse, their ancestors must also have screwed their eyes up in the snow when they came as invaders from the steppes in the sixth century and drove the Illyrians, ancestors of the Albanians and the oldest inhabitants of the Balkans, up into the hills. This was land to conquer, and they did conquer it, but they could not conquer the human spirit.

Daily politics of a non-military kind wobbled uncertainly forward. In Prishtina talks were supposed to be taking place between leaders of the Kosova Albanians and the Serbian opposition, but Adem Demaci, the famous leader of the older generation of Albanian politicians recently released from gaol, and Ibrahim Rugova did not bother to come at all, nor did any of the other Kosova Democratic League leaders. A then little-known Serbian leader, Zoran Djindjic, was attacked in the newspapers as a traitor to the Serbian nation for claiming he was willing to talk to the Albanians (he became Serbian Prime Minister after the fall of Milošević and was assassinated in March 2003). A gathering was organised, but only two Albanian intellectuals—Skeljzen Maliqi and Veton Surroi, both from Prizren families—appeared. For once *Politika* reported something accurately, saying: 'In common with members of the Serbian intellectual élite, they have very little influence with the masses.' Their discourse was typical of the high-minded European liberal, and everyone disappeared to the conference bar.

The human spirit was in slightly more generous supply in Prizren than Prishtina. The historic capital of Kosova, then partly Serbian, was only a two-hour bus ride away. It was generally quiet, and still supposed to be a tourist centre where the police were not too obtrusive. A correspondent could just pass as a tourist in those pre-war days, particularly if accompanied by a non-Yugoslav friend, preferably female, during the spot-checks, in order to distract the police. The south-west is a magical part of Kosova, with its broad fertile fields running up to the edge of the wooded lower slopes of the Sar range. Above the town was the castle and beyond it the old trade route to Albania and the Adriatic. It seemed to belong to a different world from the claustrophobia and illusions of Prishtina and its unbearable wartime tensions and windbag communist intelligentsia. The narrow Ottoman streets are full of wonderful religious and secular buildings, Christian and Muslim. On the outskirts is the monastery of the Archangel at Dusangrad, in ruins since the Turkish conquest, but in the early 1990s part of it was rebuilt with money from the Karić banking and business dynasty. The Greater Serbia project included restoring Kosova churches, and some valid work was done, as at Dusangrad, while in other places new Orthodox churches were built where there had never been a church before. These were colonial rather than religious buildings, built as a political statement, and it is not surprising that many did not survive in the aftermath of the 1999 conflict.

Although Prizren did not do badly out of Yugoslavia in some ways, particularly since the old town was preserved, it was only twenty miles from the acutely sensitive main border crossing between Albania and Kosova at Morina, and had a long history as a fountainhead of Albanian nationalism. Under the solidly respectable middle-class exterior was a radical political underground, but it was impossible to stay the night there and there was never time to do more than study the historic mosques and churches on a day visit from Prishtina. One's work was very similar to early days of tourist visits to Albania in official tour parties, when you studied the buildings in Ottoman towns like Gjirokastra if you wanted to keep out of trouble with the guides, and tried to grab a chat with possible dissidents if the police were not looking. Journalism and academic research had to hide like thieves in dark corners of historic buildings.

Prizren had not always suffered this isolation. During the years of improving relations between Albania and Yugoslavia in the 1970s and '80s, when the great hydroelectric dams were being built down the Drin valley thirty miles west over the Albanian border, there were openings to the Albanian nation, and people, books and the magical, severe music of the region began to interact. They had always met at Kukes (Ottoman Kukush) fifteen miles down the mountain inside Albania. The White Drin had cut a deep cleft through the limestone rocks, and the road wound through the gorge. The original settlement at Kukes was drowned in the hydro-electric schemes, but the town had been part of Kosova *vilayet* before the end of Otoman rule in 1918. The modern border came into being when Albania was betrayed by Britain and France at Versailles, and the Albanian lands were divided to benefit their war ally, Serbia. Natural geographical, trading and cultural links had developed under the Ottoman civilisation which royalist and communist Yugoslavia had broken by the imposition of the national Yugoslav borders. In the nineteenth century the League of Prizren was founded in this region, the first real campaigning organisation for Albanian independence; at that time the unity of the Albanian lands was being planned and developed mostly in Kosova. But some Serbs had always lived as a minority in Prizren, and had one of the longest histories of continuous occupation in the region—over five hundred years. Most of them were poor and docile and sat smoking cigarettes in a café by the rushing river. There is also a strong Turkish thread in Prizren: several thousand of the inhabitants can speak Turkish, and acted as intermediaries in some of the complex and ambiguous ethnic politics of the town.

On a fine day Mount Pashtrik emerged from its normal clouds and dominated the view to the west, a severe peak snowbound for nine months of the year. The western side of Pashtrik was Albania, the east Kosova. The border was way above the snowline for most of its length, or ran through vast, tangled and mostly inaccessible forests. Years later the seeds sown by the founders of the Kosova Liberation Army would result in many young men and women dying for Kosova on those slopes. Their commander Ekrem Rexha (Captain Drini) was to die in a hail of foreign bullets in the street outside his house on 8 May 2000. But in the remote time of this narrative these events were far ahead. Prizren was timeless, a vision of how the Slavo-communists thought an Ottoman museum town should be. The glorious mosque of the Pasha had been turned into an 'Oriental Art Gallery'. The Dervish monks had long since left the *tekke* with its blue Iznik tiles and exquisite courtyard and fountains, and the place was a shadow of how it had been. A few old men sat smoking on the long sofas covered in sheepskins, seeming not unlike lost sheep themselves. The human rights of the Islamic believers were being trampled on, and nobody stopped the Christian nationalism of the Serbs from benefiting from Karic money and rebuilding Dusangrad in the bend of the Bistrica river a mile away. The communists could not actually demolish the mosques and *tekkes*, since that was what the foreign tourists came to see, when there were any, although in 1998 a mad, cruel town plan was produced in Belgrade that would indeed have flattened the Otoman heart of Prizren. Hearing about it then made me feel that a major war was inevitable. Historic buildings are symbolic structures in the Balkans, if anything more than elsewhere, and even the most passive and conservative professional or commercial residents would have died for their historic city.

But all this was to come. The days of the late 1980s and early '90s were hard, and there were many known and unknown men and women who found heroism in prison and exile, protecting their dignity and humanity in small acts, smuggling a banned newspaper into prison folded up small in a bra, or the drudgery of going round the Albanian cafés of Geneva and Aarau trying to persuade disillusioned young exiles that the cause was still alive and that they should give some hard-earned Swiss francs to support it.

A spirit they did not break was Adem Demaci. The Nelson Mandela of the Kosovar struggle, he was first arrested and charged with offences against the state in 1956, and first went to prison in 1958. In total he spent twenty-eight years of his life in Yugoslav prisons. I first met him in 1991 through a friend of my friend Miranda Vickers—Lala Meredith Vula, a brilliant young photographer already exhibiting in London whose father was from Kosova and was in trouble with the authorities. She gave me a secret contact method to use when I arrived in Prishtina. It worked.

I went to visit Adem Demaci. He was a legend of resistance. The people of Prishtina had bought him a house, so that he had somewhere to live after prison. It had high white walls, and a pretty courtyard; in the past it could have been the house of an Ottoman bey. I was sat on a wooden bench in an outer room to wait for the hero of the illegal underground struggle. He came to the door himself, there was no security for this small, tough, intensely compact man, wearing a lumberjack shirt and worker's trousers. His head was almost shaved and he had spiky grey hair an inch long left behind. With his penetrating flinty blue eyes behind big glasses he exuded the presence of the revolutionary, a man who dealt in political danger. In a different life and a different place he could, with his fierce compressed energy, have helped to organise the defence of Paris in 1870 or the battle of Dien Bien Phu, or reached the Bolsheviks' central committee or gone on the Long March. Material things were clearly of no importance to him at all. I understood he was a great intellectual, and that his novels had inspired the young to resistance. His spirit was clearly unbroken, a miracle after so long spent in Tito's gaols. He seemed kindly but impatient, probably with my questions, which he could not answer in a way that would make good quotes. Most of what he said was about the increasing police repression and endless arms searches to intimidate families. Had the Slavo-communist war against Balli Kombetar* anti-communists after 1944 ever really stopped? The Serbs claimed to have 'pacified' Kosova by 1949, and this was certainly what the West believed, but was it true? Demaci had been working in the political underground and forming small armed groups in the 1950s. It hardly seemed a society at peace.

I felt a happy sense that it was a great privilege for me to meet him. He had about him a distinct air of élitism. Like many people who have been in prison for a long time, he found the outside world lacking in intensity. There was no room for doubt about his personal stature and moral authority, but he came from a political culture way outside the understanding of most Westerners, and was not likely to appeal as a leader. It was one of the great political strengths of Ibrahim Rugova that he understood this: Kosova would need outside help to achieve freedom, and the spiritual intensity and power of the tough Demaci personality might repel rather than attract potential supporters.

Who were the Spirit Breakers? How was Slobodan Milošević able to rule with so few Serbs in Kosova, many of them privately unenthusiastic about his government? The Kosovar Albanians, like many

---

* Balli Kombetar (National Front) was the main nationalist opposition party to the Albanian and Yugoslav communists in the 1943–9 period in Albania and Kosova.

similar societies, had their enemy within. I have only written one
obituary for a British newspaper, the London *Independent* of 19 October 1990, on the death of a Kosova leader, and it was that of the vile
Rahman Morina, one of the Albanian secret policemen and collaborators in the Kosovo Albanian community whom Tito and his successors relied on. Collaborators are the scorge of the resistance in an
occupied land, and the Albanians had a number of them in those
days. Perhaps Morina was poisioned at the Party Congress. Some
have speculated that be might have had a heart attack. Who knows?
A common cause of heart attacks is said to be endlessly saying things
that you do not believe. My obituary of Morina read as follows:

In the eyes of recent Yugoslav governments in Belgrade, Rahman Morina
was a good Albanian, one of the few people at senior level in the old
League of Communists from Kosovo Province who could be relied upon.
His early death, aged 47, in melodramatic circumstances last week at the
founding of the Kosovo Socialist Party of Serbia is likely to have a symbolic
importance quite out of proportion to the modest qualities of Morina
himself.

A career party official and policeman, he worked his way up through the
Ministry of Interior in Belgrade and the provinces in various routine security jobs, but would probably never have achieved prominence of any kind
had the ethnic relationships between Serbs and Albanians not begun to
deteriorate sharply in the early 1980s. Morina was one of the very few
strong opponents of the separatist tendencies in the Albanian community,
and after the 1981 disturbances in Kosovo under the Vlashi regieme found
himself appointed first Interior Minister for the Kosovo province, then sub-
sequently leader of the communist party there.

Morina attempted to reconcile by political means the Albanian community to an increasingly hated central authority in Belgrade, and to defuse
tensions between the Serbs and Albanians. But his efforts were doomed to
failure and any personal hopes he may have had of a return to a more liberal
regime were dashed by the increasingly military and authoritarian methods
laid down by central government. His own rather doubtful role in these
events has been documented by Amnesty International and other human
rights organisations. Morina was a key figure in Belgrade's efforts to keep
the turbulent province under control, and last week he still spoke as President of a ruling party, in name if not in substance.

It was entirely characteristic of him that when his heart failed he was in
the very difficult position of being an ethnic Albanian, but speaking in
support of Serbian nationalist proposals to change the name of the party
from Communist to Socialist; a party trying to assert authority over a

people most of whom had long since abandoned it, whatever their political views, and where his own political power depended entirely on Serbian sponsorship.

It is symptomatic of the condition of contemporary Yugoslavia that the post mortem verdict of a heart attack has already been widely criticized by ethnic Albanians who believe he was killed by ultra-rightist Serbs, and by Serbs who believe he was killed by ethnic Albanians because he was a Quisling.

A charitable view of his career would be that he was a man who put his socialist principles and the unity of his country before the interests of his own nationality, and who in happier times for Yugoslavia might have been seen as an example of a successful career politician within the multicultural system. Whatever truth there was in this view of him a few years ago, his death removes from the scene one of the very few Albanians the Serbs were prepared to trust, and it must increase the divisions between the two communities.

Morina seriously believed that unity with Serbia was the best policy for Kosovo. Not many Albanians agreed with him in the past, and there is little reason to believe that more will do so in the future, but he understood the force of the Serbian attachment to Kosovo, and the potential for bloodshed in the area.

Rahman Morina, politician, born Pec, Yugoslavia 1943,
died Prishtina, Yugoslavia, 15 October 1990

It is easy to see the mistakes now, to deconstruct something written twelve years ago. I made Morina into something he never was, a real politician. It was all really much simpler. He was a criminal police collaborator, employed by a criminal regime. The obituary sub-text is full of Titoist assumptions, words like 'separatist', an unconscious use of Serbian political vocabulary, a product of the Yugoslavist atmosphere in London at the time that I had unconsciously imbibed. He did not 'reconcile' anybody with anybody, he divided, arrested, lied and tortured, and was an empty cipher for evil men in Belgrade who manipulated him like a puppet. Above all, my obituary does not mention the name of the President of Serbia, Morina's boss: Slobodan Milošević. It was an irony given the circumstances of his death. Morina was one of the regime's first victims within the Socialist Party of Serbia, and one of the first victims of the Kosovo war. The new party was only just being founded but there was a stream of blood running through it like water down a hillside. I believe now that Rahman Morina was probably murdered, a revenge execution. I have a photograph of him sitting next to Milošević, and a bad black and white shot of him at a table with Milošević henchman Tomislav Sekuliq, and laughing as he got his instructions from Belgrade on how to crush the miners' strike, how their leaders should be double-crossed, how the rank and file should be reduced to poverty-stricken submission. In Stan Terg, the vast cavern of a mine that had been worked for its rich lead and zinc ores since antiquity, the miners were sleeping down the shafts, there was a makeshift underground hospital, and Prishtina citizens donated blood for the miners.

I began to understand that the Kosovar Albanians were the toughest people I had ever met or was likely to meet. They have extraordinary qualities of physical endurance and indifference to discomfort. There was an echo of this thought many years later in Hashim Thaci's moving speech to the final election rally in Prishtina in November 2001. He told his audience of thousands in Prishtina football stadium that they were only there and able to vote because so many had been prepared to stand in the hail and rain and die if necessary. It was true.

A month earlier I had been in Prishtina, and ancient Kosova wounds were reopening, according to the headline the *Independent* subs put on my story. Even the most openminded and sensible newspaper, as the *Independent* was, believed in the 'Balkans rent by ancient hatreds' school of thought. The main headline on one story was 'Serbs sweep Kosovo for hidden arms and deserters'. That was accurate. The ripples of the war in the northern Yugoslav republics were spreading south.

Cuci Rexha, as I called him, was a printer before he fell foul of the emergency regulations imposed on Kosova by Milošević in 1990. I spoke to him a few days after paramilitaries had descended on his house, beat him up and sexually abused his wife. Sitting by a little dusty laurel bush in his garden, he recalled his terror. 'They said they were looking for hidden weapons. And they wanted to know if I'd seen my son, who is in the army. I told them I hadn't seen him for two months.'

The Yugoslav national army (JNA) was still battling against Croatia in the north, but Milošević still had men to spare for Kosova, and the JNA was on the hunt for ethnic Albanian deserters. Kosovars were then very poorly armed, having been stripped of their traditional arsenal years before by Tito. But it was important for Milošević's image in the West to present the Albanians as armed to the teeth, to justify his repression. He feared that the ethnic Albanian soldiers might desert from the north, return to Kosova with their weapons, and start forming paramilitary militias, as other Yugoslav nationalities had done or were doing. Even worse, they might join the rumoured national army of Kosova. The Kosova Democratic League had formed a 'Ministry of Defence', although it was uncertain what substance or military capacity it would have. Daily searches tore homes and shops apart in Prishtina, and whole lives and bodies were broken in the villages, where we knew even then that no holds were barred. The roads linking Kosova with Albania were closed to prevent arms smuggling across the border. I interviewed one Milorad Djokić, the head of border security in Prishtina, a gloomy Serb official, who told me the measures were to stop ethnic Albanians illegally crossing the border into Kosova in massive numbers. It was not clear how many Albanian shepherds or Serb soldiers were being killed in these obscure clashes in the hills. Mr Djokić only drew a Bejour cigarette from the old Niš factory out of its famous red and white packet and said 'Some liquidations of persons have taken place.'

Elsewhere in Prishtina a contact told me that Albanian politicians in Tirana were claiming that the JNA was allowing local Serbian paramilitary militias across the border to fire on Albanian peasants with the aim of producing a wider conflict between the two countries. There had certainly been regular reports of shootings in *Albanian Daily News*, the government wire service in Tirana, but as Albania was still more or less communist and in chaos, and it was a Tirana government wire, British foreign editors took no notice. Open Albanian resistance in Prishtina was confined to a feeble education boycott that collapsed within two days.

The last paragraph of my story that ran in the paper on 22 September 1991 was more perceptive than the Morina obituary, and does not need deconstruction:

Underlying it all is the Serbian determination to hold on to Kosovo at almost any cost. Although a minority now, the Serbs see the province as the heart of the old Serb domain. The Albanian leaders know, too, that the most extreme Serbian nationalists recommend not merely the absorbtion of Kosovo into a Greater Serbia, but the physical expulsion of Albanians from the province. In these circumstances, a renewal of the clashes that killed dozens of people in Kosovo in 1981 and 1989 cannot be ruled out. This was the best work I did that year. In essence it forecast correctly the nature of the politics of Kosova and the war that the Kosovo Liberation Army would eventually fight several years later, after 1996. It called the pacifist education-based civil disobedience of Dr Ibrahim Rugova's Democratic League feeble, and as a result the Foreign Office hated it. A complaint was made from Whitehall to the *Independent* foreign desk that Cuci Rexha did not exist. This was certainly true, since I had changed the name of the tubby leather-jacketed man in order to protect him and his victimised family from further reprisals. This was normal practice in the region, and elsewhere. But I was naïf then, and it did not occur to me to ask how they knew this. In fact it was the result of collaboration between the British and Yugoslav foreign and intelligence services. The pro-Serb hidden wiring linking Whitehall and Belgrade was unknown to us then, but it would haunt and distort media coverage of the conflict in Britain for many years. Some of the leaders of the Kosova Democratic League in London, a generally dismal bunch, were also collaborators in this mystification process. I was told that one of them had contacted the Foreign Office and complained that my story was an attack on the Democratic League. The Foreign Office liked them because they were no real threat to the Yugoslavist *status quo*. It was not long before my relations with the then foreign editor of the *Independent*, Godfrey Hodgson, a distinguished correspondent who had spent most of his time in America, began to deteriorate. One of the chief editors apparently told him that Kosova was a 'difficult' story and needed 'expert' handling. Elizabeth Young was appointed as the paper's Balkan expert, and she wrote an article claiming that the Kosovar Albanians spent all their time in blood feuds. This satisfactorily reinforced the Foreign Office's racist stereotypes of Albanian culture; it was also the exact opposite of the truth. A large national movement for blood feud reconciliation had been in progress under Professor Anton Cetta for more than two years.[1] The better people on the desk did what they could, but the top brass

[1] See 'Levizja Gjithë popullore Shqiptare për Faljen e Gjakere, 1990–2' by M. Pirraku, Prishtina, 1998.

were like putty in Foreign Office hands. To try to redress the balance Steve Crawshaw, the paper's East European editor, went to Kosova himself and did a good story about the secret police in the Grand Hotel in Prishtina, but I had a clear message that the story was considered too sensitive for me to handle. There was a sense in the pit of my stomach that I might not be writing news, features and travel pieces from the Balkans for the *Independent* much longer. It seemed as if 'Independence' was a relativist concept if reality strayed too far from the prior Europeanist agenda. At the same time, Steve Crawshaw started to take copy from a young man called Liam McDowall in Albania. I knew and liked Liam, who worked in the Albanian shop in Covent Garden in London. Unmistakably doors in the *Independent* were closing. Then there was an internal upheaval which led to Godfrey suddenly leaving. It was not clear why he had done so, but the atmosphere was bad and I hated having to go into the office in Bunhill Fields in the City of London. Crawshaw and the other *Independent* people had a clear vision of what they wanted to report about Albania: progress in the overthrow of the one-party state, and a rapidly developing 'European' future. I was all in favour of the first but felt the second was most unlikely, and when I could get nothing into the paper about the closure of the Kosova Parliament in June 1992 I started to look for another paper. It is always easy to think of points of principle to stop writing for a paper, whether as a freelance or a staff writer, but often harder to act upon them, for economic or other reasons. As in cabinet government, there is never a right time to resign. However, the closure of the Parliament was a defining moment.

At about this time, in July, Hashim Thaci, as leader of the Prishtina students, gave his first major interview to *Bujku*, the Albanian-language paper in Kosova, and emerged in a small way on the public stage. In retrospect the timing was symbolic, as was the language. He called Kosova an 'amphitheatre', and combined a call for university reforms many others would support with a call for activism of a new kind. A gauntlet had been thrown down, both to Rugova and to the Serbs.

Deconstruction: The nightmare begins in the Grand Hotel

Another visa had come through, and I returned to the Kosova amphitheatre. The Milošević system was now totally entrenched, after a

INSTRUCTIONS FOR GUESTS RESIDING AT THE GRAND HOTEL PRISHTINA

Hotel guests are kindly requested to keep this booklet with them.
GRAND HOTEL PRISHTINA—Address Marsala Tito 65, Prishtina, Hotel Enterprise 'SLOGA', Phone 20–200, 20–111. Telex 18222, 21615 yu hotju. 'A' category, in the city centre, 32,000 sq.m. available area, 764 beds, 84 single rooms, 265 double rooms, 10 three-bedded rooms, 8 suites, 2 residences. Air conditioning, with individual control switch in each room.
Hotel distance from airport, 17 km., Railway Station 8 km., Bus Station 3 km., Town Bus no. 7.
Check-Out Time 12 noon
GRAND RESTAURANT PRISHTINA, indoor 450 seats, outdoor terrace 180 seats
GRAND TAVERNA GRILL, indoor 250 seats, 180 seats on the terrace, aperitif bar, national cuisine
GRAND CAFé FONTANA, 250 seats indoor, 180 seats on the terrace
GRAND RESTAURANT PANORAMA, 200 seats, unique cuisine
GRAND SNACK BAR PANORAMA, 200 seats, unique cuisine
GRAND CONGRESS HALL, 400 seats, facilities for simultaneous interpreting in five languages, wireless system
GRAND BANQUET HALL, 80 seats, aperitif bar, banquet hall
GRAND COLLEGIUM HALL, 30 seats
GRAND NIGHT CLUB, 200 seats, international artistic program
GRAND CASINO PRISHTINA, roulette, black jack, aperitif bar
GRAND BOWLING CLUB, three automatic tracks, table tennis, flippers
GRAND SALON 'EVA' AND GRAND SALON 'ADAM', with available medical care
GRAND TOURS OFFICE, on the ground floor
GRAND HOTEL GARAGE, indoor parking for 100 cars
Also newspaper shop, laundry, souvenir shop, post office, safe-deposit vault.

mass demonstration of Albanians on 13 October of that year had been teargassed and crushed, and Ibrahim Rugova had started negotiations with the Serbs, in the odd shape of the Prime Minister

Milan Panić, a Serbian-American multi-millionaire, who had made his money in the pharmaceutical industry. Panić was more American than Serbian, and was no match 'for Milošević. But it suited the dictator to have the apparently more reasonable and 'moderate' Panić draw the Kosovars into the swamp of false negotiations and bogus promises from Belgrade.

Rugova had enraged even his closest supporters by holding the talks in the ill-fated building of the Kosova Parliament, so recently closed by Milošević. The LDK leadership seemed to be dancing on the grave of Kosova democracy. In every Kosovatrans bus there was the rhythmic accordion and regularly banged drums that had accompanied so many blood-soaked Serbian nationalist dreams. It was not difficult to understand the bus music. The message it sent to the Albanians was that we are the master race here, at the moment we are only playing music, but if Milošević so decrees and the drummer bangs his drums hard enough, we will come to kill you. The master of the orchestra is in Belgrade and his representative is Mr Arkan. The nightmare had begun in the Grand Hotel.

By now I was getting to know Prishtina better. The centre of life was certainly the most badly-named hotel in the Balkans, if not the world. The only thing Grand about it was the name on the sign, a yellowing neon row of letters high above the street where the electricity had long ago been cut off. The war in Croatia had brought someone new to power in Kosova, Arkan. Zeljko Raznjatovic, Arkan to the wider world, was now deputy for Kosova in the Belgrade Parliament, perhaps one of the most unsuitable people ever to have been a member of a democratic assembly. He was wanted for bank robbery, extortion and murder in various European countries, and had escaped from gaol in Holland. Blood brought political power on this cursed soil, as it did in ancient Argos; Arkan meant spilt blood. In a land of powerful myths the master-politician in Belgrade had introduced his own mythological hero, the charming paramilitary leader who would be the Kosova Serbs' Robin Hood and like a magical avenger right the wrongs done to them by the Albanians. In real life Milošević had done nothing for Kosova since 1989, and had scarcely set foot there, so a myth was needed. Serbs were continuing to leave Kosova, as they had been doing for the previous fifty years.

Arkan's election posters stood twenty feet high in the doorway of
the Grand Hotel. He loved to wear colourful old Serbian military
uniforms. He was a superstar, someone who could lift the average
Kosova Serb out of his usual depression and gloom. Arkan was
action, someone to do the Kosova Serbs' fighting for them with his
'Volunteer Guards'. Arkan was also razzmatazz, part of the entertain-
ment industry. Arkan increased the fear factor in Albanian life. Arkan
was a sportsman, he sponsored the Prishtina team as well as Red Star
Belgrade, his own team, and flew in to watch matches in a military
helicopter like a god. Arkan could fulfil almost every human need, it
seemed, from murdering your enemies to amusing your children
when his Tigers decided to parade somewhere and make them feel
they were part of the 'defence of Serbia' in the war to the north.
Arkan pleased your wife with a new fridge from a looted Croatian
house. Arkan fascinated spies, who could not decide how important
he was. He was friendly and easy to get to know, readily available to
journalists, and always made a good story. For Milošević and the
Socialist Party of Serbia he was extremely useful. The awful communist concrete pile of the Grand was something special in its way, a
suitable place for Arkan's state terror machine to base itself. The outside was terrible, but the inside had poetry, the poetry of real danger
and fear. The glass entrance porch was small; a Roma scraped a living
cleaning shoes there. Then there was a vast cavernous hall, low-
ceilinged with a long reception desk to the left, and lifts in the far
distance. A large map of the Prishtina region hung on the wall, but
with the numerous military bases around the city airbrushed out.
Everything was black in this hotel-tomb. A generation ago the
Serbs had run the Black Hand as a feared terrorist organisation in
Europe. Now we had the Black Hotel. There was a black floor, black
walls, black furniture, black curtains, and the waiters wore black
trousers and jackets. It was all badly lit, if at all, by small wall lights
with many bulbs missing. The place that Mahmut Bakalli, last Albanian chairman of the League of Communists in Kosova, had seen as
a major achievement was now a gloomy nightmare. The workers
there were like Plato's shadowy figures in his cave, chained to the
Serbian past, faces to the wall, as much prisoners as the Albanians.
Rightly, for a Kosova hotel built by the Titoists, it was like going into
a vast mortuary, a place for those who were dying and dead in spirit.

As always in Kosova, the war was very far away, yet near. There was war in Croatia, and it was waiting to spark in Bosnia. What would happen in Kosova? The only obvious Kosova evidence consisted of the old trucks loaded with fridges and stoves being sold near the entrance to the JNA base on the Pec road. Arkan was moving into Kosova, his thugs in black leather jackets fingering rolls of Deutschmarks. They were taking control of the diesel oil smuggling from Albania that kept the Kosova power stations on the plain functioning. They visited some of the Serbian Orthodox monasteries and told the priests they could help by storing weapons and munitions for a future war against the Albanians. Some of the priests and nuns now living under difficult conditions in post-1999 Kosova were then open and eager supporters of the Arkan regime in Kosova politics, such as a priest whom I met then at Devic who told me enthusiastically that Arkan would stop the Albanians from stealing his animals. This is not something that justifies the human rights problems for the Serbs ten years later, but it helps explain them.

An Albanian friend who ran a draper's shop said to me: 'When Arkan was in Serbia there was war, when Arkan was in Croatia there was war, and when Arkan comes to Kosova there will be war'. It was one of those gritty little Kosova peasant sayings that are difficult to argue with. I put it into an *Economist* piece, and the paper ran it. People on the London tube would read what the Prishtina draper said, it was journalistic work at its most satisfying. But in retrospect it also built up the myth of Arkan, something that harmed the prospects for freedom in Kosova. Kosova was a popular field of activity for many intelligence agencies then. The MI6 officers around the region and in London were obsessed with Arkan. My contacts in the intelligence world were endlessly debating whether or not he was directly controlled by Milošević. Although it was a legitimate and important issue to be thinking about, some of them made it a new theology, and built Arkan up into a new Satan. This was a very British tendency from the beginning, based on the erroneous view that the Yugoslav system was basically valid, but that some rotten apples had taken it over at the top.

American journalists who had met Arkan were less blinkered. Someone who worked for the *Wall Street Journal* once told me in the Grand Hotel bar that he had met Arkan in Belgrade and he was a jerk and people should stop taking him seriously. From a philosoph-ical point of view he was right, but Arkan also in many different ways represented the practical power of the Serbian state. The re-frigerators his people sold out of the backs of lorries were, no doubt, from the homes of dead Croats, far from Kosova. His arm was long, yet he was also near, in the echo of the music at the wild parties in the Grand basement, the long chains of Serbs dancing the *horo*; it was the party with a hundred guests that is always held when some-one's son goes off to join the army. This lost and disappeared world merges in memory with the crowds of Serb girls watching the recruit, perhaps for the last time. The room they danced in was dark and gloomy, a touch of the barracks even at the going away party. A tall raven-haired mother with long arms and thin fingers clutched her small absurdly young-looking son going to the war in the dan-gerous north, away from the safety of blessed Holy Kosova.

There was death in her eyes, a black mist was spreading in front of her. She was afraid she would lose her son for ever. Arkan might have the image of the magician, but the reality of war is different. A bullet from a sub-machine-gun travels at 705 metres a second and des-patches whoever is in its path. Not for nothing did Joe Bananas invent the term 'the equaliser' for his gun in gangster Chicago. The little band thumped out Serb nationalist songs, with the incessant drive of the accordionist and his fat grubby fingers moving over the black and white keys holding everything together. There were homely touches, as always in Serbia, the solid middle-aged women bopping, with sensible middle-aged woolly sweaters, but holding on to little girls no more than five or six years old. There was defiant sexuality, a flash of black knickers below an ultra-short skirt and dreaming long legs. This was a real war, you do not turn down any available pleasure, you may not be around much longer to enjoy it. Later female voices would be heard crying out, bedheads would knock repetitively against bedroom walls, and more Serbs might be made. One of the Serbian slang words for a prick is *voika*, soldier. The soldiers would be marching to war inside women's bodies tonight. Yet the war was also everywhere else—in the dark hotel corridors, in the sinister restaurant, in the roof tiles, down the drain-pipes, in the beds, in the carpets, hiding behind the mirrors like the cockroaches that hid behind the heating pipes. Grand Hotel roaches are tough and difficult to kill, and eat the toilet dirt at night. If you squash one it oozes brown out of its rear end as it dies. Life is war for a Prishtina roach. Life is war in Milošević's and Arkan's Prishtina. It was a war the Serbs believed they could not lose. The Grand Hotel was the hugely outnumbered Kosova Serbs' safe island in hostile Albanian Kosova. In less than ten years they would be gone.

The Serbian Orthodox church is an archipelago spread through Kosova, buildings of majestic calm and dignity such as the Patriarchate at Peje, smaller jewels like the church of Milutin at Gracinica, and hundreds of other buildings of varying pedigree and antiquity. The authorities approved of interest in these buildings, an echo of a largely vanished foreign tourist trade for which the only buildings mentioned in the Kosova guidebooks were Serbian churches. A car travelling to a church in Drenice came along, and it was worth taking a journey to the heart of Kosova that could be made in relative calm and safety.

The church was deep in a forest far along a remote cart-track. It was occupied by a few nuns who offered strong coffee and wooden spoons carved from holy wood as gifts. They clustered in the gloom of the refectory and reeled off allegations of violent acts—attempted rapes, theft of animals, attacks on their building and numerous minor and major humiliations at the hands of the Albanians when they controlled the government in the aftermath of the 1974 Yugoslav constitution autonomy decision. They needed protection from the Albanians, they felt, and whether anything they said was really true or not, it was undeniable that they were vulnerable and worried. A priest was less reassuring, a tall black-bearded man who seemed something of a tourist too, revealing that he lived in Belgrade for some of the time. He was a strong supporter of Arkan who, he felt, would protect the church effectively. This was perhaps to be expected, but he then leaned back on the long bench by the refectory table and boasted of the number of weapons he had just stored in the outbuildings, so that if any Albanian uprising or separatist insurrection happened, he was sure the church could be defended. Was he a real priest at all, or just an arms dealer in disguise? The nuns seemed to see him as a stranger just as I was. It was hard to think of the nuns fighting a pitched battle, but he had no problem with the concept.

I was trying to think of something adequate to say in response when there was a minor commotion outside and two of the old women scuttled outside, hitching up their habits so that they could move fast. We had just been looking at a bent and cracked picture postcard of Fountains Abbey sent years earlier by a well-wisher in Yorkshire who had visited them. The nunnery pigs had broken out of their pen, and were streaming up the track menacingly towards the church door. They were half captured and herded back, then one of the nuns slipped in the mud and fell, while a pig took a flying leap through the hedge and disappeared from view. There was always the perennial problem of conveying the reality of the conflict in rural Kosova to the Desk, but it would be even more difficult to convey the material world in which most of it was taking place. No doubt in thirteenth-century northern England there were monasteries armed to the teeth against the Scots, just as monasteries were munitions stores in Greece in the early days of the War of Independence against the Turks, but could a modern war be fought that way? If I filed, would they believe that an Orthodox priest could be an enthusiastic supporter of Arkan? We went to look at the beautiful frescos, some in which the eyes of saints and apostles had been gouged out by the Turks. A nun tried to read my name under a story for the paper I happened to have with me, but her glasses were not really up to the job. I wrote it out in large Cyrillic letters. All that was certain in the lives of the people here was that the Past was Glorious (imperial medieval Serbia and Byzantium), the Present was not up to the Past (Milošević), and the Future was Uncertain and probably Bad (Albanian, in some form). But their graves were waiting for them, ready dug beyond the piggery. There was certainty in that.

I went for a walk and made some notes. The forest was very still and dry, the oak leaves crackled underfoot, motionless on the branches, every speck of green turned to a dull brown. The forest always holds memory, the trees the height of a man march up the shallow slopes of the hills. It was a very human embracing woodland, a comforting setting for an inhuman war.

2. Days with Arkan

The days of Arkan as Kosova deputy in 1992 coincided with social and economic disintegration. The pretence of normality in 1990 and '91 was being abandoned. It was not long before the general Yugoslav hyperinflation came to Prishtina. Hyperinflation damages perceptions of the future, life can only be lived from one moment to the next. Madness is normal, and no action is irrational. Kosova started to go bankrupt. Money was always difficult and uncertain in the old Yugoslavia, and for many years people had kept their savings in German marks. The dinar was still the currency of everyday life. But with the war machine running at full blast in the north, Milošević was losing a lot of money, and he printed more and more of it. Returning to Kosovo I met my contact and sometime minder, Miki Vasic, on a sunny winter morning in the dust and mess outside the Grand.

'Lunch?', he asked, his dark warm face expectant as he rubbed his stubble. 'Lets go to the Blackboard.' He pointed at the Restaurant America. This was going to be a strange lunch.

Across the street the old Restaurant America had the best pork in Kosova. It was a Serb stronghold, half underground, a useful hideaway for the party functionaries who used it as a watering hole when they came out of the Yugoslav League of Communists offices nearby. They usually wore long beige macs, whether it was raining or not. 'Why is it called the Blackboard now?' I asked. It did not take long to find out. At the end of the dining-room a large blackboard had been placed on a table, and a devoted waiter recalculated the prices on the menu as the day went on; they went up maybe six or seven times in a day. We had not yet got to the completely manic days of January 1994, when inflation was over a trillion per cent annually, but we were on that road. My pork cutlet, rich and nutty from the forest pigs fed on beechmast and acorns near Prizren, was perfect, but it cost nearly two million dinar. A room that night cost eighteen million; the days of madness were approaching. It was a good idea to pay for your meal before you ate it because it might cost a lot more half an hour later when the bill came if the blackboard scribe had been at work, carefully writing rows of zeroes in white chalk. Like all waiters in Yugoslav state restaurants, he was formally dressed in a black jacket, grubby bow tie and white shirt, but he presided over chaos, with a stick of white chalk. As Hegel says, number is the first power over the flux of things.

A meal at the Grand Hotel restaurant involved different but equally Byzantine and complex financial procedures. As a Titoist establishment it could not stoop to anything so simple as a blackboard or a market price. You arrived, sat down and stared into the distance, and then a waiter brought the menu. The restaurant was one of the few rooms with adequate electric lighting. You selected what you wanted to eat and ordered it, but that was the easy part. The waiter disappeared and returned with bad news.

'Your order, sir, Gospod, would be twenty dollars.'

This seemed a lot.

'How about fifteen?

'No, sir, it is three hundred thousand dinars an item.'

You give him twenty dollars and possibly the meal would arrive. In time it did, but with two huge piles of dinars on a side plate, which the waiter indicated you were not meant to touch. You ate your meal, and then a bill came for a nominal amount in millions of dinars equal to twenty dollars. Slowly the waiter removed the Yugoslav money, still untouched as if it were a plate of cold brussel sprouts. Money was not a means of exchange, but a symbol of the state. Honour had been preserved, and Yugoslavia was still going forward.

Up in the north, at Osiek and Vukovar, the mass killing was going on and here, down south in Kosova, we had to pick up the economic pieces. Serbs as well as Albanians were getting poorer as every minute passed. The government had stolen everyone's savings. It could have been the 1920s in Weimar Germany but it was stranger still. We did not go to work seeing people pushing wheelbarrows full of money to pay for their shopping. There was simply nothing to put in the wheelbarrow. The government in Belgrade had stopped giving the banks any cash. That was a novel way to control inflation. Money just disappeared, like rain in the desert. This was a strange, draconian way of confronting the problem of looming hyperinflation: without any money there could be no inflation, but equally society would slowly cease to function. Serb bank clerks dressed in neat and formal but often shabby clothing sat all day without serving a single customer. With no money in their tills they had nothing to do. The Serbs were as badly affected as the Albanians. One mad old man occasionally came in and shouted at the carefully manicured girls behind the counter: 'I fought in two world wars for Serbia, and now this!' He would wave his walking stick at them and go out into Prishtina's mean and pitiless streets, unkempt grey curls over his old macintosh collar.

A reporter in Kosova then spent a great deal of time at the Grand, where I set up a safe way of meeting people at the back of the sepulchral downstairs bar. One slept at night in a plain bare room, with pale blue blankets (never enough in winter) and the threatening list of rules on the wall making sure that the hand of the League of Communists was never far away. There might not be any water, but any that might come forth was usually stone-cold and foul-smelling. The windows did not fit and a winter gale blowing straight from the Sar mountains froze your leg. The most important thing in the room was the quarter bottle of Johnny Walker on the table; you did not have to be an alcoholic for it to offer hope and solace by its very presence. Sometimes at night you heard a rattle of gunfire nearby, a Serb sending a message to his Albanian neighbours: We are in charge and you are not, We have the guns and you do not. The bugs in the wall and in the lights sent anything you said straight to the secret police. I have always slept well in Kosova, but the Grand had fear coming out of the cracks in the walls and running around the filthy bathroom floor with the cockroaches.

The Serbian myth the management wished to encourage was of loyal peasant heroism. A life-size wooden statue of a Serbian First World War infantryman stood in the hall; but although well carved and giving a humane and pleasant impression, he kept moving around; the wideboys and gangsters from Arkan's entourage who ran the place could not make up their minds where to put the old statue. He represented legitimacy for them, but in the sinister dark cavern of the reception hall he was as lost as we were. I often felt that non-religious Serbian art in Kosova seemed lost. This was the case with the 1389 monument on Kosova Polje.

Beyond him in the winter snow outside the town lay the Unknown, the villages where we knew the war was being fought, even
then. The simple white news-sheet that came from the Kosovo
Information Office spoke of torture and deaths in gaol and it could
not all be propaganda. It was not lack of courage or energy or commitment that kept you in the Grand. No taxi-driver would take you
from there into the rural heartlands, often the roads needed a four-
wheel drive, and there were police checkpoints at every cross-roads.
Milošević's terror machine was basic but efficient, and it limited
reporting. We were not collaborators with the martial law 'government', but we were reined in; and there were a lot of people to see in
Prishtina. But if you got to the villages? The violence took place in
gaols and rooms, there was nothing to see in the village street to
impress a foreign editor. This was a hidden, secret war. There was
always the same question at the Desk when you came back—is it
going to blow up like Croatia, and then Bosnia? How many dead?
And after 1992 if you did not have a figure for the dead to report,
there was no story.

One way of trying to make a story was to go and interview
Dr Ibrahim Rugova, the pacifist Albanian leader who had been
elected President of Kosova in 1991. This Sorbonne-educated literary critic—head of the Kosova Democratic League, the main ethnic
Albanian political organisation—was widely felt even then to be an
increasingly ineffective figure despite being worthy and honourable
and gaining many plaudits for his pacifism. The League was run in
an obscure and impenetrable way by a group of families, and it was
known to have many critics in the Albanian political underground,
mostly in the diaspora—people who had been forced to leave
Kosova to escape the police or find work. But at this stage their
movement was limited and fragmented, and appeared to have little
practical influence.

An interview with Rugova had similarities to visiting an oracle in
classical antiquity. The President operated from a small group of white
sheds beside Prishtina football ground, on one side of a muddy and
rubbish-strewn car park. He was surrounded by a group of fanati-
cally loyal retainers who for most of the time were successful in preventing access to him. In the main building there was a meeting
room with a semi-circular table and a picture of Rugova meeting

the Pope and Mother Theresa. Although he was a Muslim from an underprivileged family near Istog, for the strong Catholic, Italian and Vatican lobby he was a favourite son, said by some to be under the *de facto* control of the secret intelligence service in Rome. If you were allowed an interview, access was controlled by his driver and bodyguard, Adnan Merovci. This overbearing and tough man had an extraordinary power over the President, and inspired awe in many of the kitchen cabinet members who were genuine intellectuals.

I saw Rugova for the first time that year on 16 May. He spoke French, and one might have been in a Left Bank café. Yet despite the odd surroundings and the strange entourage, there was integrity there; in British terms he was akin to someone from nineteenth-century Cambridge University, all intellect and words. Action in the practical world was something he found difficult. With his famous silk scarf around his neck, he waved his cigarette at me through the thick clouds of smoke. Was there a larger number of Serb troops in Kosovo than usual—or just more activity? He drew in smoke and condemned the provocations by the Federal army against villages, the imprisonment of Albanian militants and the increased police presence in Prishtina; a UN peacekeeping force was needed in Kosova. He rejected the current discussion of a future partition of Kosovo in the Belgrade press, in *Borba* particularly. There was no question of Kosova being partitioned.

He spoke like an oracle, and in a way he did foretell the future. The imprisonments and beatings went on and bred a generation who would be looking for military solutions. The Federal army did carry on violating the little wooden farms of the villages, until they shelled them to destruction. A UN peacekeeping force did eventually arrive; he foretold the war of 1998 and 1999 quite accurately. The people his 'villagers', as he patronisingly called them, did support him, despite all his obvious faults because he understood the situation so well. But there was no strategy for them to try to change their fate. Thaci, Demaci and the other radicals in the underground had such a strategy, but at this time they had no way of communicating it to many people—such was the strength of the police terror machine.

The situation in Kosova was of the kind that inspired ancient Greek dramatists: tragedy was inexorably coming, the old order was doomed and a new order would be born in blood. Sleeping in the nightmarish world of the Grand we knew it, just as we knew it in our bones when we walked in the streets. The writer or journalist had a role, to bear witness, to try to find out and understand what was happening and write it down, but in our hearts we knew it would make little difference. Rugova probably knew that too, that in the end he would be overtaken by great inexorable historic forces that nobody could control. Although I thought his outlook was mistaken and once the Dayton Accords ending the Bosnian war were signed in 1995, deeply flawed and certain to fail, I do not belong in that camp who feel his whole political life was totally wasted. At that time, in the early 1990s, when Serbia was still very strong and Milošević had the West in his hand, there was a power and value for Kosova in silent peaceful witness and dignified rational quiet opposition. But he kept on with this policy for far too long and became a prisoner of his own image with the West. And there was a complete absence of effective civil disobedience, strikes or non-military forms of struggle that could have mobilised the population against the Slavocommunists, and also forced the international community out of its role as passive bystander.

After the defeat at Trepce, this was beyond the LDK leaders. And in his self-delusion Rugova considered himself to be the head of a real government, but it was not one. As Adem Demaci pointed out, Rugova and his entourage headed the phantom government of a phantom state that did not exist. In that sense he was a tool of Milošević, and profoundly dependent upon him, as events in the wartime period showed, and this was why the West liked him. Kosova and its politics have a vast and endless capacity to create myths out of history almost as soon as it has occurred.[1] Perhaps, again echoing ancient Greece, Kosova soil itself has this mythmaking capacity since so much blood has been spilt on it. Within a year or two of taking over the leadership of the Democratic League, Rugova's actions—or lack of them—and his political role became mythical, and rational analysis or discussion of other political options with his close entourage became impossible. He was a different man in a foreign country, much more confident and effective, and a more practical politician—as I discovered a couple of months after that interview when

---

[1] See 'Three Elegies for Kosova' by Ismail Kadare, Tirana, 2000.

I attended a Balkan conference at the Jimmy Carter Center in Atlanta, Georgia, and was a session speaker. Rugova and his kitchen cabinet came, and were a dramatic focus of concern about Kosova— they made a great impression on the Americans. They were petulant and cross when I said that the Serbs were currently winning in Kosova. This seemed a self-evident fact, whether one agreed with it or not, but they disliked it being said in public.

Other future leaders came, like the future Macedonian President Boris Trajkovski, then totally unknown, a tall, wild, madly gesturing man among a group of even more extreme Slav-Macedonians from Canada and Australia. (He was to die in an air crash in Bosnia in March 2004.) They were believed to have a secret IMRO army in training and be planning the overthrow of President Kiro Gligorov in Skopje. Trajkovski lost his temper and waved his long arms like a windmill in a high wind and fell out with everybody—with the Carter people over speaking rights, with me over Macedonian history, with the large Greek presence there over the name issue. He did not make a good impression at all. The Albanians did somewhat better. In the end much of the Kosova Democratic League in that period was diaspora-based, and one of the many errors I and other journalists and academics made then was to believe that the LDK had the same kind of more or less universal support within Kosova as it seemed to have outside it. This was far from the case but there was no way of knowing it at the time.

Back in London, life as a regular writer for the *Independent* was getting more and more difficult. After the good days of 1990 and 1991, I found getting material into the paper more and more difficult, and my relationship with the main Desk people was increasingly tense. Although the paper was called the *Independent*, and Godfrey Hodgson, the foreign editor certainly answered too that description, there were other people around who seemed to spend more time looking over their shoulders at the Foreign Office with its dogmatic and manipulative Eurocentric outlook than listening to what their correspondents told them about what was actually happening. All Balkan peoples wanted to build nations after communism, but the *Independent* Foreign Desk thought they ought to want Europe. 'Europeanism' has been a millstone hindering the *Independent* for many years. After a good time in the previous two years, I found working for Steve Crawshaw problematic. He was a very talented journalist but held a strong personal view about the development of eastern Europe after 1989 that seemed to me excessively optimistic, and he found my general pessimism about the Balkans post-1991 difficult to accept. With all the news interest moving to the wars in Croatia and Bosnia, I was beginning to place more and more material elsewhere.

The Albanian and southern Balkan world had suddenly become uninteresting for them, and enough of the smear the Foreign Office media people had made on my Cuci Rexha story had stuck to make the paper unwilling to pay any expenses for me in Kosova. I was not sure how much this was to do with me as an individual. After the wildly expensive Gulf war, money was certainly short in City Road. The retreat from a possible Kosova uprising with the tightening grip of Arkan was also a factor. Most informed people in London assumed that the Serbs would always be able to hold on to Kosova, an opinion the Foreign Office strongly encouraged. It seemed time for a change. The *Independent* may well have been independent organisationally from any other group, and I greatly admired Andreas Whittam Smith and the other founding fathers, but their heritage was rapidly being corrupted by the Eurofanatics, never more so than in the key area of foreign news-gathering and onward publication. I had met Richard Owen, foreign editor of *The Times* and today its distinguished Rome correspondent, and he encouraged me to file for his paper. It was an immediately uplifting experience. Although the paper was and is owned by Rupert Murdoch, his people did not interfere except to prevent an editorial sellout of our country to the Brussels bureaucracy (a view I strongly agreed with in any case).

There was a hard core of dedicated people on the desk and among the foreign staff generally who were of the old school and open-minded, and some seemed generally interested in the Balkans. They did not have the political difficulty that affected the *Independent*, which saw the world through such Euro-optimistic spectacles and found the tragic evolution of events driven by competing nationalisms so hard to cope with or understand. There was also a tradition at *The Times* of the gentleman expert, a category in which they seemed to place me. I do not know about the 'gentleman' part, but

I did feel I had built up some expert knowledge of the region, and there was more chance of it being respected and utilised in Wapping. I went to Tirana, the Albanian capital, a month later in December 1992, and immediately walked into a big story. In response to the high tension in Kosova the Albanian army was moving forces up to the northern border at Kukes. Although hopelessly antiquated and badly trained and equipped, it did have some defensive capacity, and in company with an Albanian army officer I knew, I saw tanks and artillery being moved out of Tirana depots to be taken on transporters to the north and dug in as fixed artillery beside the main road from Kosova to Albania. The old green-painted tanks of the Soviet era lumbered, through the olive trees and maize fields on the road to Lac and to Kukes in the White Drin valley. I had good sources in the army and had seen tanks and other hardware on the Elbasan road. It would be a major landmark in the Balkan crisis, with Tirana showing, under its newly-elected President Sali Berisha, that it was not prepared to stand idly by if the Kosovars made a bid for freedom. I also discovered what was alleged to be a Kosovar military training camp near Elbasan, the main town of central Albania, with hard-bitten young Kosovars, who had jumped the JNA in the Croatian war, assembling and looking at military options. One man had a wound in his forearm from shrapnel at Vukovar. They were more or less sleeping rough, and it was not clear what would happen to them, but I learned here that there was more to the Kosova movement than the pacifism of Rugova. I was looking at men some of whom were to become part of the future Kosova Liberation Army. Most were very serious, with that abstracted look of those who have recently seen heavy combat. But these were difficult early days. Some would betray their cause, being bought off by Western intelligence agents and never taking any further part in the Kosova struggle. It was typical of the incompetence of the Democratic Party government in dealing with Kosova that this happened, but it did. I did not learn till several years later that future KLA heroes like Zahir Pajaziti, who died in a hail of bullets near Vushtri in 1997, had received military training at the military academy in Tirana, and that this had begun well before the emergence of Sali Berisha. Several key leaders were to be arrested by his government at different times—Adem Jashari in 1993, Zahir Pajaziti in 1995 and Hashim Thaci in 1996—and the government that collapsed in 1997 did as little for the military struggle in Kosova as it did for most of the citizens of Albania itself.

As far as *The Times* was concerned, on that day, 24 November 1992, there was only one story. On Army Day, which happened to fall that week, I reported the movements of heavy armour and the fact that Berisha had 'reassured citizens that the country's defences were adequate'. The story was first picked up by the BBC World Service, and I duly filed next day, confident that I had a small scoop, since I was the only Western correspondent around in Tirana. I spent another two days there, and when I phoned in to the Desk on the way home, from Zurich airport, I was assured by Eve-Anne Prentice, the Foreign Desk editor for that day, that it would be in the paper the next day. It duly was, and the shit hit the fan in no time.[2] The Foreign Office was apoplectic and said it was all exaggerated. The Berisha people put out a denial and in no time there was a general attack on my journalistic credentials. The Desk were very good, and pointed out that I was not imagining things, as the BBC World Service had run a similar story on the subject.[3] I began to appreciate the solid integrity of *The Times*. But it was an interesting illustration of the lengths to which the FCO would so to try to control and as far as possible exclude any media coverage of anti-Serb aspects of the Balkan crisis. Anything to link the future of Albania and Kosova produced total paranoia. The difference between the *Independent* and *The Times* was that the *Times* people were prepared to back their correspondents more against the FCO in these often acerbic exchanges. On the *Times* Desk Denis Taylor in particular was a master of diplomacy when dealing with the irritating phone calls from the complaining parties.

I remembered my father's descriptions of fighting against the appeasers of the 1930s in the ruling echelons, and it was clear that we were seeing the birth of a new appeasement, this time of the Serbs. The craven response of the Tirana government people was also interesting, and set me thinking. In the next five years we were all to discover the extent of the hidden wiring between them and the pro-Serb Conservative government in London, which led to the betrayal

[2] For an interesting if controversial account of 1999 events in Kosova see Eve-Anne Prentice, *One Woman's War*, London: Duckworth, 2000.
[3] See *The Times*, 9 December 1992.

of so many fundamental Albanian realities and national interests before 1997.

At home that Christmas I walked round Lansdown Crescent in Bath thinking that I would have to develop my academic work if I was to survive as a journalist in the region; it was a strange situation. All this should be seen in context. The sinister nature of the war was beyond the imagination of many people at that stage. The same paper that carried my Tirana story on 9 December 1992 also reported the Serb elections, and Slobodan Milošević saying that he would win on 20 December, in only nine lines. *The Times* also carried allegations by Médecins Sans Frontières that 'it had evidence of several so far unpublicised Serb-run concentration camps in Bosnia' in just eighteen brief lines, where 'in filmed interviews, the group also presented' testimony of widespread tortures, sexual mutilation, rape and violence against children.

The full horror of the Serbian attack on European civilisation was not yet really in the public domain. In my Tirana story for *The Times* I had put the phrase 'ethnic cleansing', which was only just beginning to come into general use, in quotation marks. Nobody except a few Yugoslav specialists had ever heard of place-names like Prijdor, Omarsk or Srebrenica. Old Anglo-Yugoslav links and prejudices were still strong, particularly on the British political right. Serbia was seen, quite wrongly, as a bulwark against Russian influence in the Balkans. In fact British collaboration with Serbia in trying to prolong Titoist government allowed the Russians a role there that had long since disappeared elsewhere in Eastern Europe.

At the wider political level I was also unaware, like most other people, of the bitterness in the transatlantic relationship over Bosnia, and the way the Foreign Office and Ministry of Defence media machines put intense pressure on leading journalists from every paper in exchange for alleged 'inside' information. I had not visited the United States for a long time, and did not know that there were wonderful people there in the administration and the Congress who knew, through their immense and astounding technical intelligence collection capacity, the full extent of the horror the Europeans were prepared to tolerate in their own backyard. A great strength of the Serbs in those days was the isolation and intermittent self-doubt of their potential opponents.

A couple of weeks later I wrote an Op Ed piece for *The Scotsman*, where the brilliant features editor, the late Bobby Campbell, was an old friend. Headlined 'An Army which is ill-equipped to fight', it went into the border conflict situation in the north-east of Albania in more detail. The paper ran it in a prominent position on 22 December. It was sweet revenge on the Foreign Office and intelligence service media machine, and made the point clearly that the military reforms of the Berisha government had 'seriously damaged the capacity of the armed forces to defend the country'. It was accurate in predicting the decimation of the Albanian army under Berisha that was to lead to the chaos of the 1997 uprising in Albania.[4] Revenge was possible, but often complex, tiring and frustrating.

It was clear that there were many hardships, difficulties and dangers of work on the road in the region, to the point where I often carried bags of my own food because in rural Albania you could never be sure that there was any, and if there was, the local people needed it for themselves. Work was always run on a financial shoestring, and the general social environment was difficult and sometimes hostile and dangerous. Hotels were filthy and derelict, often there was little or no reliable water supply, and the only light came from the candles we carried. If you fell and broke a leg, the nearest decent fracture clinic was in Rome or Thessaloniki. All this was manageable, but a much more subtle series of dangers loomed at home. I felt I knew how to cope in the Balkans, but in London the enemy was often invisible, consisting of faceless pro-Serb mandarins ceaselessly plotting in the Foreign Office and MI6, and with all the resources of those institutions, against individuals in journalism and academia who were trying to discover the truth. However, there were a very few people of integrity in those official British institutions, and helpful American colleagues who were already showing concern over the direction of British policy, and it slowly became possible to pick up, with great caution, highly-placed sources which well understood the Serbs and their genocidal plans and were prepared to put their careers at risk to inform us of what was really happening inside the Tory government. Those in the intelligence and military apparatus even risked prosecution and possible gaol

---

[4] For a detailed analysis of the 1997 uprising see Miranda Vickers and James Pettifer, *The New Albanian Question*, London: I. B. Tauris, forthcoming.

sentences under the Official Secrets Act. They are moral heroes, and have often provided confirmation of perceptions and knowledge laboriously gained on the road in the Balkans. The winter of appeasement of 1992–3 was a dark time for British foreign policy but, as with the appeasement of the fascists of the 1930s, some brave individuals swam against the stream and did what they could. I hope that in time it may be possible to make their names public, and those of two individuals in particular.

The spring of 1993 was beautiful—warm and with a deceptive calm. Visiting Gracanica monastery one sunny May afternoon was a poetic dream, with swathes of wild flowers in the deep sea of long grass inside the monastery courtyard and the exquisite, painful beauty of King Milutin's church lost in the centre of the scene. There was a light breeze that made the dandelion seeds fly. A group of agricultural workers were drinking wine on wooden benches, and one of them, wearing a filthy old suit, offered me a glass. Working for the Orthodox monks in Kosova then was not strenuous—a poor, simple, credulous life, trusting God, the church and, a very misplaced trust, the authorities in Belgrade. With the war going their way in the north, Serbs were quite relaxed in Kosova. They knew that the diplomats in Belgrade would collaborate with the Milošević police state. Perhaps, in retrospect, it was the time of their greatest advance. The fears of an Albanian uprising that dominated 1992 had receded, and Kosova Serbs had got used to Arkan as deputy for Kosova after they had successfully installed him. The paramilitary leader hardly ever visited Kosova except to appear occasionally like a god from the sky landing his helicopter on a soccer pitch on a Saturday afternoon. Belgrade as a city was full of energy, which it imparted to you in turn so long as you suspended all moral sense. As in the old Yugoslavia, you went to Belgrade to have a good time, spend money, lose your virginity, get drunk or whatever. Belgrade was driven by the mad party of the war, and Arkan was the host in Kosova. Today that name brings a sense of fear and loathing, murder, rape, organised crime and death, but then it did not. Kosova Serbs regarded him as a patriot who had done good things in the north and was now coming home. His mother was from Kosova, and still lived somewhere or other—his people would not tell a *stranatz*, a foreigner, exactly where. But he was a good local boy and he was coming to help Uncle Slobo in Belgrade with one or two things on the home front, the Muslim problem particularly. That is how they saw the situation.

I went for a few days up to Belgrade where Serbs were happy, celebrating victories in the Bosnian bloodbath. In the Hyatt Hotel Arkan held court, while his staff monopolised the downstairs swimming pool and baths. The manager Richard Steadman, a huge laughing half-English Parsee who had been to school at Marlborough, traded whisky with Arkan's business people to keep the hotel in milk and sugar. A Chinese diplomat who was coming to negotiate with Milošević was tapped in a bugged room with a prostitute. Unlike the weird and sinister Intercontinental, dominated by Radovan Karadjić and his entourage gambling all night to celebrate Bosnian victories, the Hyatt kept its dignity during the Weimar-style hyperinflation period, and had close links with Western intelligence agencies. In return its staff were loyal to a fault, walking to work at four in the morning through the snow when all public transport was at a halt because of power failures.

Returning to Kosova on the bus, every time you rediscovered the forests, the wildness and remoteness of southern Serbia, the sudden fitful lights of small villages at night and towns lost like islands in a vast green sea. In Belgrade even the bus queue, containing Serbs and Albanians in about equal measure, was relaxed. Mr Milošević was on a winning roll. But the street rate for dollars was going wild, about 3 million dinars for a 20-dollar bill. The warry party would have to be paid for. A train ticket from Titograd to Belgrade was about one and a quarter million dinars. I attended a Conference on Security and Cooperation in Europe briefing, given by a Swedish colonel with extreme pro-Serb sympathies. No, the Serbs were not involved in a military build-up in Kosova. Yes, there were normal 'policing problems'. No, there were no unusual movements of troops—conscript training was normal for this time of year; no, there was no artillery around the towns. But I had already seen it. The Serb military intelligence officers with whom he probably spent a lot of time in Belgrade pubs were expert at handling such types. Although there have been exceptional individuals, the Nordic countries have generally had a poor record in Kosova, Norway in particular. Truck-mounted light artillery pieces could be seen on any Kosova road, particularly in the west. I thought *The Economist* would take a piece on it, since it was one of the few strongholds of fair reporting and comment and resistence to Foreign Office pressure. I knew that the generals in Belgrade were shuffling the Kosova pack, there was a noticeable absence of the usual fresh-faced young conscripts and plenty of hardened, even recently wounded men in Kosova, heading for the artillery ranges on Kosovo Polje. I thought he was just an unintelligent Swede, little did we know then how the British government media machine was working with the Serbs to conceal the truth.

On 15 May Rugova held a very long Friday press conference, at which he was more articulate and forthcoming than usual. These events were usually the Prishtina Friday Follies, dull and platitudinous recitations of what everyone knew already, Rugova at his worst. This time he said that more Serb troops were coming into Kosova, that the military command in the countryside was being reorganised, and that Serb provocations were increasing. He condemned the imprisonment of Albanians. The Serbs were having a particularly severe crackdown in Mitrovica, with more troops. He believed Milošević was thinking of partition.

My story on this ran in *The Economist* on 29 May, saying *inter alia*: 'The Serb minority in Kosovo has a monopoly on local firepower, and uses it to intimidate the Albanians. Prishtina is surrounded by artillery ranges that belonged to the old Yugoslav army. The ranges are much in use at the moment. The Serbs say this is normal at this time of year. The monitors from the Conference on Security and Cooperation in Europe say they agree. The Albanians feel that the CSCE has been hoodwinked, and believe that guns are being dug in round the city.'

In those days the internationals in Kosova did little more than provide a cloak of respectability for security apparatus repression and, as the story went on to say, 'the sealing of Bosnia's fate makes the people of Kosova feel vulnerable.' This was true, but it did not make most of them very confident or able to organise opposition.

I met my lawyer friend Blerim Reka outside afterwards. This astute Albanian from Skopje was involved in regular contacts with Macedonia, mostly over economic matters. Albanians made up about a quarter of the population of the new Macedonian state that had come into being after an independence referendum in September 1991, and suffered various human rights problems and discrimination. He said that the radicalism of the young there was causing problems for the leadership of the Macedonian Albanians, and that Abdurrahman Haliti, boss of the ex-communist PDP party favoured by the international community, was losing control. It was the first sense of a coming deluge, from a direction we did not expect. Events there six months later were to change my life. It was hard to grasp that if you left Kosova to go to Macedonia you were now travelling to an independent country; your visa then expired and you could not come back, possibly for a long time.

1993 was a terrible year for Kosova. It was also a terrible year for anyone in the Balkans who was not a Serb, particularly in Bosnia. The crucifixion of Bosnia was at its height, with the government back in London blocking American peace intervention plans. Whole communities were starving. Radovan Karadjić and his ilk in the Bosnian Serb leadership were regarded with awe in Western chancelleries, British soldiers swilled whisky at Pale all night. It was not even a very good year for Arkan, in Kosova at least. In the dark cavern of the Grand bar, Ranko Babić, the local leader of the Serbian Radical party, mused into his drink and told me: 'The Cult of Arkan is dying in Kosova. Four Prishtina boys have been killed fighting in Bosnia. That bastard Milošević wants more of us to fight for him up there.'

Ranko was then Vojislav Seselj's man in Prishtina, a designer-label ultra-nationalist and a brilliant computer designer, with a penchant for Pierre Cardin monogrammed shirts and silk socks. Seselj and his party were effectively a neo-fascist force that openly proclaimed the need to remove the Albanian population from Kosova. Babić was a profoundly middle-class man. When visiting his party headquarters—rooms commandeered from the League of Communists in a little tower block—I thought that he looked incongruous among all Seselj's unshaven working-class toughs, most of whom never wore anything but paramilitary uniforms whether or not they were intending to join in the war, and whether or not they felt like murdering anyone on that particular day. Some of them had been killing people recently on an industrial scale in Bosnia, and used to come down to Kosova for rest and recreation and to impress the local Serb girls with tales of mayhem and blood and their national heroism within it.

In the Serbian Information Office Miki Vasic agreed: 'Arkan is a rip-off merchant. He made money for people up in Voivodina. But not here.' That was how the Kosova Serbs saw things in 1993. As usual, Kosova was at the bottom of the Yugoslav heap, even in the benefits of carnage.

The rest of us learned that war *was* different from peace in Kosova, but not by very much. It all depended on what you meant by 'war'; Milošević regarded Kosova under Arkan as at 'peace' and 'normal'. Arkan thought the rule of 'law' was in operation there, but in reality there was a war against the majority of the inhabitants going on every day—a state of war in society means not necessarily violent anarchy and chaos everywhere, but life merely carrying on as best it can under alternative conventions and regulations. The whole development of the Serb army for a hundred and fifty years had been based on small colonial wars, and patterns of local terror. I was of the generation brought up in the shadow of the Second World War, in which my father had worn a uniform with distinction for six years, through Dunkirk, North Africa and finally, in the best days, with the Eighth Army in Italy. This had given me the impression that war was a total, all-embracing experience with a starting time and a final whistle like a football match. Terrible events occurred, like the occasion when he ordered his tanks to flatten an inhabited Italian village because there seemed no alternative, and the battle for Monte Cassino with the destruction of the Benedictine monastery, which even fifty years later he found difficult to discuss. But these events began and ended in a finite way. War in Kosova seemed elusive and endless, and peace indefinable.

EQUIPMENT LIST, 1992—SOME ITEMS FOR
THE GRAND HOTEL GUEST

Sellotape to mend the broken window before going to bed
Toilet paper that works, unlike the Hotel product
More thermal underwear
Babybell cheeses and Pepperami for emergency food supply
Glucose tablets
Sleeping bag
Swiss Army knife

Travelwash
Balaclava to wear in bed
Spare torch
Pegs and washing line

A television venture

Later that year a BBC producer, Catherine Seddon, approached
Miranda and me and asked for our help with a film she was planning
to make in Kosova for the 'Disappearing World' series. It involved
comparing the lives of an Albanian and a Serbian family in Prishtina.
We duly got involved and in the end a worthy if somewhat limited
result was transmitted. The approach was anthropological, which
meant the almost total exclusion of politics, with neither the name
of Arkan, then the dominant political presence in Kosova, or his
master Slobodan Milošević ever being mentioned. Both families
were dull as ditchwater. However, it was an educational experience
because the research illustrated the profound and abiding interest the
Roman Catholic church has taken in the fate of Kosova, with the
role of the Mother Theresa organisation and its charities in the
background. Mother Theresa was then the most famous Albanian in
the world, and she had recently visited Tirana and met the remnants
of the communist party leadership, including a surprisingly warm
and cordial meeting with Enver Hoxha's widow Nexmije, whom
most of us who knew anything about Albania considered a harder-
line Enverist communist than Hoxha himself. But the two elderly
ladies got on well. Mother Theresa also had successful dealings with
the Milošević regime in Belgrade later in the year.
  It was clear that Milošević saw the Catholic church as a positive
force against the Muslim (nominal) majority in Kosova, with about
one in ten Kosovars being Catholic. It was equally clear that although
many individual Catholic Albanians were and always had been outstanding patriots, and Mother Theresa herself fell into this category,
the role of the church would become (and perhaps already was)
politically ambiguous, something that emerged clearly into the public domain a year or so later when Milošević allowed an organisation
using the Mother Theresa name to open the only independent
NGO that ever existed in Kosova before 1999. This organisation
provided humanitarian aid and some medical help to the poor in the

villages. Mother Theresa herself had grown up in a strongly nationalist Albanian family with Kosova roots in a village outside Skopje.
When she was born before the First World War, Skopje, now the
capital of Macedonia, had been capital of the Ottoman *vilayet* of
Kosova, and her father had been an active supporter of the League
of Prizren campaigning organisation.

In 1996 the Catholic church—through an offshoot organisation,
the so-called Sant' Egidio peace trust, based in Rome—brokered the
disastrous education agreement between Rugova and Milošević that
was supposed to re-open Albanian language education in Kosova.
It was very hard to find out what was really happening with the
Catholic movement in Kosova, then or later. Most Kosovar Catholics
were as patriotic as anyone else, but at higher levels in Italy the church
had a strong private anti-Muslim agenda that preferred Serbian control over Kosova, even with Milošević at the helm, to any new 'Islamic
state'. This view was strongly reinforced by a number of Euroid Italian Catholic politicians. Some Kosova Catholic priests were said to
be members of the secretive and élitist Opus Dei organisation. In the
aftermath of the Cold War Islam had replaced communism as Opus
Dei's main target in international politics. The Mother Theresa people were banned from talking to the press, and in general the NGO
became an accessory wing of Rugova's Kosova Democratic League
in most places. The film research work illustrated for me how skilled a
politician at tactical and local level Milošević was, in his manipulation of the different parts of the Catholic church, and the extent to
which the LDK as an institution could be integrated into the communist system of 'government' of Kosova; also in his 'special relationship' with some leading Italian politicians that was to continue
right up to the period of the NATO bombing campaign.[5]

It was nevertheless possible to learn a good deal about Kosova
during the making of the film, and to see and feel the quiet despera-
tion in which most people in most families, Serb and Albanian, lived
for most of the time.

The statistics for the slow ethnic cleansing were easy to obtain
from the Kosova Democratic League: 352 families were evicted

---

[5] There has recently been controversy in Catholic circles about the exact amount
of control actually wielded by the Mother Theresa organisation over the Kosova
organisation.

from their homes in late 1992, and Serbs and Montenegrins were given their apartments. Was 'apartments' a euphemism, or should we have been thinking about the break-up of small farms, the enclosures Sir Arthur Evans of Knossos fame had noted on his Balkan tour in the nineteenth century, with closely planted rows of plum trees, the common dwelling-house, the summer dwelling-house, stalls for the horses, sheep-pens of closely woven hazel wattle, the long wooden spike to stack and dry the maize for the cows, and the honeypot haystack? A Kosova farmyard is a human space where every grass-stalk has a name and a tradition, the name of the family that owns the land.

In the argot of Prishtina there was one key phrase: 'Refugee pressure from Serbian outsiders continued'. The Serb police looked more and more Western in their blue uniforms, compared to the white felt *pliss* hats and women's baggy trousers and other appendages of the 'eastern' Albanians. The film also embodied a more or less Serb-nationalist view of Kosova history. Events did not wait on our film. That summer 1,600 people were sacked from their jobs in Suva Reka, there were riots outside the 'Balkan' tyre factory. Men with guns and cows on their way to the slaughterhouse cluttered the street. Groups of Albanian young men in jeans—always groups, never alone—stood at street corners. A book in a Suva Reka shop window told us that Kosova in primitive times had been an enormous dried-up lake; it was how the Great Plain had started. Miranda said rightly that there was no shortage of primitive behaviour in the present.

I began to understand better the proclivity for occasional savage interethnic violence that has always scarred Kosova history, where compelling psychological pressures bore down on fallible individuals, and sometimes violence against real or imagined enemies seemed the only way out. Daily life went on in a society almost unrecognisable in descriptions by those familiar with northern Yugoslavia. It was also possible to see an evolving future. The Serbs interviewed were almost without exception trying to hold on to a disproportionate number of state sector jobs, while Albanians were beginning to see their future in private business and entrepreneurial activity. In that sense the Serbs were tragically tied to a communist past, while the Albanians were beginning to commit themselves to a capitalist future. Sometimes that commitment became distorted, with young men being drawn into crime. But in a society run by ex-Titoists who saw no legal framework for modern private business this was not surprising. It also has ramifications for Kosova in the post-1999 period, since the calls by international community administrators for ethnic Serbs who had left Kosova to return meant little if there was no job for them to go to—which is the case in the free enterprise world that has been created since June 1999. And the criminalisation of business under Milošević trained a generation of entrepreneurs with instinctive disrespect for state legislation. This was part of the bitter heritage of that era.

A short Skopje interlude: the arms plot, 8 November 1993

After the BBC work was over, I had followed the advice of my Prishtina lawyer contact Blerim Reka and gone down to Skopje, the capital of FYROM, seventy miles south of Prishtina. It was a yellow and white Jugotrans bus in Skopje from Diber, in the west near the Albanian border. The city seemed asleep, the grim modernist architecture built after the 1963 earthquake housing thousands of sleeping workers and bureaucrats. Skopje is many people's least favourite Balkan capital, but the earthquake devastation needs to be remembered. The bus station is a timeless characterful edifice just under the high walls of the Ottoman citadel, with a cavernous ticket hall and toilets run by impoverished Roma who charge 10 denars for a pee. There are metal turnstiles to enter the toilet, and a swinging metal gate to control the movement of the great buses as they leave the numbered stands where the passengers get on. Each ticket is pale blue and white, with a small tear-off strip to surrender to the turnstile operator (never a Roma) at the entrance. Throughout the entire Yugoslav war I never knew a Skopje bus that did not arrive at the correct stand. The kiosks sell cigarettes, newspapers and pornography; the food is cheap and may not be hygienic, like some of the sex acts depicted on the magazine covers. But the Skopje buses run sweetly, and they played a stalwart role in all the recent wars. There is not the same sense of excitement as when a Tirana minibus sets off on some dramatic journey into the mountains, or a Kosovatrans bus fights its way through winter snow, but a quiet assurance that the

destination is possible; cheap movement for the people in the Balkans is not an empty dream. It is public transport under enlightened
state control, along Titoist lines. Skopje has always been a central
transport hub of the Balkans, in our days of Jugotrans and Kosovatrans buses, as in the time of the Byzantine bullock cart and the
Ottoman camel train.

The arms plot was very simple in essence, although many of the
finer details are not yet public. The history of British counterinsurgency operations in support of the Milošević regime and Balkan
allies such as the Skopje ex-communists has yet to be written—
unsurprisingly. The same is true of the British secret war against the
KLA in Albania between 1996 and 1999, about which material is
only just emerging into the public domain. The renegade British
MI6 spy Richard Tomlinson has explained that a secret counterinsurgency operation was set up by British intelligence to support the
post-communist Gligorov government against the Albanians who
were thought to want an 'Illyrida' Albanian republic. A MI6 agent
seems to have been responsible for liaison with a secret SAS team
who would take out any rebellious Albanians: they allegedly rehearsed
evacuation from the Adriatic coast in a midget submarine in case the
whole operation went wrong.

In the end much of MI6's original melodramatic plan was aborted,
and instead it was decided simply to frame some of the Albanian
minority leaders whom Gligorov saw as a threat, and all the details were left to the Macedonians. This decision guaranteed chaos.
Although Tomlinson does not disclose it in his book *The Big Breach*,
his job seems to have been to set up secret food and ammunition
dumps in caves and distant hideouts. This was a serious error, and
Murphy's Law,[6] that inexorable factor in the Balkans, was soon in
full operation. I had no idea about what was happening except that
there were vague rumours of a political crisis, and went for a drink
in the Grand Hotel (every Balkan capital has one, just as every Irish
provincial town has a racecourse). The front page of the main
Skopje paper, *Nova Makedonije*, was dominated by pictures of piles of
weapons and ammunition supposedly found in an ethnic Albanian
minister's office. It seemed a strange place to hide munitions if you
are planning to overthrow a government.

[6] Viz. what can go wrong will go wrong.

In the bar I met Ian Whitehead, the recently appointed British chargé d'affaires, who told me that various senior Albanians had been arrested for illegal weapons possession. He was genuinely surprised by what had happened. The ethnic Albanian conspirators from Macedonia's 25 per cent Albanian minority were supposed to be planning an armed uprising to establish a new Albanian republic, to be called 'Illyrida', in the western Macedonian mountains. It all seemed very strange, and so Balkan as to be a caricature. Whitehead was a cheerful practical man and helpful to journalists he met. It later transpired that one half of the British government had not been talking very clearly, if at all, to the other half, and most of the Foreign Office had no idea at all that someone high in the government seemed to have authorised a top-secret counterinsurgency operation in Skopje. It was indeed a rich stew, even by local standards, comparable to the widespread allegations in November 1995 that President Gligorov had arranged for a failed assassination attempt on himself outside the Bristol Hotel. Journalism in Skopje might be crazy but it was certainly not dull. Tomlinson at this stage was on secondment from MI6 to the Ministry of Defence. It was a great story, but Richard Owen on the *Times* Desk, then the foreign editor, said space was difficult that day, and so I gave it to *The Economist*, which ran it immediately.

At the time nobody had ever heard of Richard Tomlinson, and in retrospect my *Economist* story was fine as far as it went, but with hindsight it could have been accused of pulling some punches. It ran as a 'classic Balkan plot', but at the time I had no idea of the degree of British activity involved, and the public at large knew nothing of the extent of collusion between the Yugoslav and FYROM governments on the one side and the Conservatives and the Foreign Office in London on the other. Over the next few years I gradually found out more, but even then it was clear that a major political objective was to prevent Arben Xhaferi and Menduh Thaci from assuming the leadership of the Albanians based in the western Macedonian city of Tetovo. These were seen as 'radical' new leaders. Whitehall preferred a pliant network of Skopje ex-communists.

November 1993 marked the beginning of the real Tetovo factor in the Albanian national movement. A fierce internal argument in Whitehall followed over the debacle, and something of an internal purge and security inquiry in MI6 followed. I was thought to have been tipped off about what was happening, which was not the case. However, hearing about the allegations did have one important longterm result: it seemed to me that if there were going to be secret operations of this kind, it would be worth trying to pick up some contacts who might tell me about them, and good stories might follow. This turned out to be possible over the years, and bore fruit during the Kosova ground war period between 1997 and 1999.

In the short term Stephen Nash, British chargé d'affaires in Tirana who was streets ahead of any of his colleagues in his understanding of Albanian issues, introduced me to Bob Churcher, then head of the European Union border monitoring mission in Skopje. Bob is a vastly experienced former Royal Green Jackets intelligence officer, a giant of a man both in his size and in the depth of his understanding, who had been decorated for his work in Northern Ireland and then seen much action in Croatia and Bosnia with various international organisations. In the Green Jackets he had been the company commander of the *Times* war correspondent Antony Loyd when the latter was still a soldier. We met secretly in the back room of a Bristol pub when I returned to England and discussed the technical side of the plot, particularly matters such as the calibration of the planted weapons. He shared my analysis of what had happened—essentially that war had been declared on the right of the Albanians to elect their own leadership democratically—and it seemed as if Whitehall policy and political practice were being determined by MI6 collaboration with barely reconstructed Slavocommunists. In the Ottoman empire there was a famous iron mine just above Tetovo in the Sar mountains, and from that month a little iron entered the soul of everyone affected by the arms plot. Political alliances were formed in many quarters that have had an effect on later events in the Albanian world.

3. Interlude, 1994–5

The year 1994 was a quiet one for Kosova in the newsrooms. On the great plain the fields were as beautiful as ever. The maize grew high, and mice scrabbled around feeding under it. Crested larks hopped across the dried winter mud. Wild flowers bloomed, splashing the verges with colour, seeded and died. Millions of frogs croaked all night. The little stumpy willow trees sprouted out of the field ditches on the Kosova plain much as they must have done when the vast Ottoman army of Sultan Murad marched on Europe in 1389. Massed *zurna* horn players marched in front of that army to announce their approach, the painful howl of the horns enough in itself to make strong men flee. Six hundred years later the broken drain on the hill in Prishtina ran away as usual, the asphalt cracked wide open over it, in Prishtina, still at heart the largest village in Kosova.

No newspaper reader in the United States or Britain was any the wiser about Prishtina or what was happening there. The foreign desk of *The Times* showed no interest in what was happening 'down there', as it was usually called, while the agony of Bosnia was the Balkan story of the moment. This was entirely reasonable from the news point of view, but frustrating for me. I had a commission to write a book with Miranda Vickers about what was happening in Albania and did not want to get involved with Bosnia. This was a major commitment that would need a mountain of work, much of it in arduous, uncomfortable and sometimes dangerous conditions. We discussed the situation one sunny May afternoon walking in Richmond Park and decided to stick to our last. I had begun to discover how much most of the Foreign Office and MI6 hated us, and the book had to be written as a survival strategy.[1]

The Bosnian war had reached the point where the cemeteries of Sarajevo were full, and public parks were used as places to bury the

[1] Miranda Vickers and James Pettifer, *Albania: from Anarchy to a Balkan Identity*, London: Hurst, 1997.

dead. Serb artillery fire from Mount Igman tore people apart. Martin Bell was wounded in 'Snipers' Alley', in full view of British television viewers. Whether, in Kosova, Ibrahim Rugova would or would not issue a statement about something or meet some human rights activist was of little general interest by comparison. Yet hopes were raised that year, deep in the Albanian world, quietly and gently, as the United States became more and more involved in Bosnia. The great northern Albanian poet Gjergj Fishta wrote in a poem many decades ago that Europe is a whore. He was referring to the failure of the European powers to do anything to restrain the Serbs from one of their periods of expansionism in the Balkan wars in 1912–13. The English traveller Edith Durham watched Peje and Gjakova being laid waste in 1913.[2] For many Albanians in the early 1990s he could have been writing of the failure of the European Union to help Kosova.

If salvation for Kosova were finally to come, it would be from across the Atlantic. Important leaders of Kosova Albanian opinion like the journalist Veton Surroi started spending more and more time there, and came back with feelings of optimism which, considering the Serbophile discourse in England, I found difficult to share. An end to the Bosnian war had to come, and the United States would now be the key power to enforce it. A deal for Kosova might come at the same time, or so the Kosova Democratic League believed. The League had profound and close links with the United States. Ibrahim Rugova stayed with a Kosovan Albanian diaspora family when he visited New York, one of the magic circle of five or six very wealthy New York families who were the financial backbone of the Democratic League.

The Albanian lobby on Capitol Hill, organised by the dynamic Joe Dioguardi and Shirley Cloyes, was a powerful and well organised force. Antony Athanasias, the richest Albanian of all who made his fortune through a chain of restaurants and property companies lives in Boston. Years of patient work and endless rubber chicken dinners for Joe and Shirley were quietly bearing fruit. In official circles, apart from the Pentagon where progress then was slow, it was becoming clear that—in theory at least, and after the overthrow of Milošević— Kosova could perhaps eventually become independent. It did not

[2] See *The Struggle for Scutari*, London, 1914.

take long for this realisation to seep into the general Albanian consciousness through the pages of the excellent New York Albanian newspaper *Illyria*. Unfortunately for the Albanians at Dayton, this change of climate also soon became apparent to the European foreign ministries, particularly in London and Paris. Kosova was not involved in the Dayton negotiations held to formulate the peace deal that would end the Bosnian war. The British Dayton negotiator, Pauline Neville Jones, was strongly pro-Serbian, and her view that the Kosova question must be excluded from Dayton because of its potential to destabilise Serbia was enthusiastically supported by the Conservative government in London. Pressure from Milošević and the Europeans ensured that Kosova did not figure in either the negotiations or the final agreement.[3] It was a terrible betrayal of the Albanians' trust in peaceful constitutional nationalism, and was to be a defining moment in their struggle. The implicit and often explicit basis of the LDK and Rugovaism was that if the struggle was non-violent, the international community would recognise a just cause and force Serbia to let Kosova go. After Dayton, however, this was a fantasy. Rugova's unique political authority began to erode, and other leaders in the unknown world of the diaspora and the villages of Drenice and the Llap hills would take his place. Hashim Thaci was a key figure in this process. It would be necessary for Kosova to take charge of its own destiny with the opening of the military struggle; the Serbs knew this, as did some Belgrade diplomats. In Kosova there was no apparent change; life for most people followed the normal path of poverty-stricken humiliation at the hands of the Yugoslav state, the hours of queueing in the rain to collect the old age pension only to find that there was only enough money in the office to pay half of those waiting, or the difficult and dangerous path home to the village with money brought in by a friend of a friend of relatives abroad. You hoped not to be noticed by the police, who would steal it; thinking of the authorities, you took care to grease and look after a precious, carefully hidden weapon, probably too old to be any use, but maybe having acquired glory by killing a Serb or two in the fighting in Kosova after the Second World War.

[3] See Brendan Simms, *Britain and the Tragedy of Bosnia*, London: Penguin, 2002.

In March 1994 a Yugoslav visa at last came through and I travelled by train from Thessaloniki to Skopje with Maria Vichou and her partner, both Greek journalists. With over 2,000 dollars stitched into the inside of my Barbour jacket to take to a Prishtina family called Dedaj, I felt nervous. Kosova Albanians could not live without diaspora financial support. Money runs into Kosova were always the most nerve-racking—although the Serbian police did not steal people's jackets, many things could go wrong. The frisson of virtue at actually being able to do something to help a poor family, along with memories of films about the way the French anti-Nazi Resistance operated, was counter-balanced by the extreme stress and danger of it all. However careful you were, and experienced in dealings with the Serb police state, there was always the chance of some random event causing things to go wrong, as had happened to a friend of mine who had a car accident near the border at Blace, and when the ambulance crew saw that he was carrying 4,000 dollars they stole it while he was under sedation. On the bus to Prishtina my fingernails dug into the palms of my hands when the police stopped it and sometimes came on board to do a search. The 'drop' meeting with the family had to be arranged very carefully to avoid the police seeing it. If they did, it was highly probable that then or later they would take the money from the Albanian family. A police raid would happen, the sledgehammer through the center of the door in the middle of the night, terror for the family, loss of all the money they had under the pretext of an 'arms search'.

The subject of a meeting could not be discussed by telephone, even where there was one, since the authorities had invested heavily in Israeli and British phone-tapping devices. A note had to be sent round to your contact's house to establish contact. A trusted friend was needed to do this, who you were absolutely sure was not a police informer or a collaborator with UDBA, the Serb secret intelligence service. I was particularly careful with Kosovo Democratic League people, many of whom were ex-communists and could still be in clandestine contact with Serbs. That was not all. A family could, and often was, charged under the emergency regulations with having illegal contacts with foreigners who were alleged to be 'financing subversion', an offence which carried a long gaol sentence. Practicalities were difficult. As a foreign journalist I was supposed to stay at the Grand Hotel, but this was the last place in the world to meet the Dedaj family who, as Albanians, were terrified of Arkan's people with their headquarters in that building, and understandably would not go anywhere near it. The Dedaj father was a nice little man, an anglophile and an intellectual, who never tired of telling you that Kosova had to wait for freedom. He was a strong Rugovaist, and my own first serious doubts about the value of the Rugova project arose from these meetings. His outlook was part of the depressingly passive world of lower-middle-class Prishtina in those days, and if everyone in Kosova had been the same it would have remained under the jackboot for ever. I did not relish the prospect of taking them money in dangerous and nerve-racking conditions indefinitely, but it seemed tactless to say anything along those lines since I could leave Kosova at any time I liked and they could not. We all knew exactly the kind of things that happened in the torture chambers of Yugoslav prisons, an unspoken bond everyone shared in Kosova. Human decency over this issue led to many Kosova organisations being slow to act on the problem of the very tiny minority of Albanian collaborators, something that was understandable but led to some disasters in the wartime period, and difficult decisions for KLA commanders in the field who had to balance the imperative to protect the security of their units against the lack of a military judicial system. I had got to know a Dedaj family member working for a publisher in London. My relations with her were not particularly cordial, but her family was trapped in Prishtina and in the front line, and had to be kept going—personal feelings could not intrude on the illegal work.[4]

I was thinking of this as we lay stretched out in the deserted night train as it crept northwards through Macedonia. Here the great open plain stretched across to the Pelister mountains, craggy wooded outcrops of limestone covered in vast forests with virtually no roads. They had been a stronghold of the anti-communist guerrillas after the Second World War. It was fighting country we were crossing, and most local people knew that it was only a matter of time before a new war would break out. As always, those on public transport were in touch with political reality, unlike the internationals concerned with Kosova in their bulletproof four-wheel-drive vehicles. In the

[4] See, for instance, the memoirs of Zijadin Qira, *Cell Number 31*, New York, 1979.

words of the title of Eleanor Karakatsidou's book on Macedonia, these were fields of wheat but hills of blood. My Greek friends were on assignment from Athens to report on the new leadership of the Albanians in Tetovo, in north-west FYROM. Already the implications of the arms plot were steadily spreading out in ripples from Tetovo and over the region—unseen but in the end lethal to the *status quo*. Earlier that month an Albanian patriot, Hamil Latifi, had died in suspicious circumstances in Skopje prison, and there had been more arrests for illegal arms possession. The struggle for Albanian freedom in Macedonia was starting to resemble that in Kosova, and for a journalist working out how to cover it would be a priority. In Prishtina I had lunch with Veton Surroi, who said that he was close to the new leadership in Tetovo, and that Arben Xhaferi hated Rugova. He thought that Menduh Thaci and the other new leaders in Tetovo were serious about the national question in a way their predecessors had not been. Possibly he would be proved right, but it was too early to be sure.

In London Surroi was the darling of the liberal establishment in the Foreign Office and was seen as a future Kosova leader within a reformed Yugoslavia. After my early visits to Kosova this could only appear as an ill-informed fantasy, but it was an *idée fixe* in the Foreign Office for some years. He was always referred to as a 'moderate'—I have never understood why, except that he was prepared to talk to Serbs when others were not. But he did not say what they wanted to hear. His father, the highest-ranked ethnic Albanian in the old Yugoslav diplomatic service, had died in strange circumstances in Spain. Most Albanians thought he had been murdered and blamed the Yugoslav secret police. Veton never talked about it.

Ibrahim Rugova was in an urbane and friendly mood when I went to interview him the next day. Through the clouds of French cigarette smoke, he described how the Serbs had wrecked Kosova's cultural heritage, building a battery factory over an ancient Illyrian and Roman site in Peje, and wrecking Roman forts in construction works near the Prishtina-Peje road. He was afraid that nobody in the West knew or cared about these things, and of course he was right. Surroi had told me of his belief that splits in the LDK were coming. Perhaps the President's mind was drifting towards the remote past to avoid thinking about the problems of the present. The streets in

Prishtina were quiet. Rugova stressed to me that the arrival of the United States in Bosnia would assist radical forces everywhere in the region, but there was little sign of this in Prishtina. A few Serb refugees from Bosnia had started to move into the dingy old Hotel Illyria, now renamed the Hotel Beaujour after the Serbs' favourite wild tulip. They hung about the main street chain-smoking, refugees in their own country, then started to scratch a living by selling illegal Bulgarian-manufactured Marlboros. In Kosova that autumn we seemed to be in an eternally unchanging backwater, while the main river of Balkan history was rushing past in the northern part of the peninsula away from us. I was marooned in a dark, often threatening and sinister town, where light faded into shadow and then into sepulchural Miltonic darkness around the dingy apartment blocks and rubbish-strewn parks. As the Ministry of Interior blue-uniformed Special Police patrolled, the fate of the Albanian people seemed lost for ever. The excitement of 1992 and early 1993, with the ascendancy of Arkan and the threat of war and popular uprising, had been replaced by a sad torpor. I felt I was beginning to understand the Kosova Democratic League better. It took time to grasp that it was an organisation born out of defeat, of the mass strikes at Trepce in 1989, the general strike of September 1990, and the huge popular demonstrations which—unlike those in Prague or Berlin—the West had failed to support properly, allowing Milošević and the communists to crush them. There was no Chancellor Kohl with a border nearby to do what could be done for freedom, as Germany had been able to do in Croatia in 1991.

Thus, although there was much to admire in Rugova personally, there was no sense at all of any capacity—or even any will—to organise practical action against Serbian rule. He had been there on the picket-line, and been defeated. Few of his foreign diplomatic guests in his strange little office by the football ground understood this, and believed that his pacifism and passivity were the result of rational choice. His own people understood how much of it was forced on him by terrible circumstances, something that has assisted his own political survival through so many vicissitudes.

I was bored with Prishtina and thought that since there was no Kosova story, I could more usefully spend some time down in Tetovo and Skopje and try to find out more about what was happening in

Macedonia. The bus sped across the south-west corner of Kosova with little stone farmhouses surrounded by the unique conical Kosova haystacks, and then climbed through the sinister dark forests under the lonely Sar mountains—its darkest and most dangerous peak of all, the aptly-named Black Nicola, to the west near the border with Albania. It was a newish Volvo coach, and the fat unshaven driver bounced up and down rhythmically on the pneumatic sprung seat, an innovation on the Volvo models of the late 1980s. The area was known for wolves, and the shepherds had enormous Sar dogs to protect their flocks. But who would protect the people? We passed through the border smoothly; the Serbs were always glad to see you leave Kosova, probably wishing that most of the inhabitants would do the same, as subsequent events were to show. We sped through the divided village of Gllobocice, half in 'Serbia' and half in 'Macedonia', but actually all in the old Ottoman *vilayet* of Kosova. You did not need to be a military genius to see that this was a key strategic road, and it would play a central role in the coming struggles— the refugee crisis in 1998 and the war in Macedonia in 2001. The actual conduct of the border post was a key sign of the capacity of the Slavs to try to separate the Albanian nation. In relaxed periods travellers are waved through; in times of tension there are thorough searches and customs checks. In 1999 it was pitted with holes from NATO bombing and Serb mines, and when Miranda and I took Sir Reginald Hibbert to visit Kosova then, he said that it was the worst road he had travelled on since the Second World War. Hibbert had been an adviser to the Albanian Partisans in the war, and was a leading figure in Albanian affairs in England after retirement from a distinguished diplomatic career.

In Tetovo everybody was talking about the need to establish an Albanian-language university. Under communism there had been over 2,000 teachers of the Albanian language in Macedonia, but now there were only 400, and they were not always paid. Under the cultural conservatism, the world of the tubby moustachioed shopkeepers of Tetovo who plodded off to the mosque on Fridays wearing little white skullcaps, it was not hard to feel a tough and resilient nationalist radicalism. Tetovo people have had much to put up with from Belgrade over the years. They are different from Kosovar Albanians, often quieter, more old-fashioned, sometimes inward-looking and harder to get to know but very firm and loyal friends once made. They had no illusions about the government of Kiro Gligorov. To the international community he appeared a moderate skillful ruler, and in its own terms there was some basis for this view. Unfortunately the history was stained with blood. On the outskirts of Tetovo are the cemeteries with graves from the 1944–9 period of anti-communist resistance, sacrifices for freedom from Belgrade rule that were made well within living memory, the skulls and bones and crushed Albanian lives and hopes on which Titoism was built. Gligorov was doing everything he could, with Western encouragement, to keep the Titoist ethos together. The East Adriatic department of the Foreign Office thought he was quite wonderful.

Then it was time to leave northern Macedonia, and take the bus down to Ohrid, the next bus to Bitola, old Monastir, then the taxi to the windswept and hostile Greek border at Niki, the half-mile walk through no-man's-land, the border of Christian Greece and Europe with the Slav barbarians, in the view of the border guards, then another taxi to Florina, Slav Lerin, then a final bus down to Thessaloniki. Most of European history had passed through the Monastir Gap, as military historians call the passage through the mountains south of Bitola, from the Dorian invaders of ancient Greece, the Roman legions, Slav invaders of Byzantium, the Ottoman Turks and the Nazi divisions invading Greece in the Second World War. The region was preparing for war again—there could be no doubt about it. The little tobacco and pepper fields seemed to smell of it as much as the vast and wild forests. The word 'war' was written on the trees, the grey stone of the Ottoman houses and the wood of the mosque roofs. But it was all invisible, and I could think of no way of communicating it to the newspaper. In Koranic terms the war was still in the world of the Unseen. The Way was Unknown.

I returned sooner than I had expected, a few weeks later in January 1995. It was a tough winter, and in Kosova the snowfield stretched as far as one could see, a vast white blanket with houses, telegraph poles and hayricks sticking up from it. The snowplough had cleared a way for the bus but drifts three metres deep remained on either side. Blinding afternoon sun shone down from a mountain on the border with Albania. It looked so intensely beautiful, but up there you would start to die of hypothermia if you were out for longer than a few hours. Little huddles of people at the side of the road waiting for the bus were swaddled like Eskimos. The bus passed through a little place called Dobra Voda, Good Water. The LDK slogans on the walls were painted out. Beyond the oak scrub at the roadside were acres of new forest, stumpy seedlings sticking out of the snow.

Gradually, with plenty of warning, the bus broke down, the diesel started waxing in the cold, the engine coughed and we came to a halt. Tension rose among the Albanian passangers, young men nipped out for a quick cigarette, older women found *burek* rolled in tissue paper and gave it to the children to eat. I might be thinking of the picturesque, but they were thinking of the danger, you could die in the cold, the Serbs might decide to turn up and arrest somebody. They would not need to kill them, just leave them outside and they would freeze to death before morning.

'The diesel is very bad now. They put water in it.' This, no doubt, was an accurate account of the diesel, but the words could equally apply to Milošević's attempts to keep Yugoslav communism going. A snowplough appeared and drove past in a white fog; it was small and nondescript, nothing compared to the great snowblowers up in the Mavrovo National Park that could shift thousands of tons in an hour.

After a few minutes snow began falling again and the men trying to start the bus engine were lost in a blizzard. A high wind blew across the road, and the drifts began to reach the bus windows, with the little farms a mile away suddenly lost in a whiteout. The press of humanity in the bus was very warm and friendly, and an old Albanian peasant smelling strongly of his goats was suddenly a reassurance not a nuisance. I gave him an English cigarette and immediately became someone of high status and prestige. Somewhere out there, through the snow, normal life would go on. The goats would be fed, somehow, even if death through cold or a Serbian bullet was out in all the fields around us.

Balkan peasants are more or less indestructible in bad weather, they have seen it all before, and more than one comment was made that if it was as bad as this, the bastards in the police would sit and drink slivowitz in the Gjakova barracks and not bother with us. Eventually, miraculously, the engine started and the old bus, all of it, shook into life. There was a bubble of laughter and an odd handclap,

our little fragment of Kosova society could travel on in the great pil-
grimage of life that the snow or the MUP could not take away from
us. We inched into the drifts, the leather-jacketed driver gripping
the cracked black bakelite wheel tight with his filthy hands. Our
lives depended on his skill. He chain-smoked, his helper ready with
another lit cigarette as each one expired, Balkan male bonding over
tobacco. It was only an old bus in a Kosova winter, but we were
going to beat Milošević's fuel crisis, we were all heroes, and the
driver was the greatest hero of all, an Achilles with a box of cheap
tools instead of a bronze shield. The people had won against the failures of the Yugoslav state. Kosova was alive in the blizzard.

Somehow, hours later, we reached Gjakova, the beautiful Ottoman town, heartland of Albanian nationalism. Milošević's police
never patrolled in groups of less than three, armed to the teeth, and
always in paramilitary fatigues, never in normal uniforms. The town
was dominated by the brutal simplicities of the front line. It had also
been a cradle of leaders of the League of Communists, starting with
Fadil Hoxha, Tito's favourite Albanian Partisan during the Second
World War. My friend Fehmi Agani[5] had come from the town, along
with many of the other party leaders from the 1980s. It had some
modern industry and a weird, overlarge modernist hotel. Why was
Gjakova so tough and lawless? The rational explanation would be
that it had lost so much, so quickly, under Milošević. Only fifteen
years before it was the most favoured town in a more or less autono-
mous republic, and now it was lost in the western hills of a Third
World-style police state. Gjakova people are proud and indomitable
and very conscious of where they come from.

The police here did not like journalists—I had discovered this
before, and now was no different. I was looking at a shop window
when suddenly an unmarked car drew up and two tough young
men got out and pushed me into the back seat. The interrogation
was short and not sweet. I was to leave town straight away. I had a
camera with me—no more photography. I must come with them.
The next thing I remember was standing outside a police station,
with a cut on my scalp that was bleeding into the snow. Then I vom-
ited the good tomato and pepper roll from the bus station café, coming back to make a mess in the snow. I was holding the railings to

[5] Fehmi Agami was murdered by the Serbs in April 1999 in Prishtina.

steady myself, when a middle-aged woman appeared and said I had
better come to the bus station with her as soon as I could, as everybody said that there was a security sweep coming from Prishtina and
it would be dangerous to be out. She probably thought I had been
drinking.

At the bus station nobody knew whether there would be a bus
back to Prishtina or not. A Kosova bus station then could be a place
of great uncertainty and tension, a place of transition from one
world to another. Kosova was like that in those days, there was a
timetable but it meant nothing. The only thing that the Yugoslav
state did with real meaning was point a gun at you or beat you up in
a police station. With millions of gallons of diesel a month being
guzzled by the army in the war in Bosnia, there was little left for
civilians, and Kosova, being at the bottom of the Yugoslav heap,
would get less than anywhere else. Buses, the lifeblood of us all with
their great shuddering, smelly diesel engines, were stranded hulks in
the snow like dead whales washed up on a New England beach. On
the positive side, it seemed that United Nations sanctions might be
working at last, fuel was so short. It was even difficult to buy a ticket.
You had to put your hand through a little glass slot and be presented
with it, or not, as the case might be. Gjakova was, in the words of the
Eddie Cochran song, something else, pure political suspense and
danger; the chattering classes in Prishtina were more privileged than
we or they knew. Up in Sarajevo the liberal élite were lamenting the
loss of a 'civilised Yugoslavia' as the shells fell. Down here in workers'
and peasants' Kosova, the Serbs didn't have to destroy their civilisation as most people had never had one in the first place in the southern mining and farming republic.

A few days later I was sitting on the luxurious wide sofa of my
friend Janet Gunn in Sofia and we looked at the cover of an issue of
Veton Surroi's new magazine, *Koha*. It was a spoof of the Absolut
vodka advertisement, with the slogan Absolut Kosova, 'Country of
Terror, 2 million, 90% Albanian, Imported from Serbia'. The vodka
bottle was shackled in chains. (I bought another copy, framed it and
hung it up in my office in Bath. Janet looked at it, shook her head,
and put it tidily into a magazine rack.) In Prishtina Veton was por-
traying the truth in images. My personal reality had been feeling sick
and humiliated in the Gjakova snow.

In Prishtina, where the temperature was over twenty degrees Celsius below, I was attended to by a safe doctor, my friend Alush Gashi, now a foreign affairs expert for Dr Rugova. It was a long way from the last time we had met, at a plush conference in the Carter Center in Atlanta. I was pathetically grateful to see and touch the shabby concrete of the Grand Hotel, and to find hot water in the pipes, even though it was the smelly Prishtina variety. A quarter bottle of Johnny Walker went quickly. I stared at my few possessions, a rucksack, a little Sony short wave radio to pick up the BBC, a dirty yellow leather bag from a Greek holiday that had been coopted into war service. This was Yugoslavia at war, but although no shots were fired till about two in the morning that night, I could as well have been standing in the snow on Mount Igman.

Next day Ibrahim Rugova held his Friday press conference. This was better than I had expected, he was fluent and relatively forthcoming. Kosova was changing for the worse, there was a large-scale campaign by the police against Albanian activists, particularly former soldiers and policemen, and a hunt for arms which meant terror for families. I asked, was there any particular reason for this? To create fear, he said, so people would leave Kosova. It was the invention of slow, steady, measured ethnic cleansing. In the meantime Milošević was building new settlements for Serbs in Mitrovica, Gjakova and Vushtri. Yes, it was a problem to be a refugee but there was plenty of room for them in Serbia, and no need to send Bosnian refugees to Kosovo. The LDK favoured 'temporary residence' if they had to come to Kosova at all.

Rugova was at his most professorial, explaining that life was getting more expensive as the economic situation got worse. The public sector had been destroyed by Milošević, and over 150,000 ethnic Albanians had been driven out and funds brought in to help start small businesses seized by the police. The jobless were in a very difficult situation, especially in the biggest industrial towns like Ferizaj and Mitrovica. But Rugova's speech was profoundly backward-looking, nostalgic for the world of ten years before.

Somebody asked if any talks with Belgrade were in the offing. I sat there thinking that this was an idiotic question—what would they be about? Rugova was good on this. No, we did not want a 'dialogue of diktat'. No, there were no policy differences in the LDK.

We were united for independence. There were very few people outside the LDK, they were not representative. On the positive side he was very pleased with the progress of the United States lobby. Mediated talks would be possible, under certain circumstances. That was all.

'Conducting a dialogue with the Serbs is very difficult. They never respect their words or promises.'

He adjusted his hair and glasses and began talking about Macedonia. He condemned the extradition of a group of Kosovar Albanian activists from Macedonia to a certain gaol sentence in Serbia, and the closure of Tetovo's private Albanian-language University in Macedonia.

'It was a very unmeasured action on the part of Macedonia. There was an agreement reached between us for those people and their stay in Macedonia.'

As the LDK press bulletin put it, it was all 'a cause for concern'. Indeed it was, but after a ripple of vague unease a series of hostile questions followed from the journalists. Macedonia was going to be Rugova's Achilles Heel. In his Prishtina-centric way, he seemed to have no inkling of the courage, organisational efficiency and ruthlessness of the new political leadership of the Tetovo Albanians and how this would affect so many regional equations. Across the bleak and snowbound mountains, the forces of Slav repression were bringing the two parts of the Albanian nation closer in a way that the international community could not see or fathom. I only felt this or knew anything because I had seen the arms plot in Skopje in November 1993, where weapons were planted on innocent people in the Albanian leadership. The British and other European states would go to great lengths to maintain the *status quo.*

In private conversation earlier that day Rugova had been much more assertive and had given me a long history lesson on how in 1981, long before Milošević's time, the Macedonians had closed the Albanian-language schools—a trial run for what happened in Kosova—and considered the Albanians who were still in the Skopje government to be communist puppets. He also said, drawing deeply on his cigarette, that the region now had a *status quo* of conflict, and everybody was getting used to it. But all he said in public was that the situation needed calming down. There was something wrong about it all, and from that January onwards I never saw Rugova in the same way again. Why was he prepared to sacrifice basic principles to please an international community most of whom were never going to do anything to free Kosova? I have never found the answer to this question.

The bus chugged slowly south through the snow towards the Macedonian border, through the maize fields north of Ferizaj, once an Ottoman *chiflik*, a huge estate owned by a friend of the Sultan. I felt unbearably sad leaving Kosova, the love affair was taking hold of me. Even Prishtina looked beautiful in the half-sun through the freezing mist. The ice by the roadside was rock-hard. The walk from the bus station to the hotel the previous night was as cold as I have ever been, minus-thirty Celsius, some said. Feet crunched loudly on the packed snow.

At an impromptu cattle market about 4 km outside town, 400 men stood in a field in the cruel cold. Trucks disgorged sad beasts, heavy steers and cows with damp staring brown eyes. They were about to stop being animals and start to be meat. Blood was central to the process, warm and steaming and flooding out under the truck wheels and across the packed snow from the killing ground behind them. A great beef cow was being disembowelled, tripes spread still quivering over the ice, feet kicking as it died, a little shit oozing out, a huge inflated stomach. The intestines are cut away and kicked, and suddenly a dog runs off with them. Here in Kosova there is fast-flowing blood, *gjak*, and endless snow.

On the bus back to Sofia to fly home, there was a strange new route. The blue and white Kosovatrans bus lumbered south-west towards the town of Gjilan, past the mines below Janjeve with their vast draglines and steel buckets running on cables high above the road. Mining is never far away in Kosovo. To the east, in the wild forests near the border with Serbia, was Novo Brde, the fairy-tale medieval castle that alone remained of the mining town that had been the biggest producer of silver and gold in the Byzantine world.

We trundled slowly towards the south-west, following a deep cleft in the hills through the Brendeli river valley, past maize fields and neat little white modern houses. This was *terra incognita*, and it was a sign of the Dayton period relaxation in Kosova that a bus ran this route without police on board. The journey had the *frisson* of excitement and danger, since it was a new route and the bus was crammed with Albanians, a few Serbs sitting at the front. Kosova society was then exactly reflected in bus seat organisation. Slavs and foreigners sat at the front, the Albanians behind them, and Roma at the back in the smelly seats above the engine. After about an hour we reached Gjilan. It was a dull Yugoslavist town, once prosperous as a showcase communist city that had benefited from Titoist industrialisation plans and investment in the food and wood industries. I knew it was mostly Albanian, but some Serbs lived there too. As we passed slowly through the outer streets it seemed un-Kosovan, unbelievably dull and pedestrian. I was quite unprepared for the scenes when we swung into the bus station, a big concrete hangar on a hill. As soon as the bus appeared, a mass of people surged round it and were trying to get on before those who wanted to get off could do so. Fights started and, a short fat woman in a purple coat was pushed away with her children and burst into tears.

The Serb police waded in and eventually some sort of order was restored. As many as thirty people crowded in as standing passangers, desperate to leave Gjilan as if some unseen power was driving them. Above the ticket office window was a picture of Radovan Karadjić, a shock of black hair falling over his face. The slogan underneath invited you to join his party. Another fight started, this time inside the bus. People were very near the edge. I wondered if anyone on the bus was armed. Eventually, the engine juddered into life on its thin diesel, and we drew out towards the Preshevo valley, then a name that meant nothing to me except as an echo from battles in the Second World War. We would soon leave Kosova, but not as soon as I had expected.

After a few miles we entered a narrow valley, with poor little farms in the fertile strip a few hundreds yards wide in the valley floor. Old couples worked in their tiny fields, making bonfires of last year's dead maize stalks. Steep hills covered with beech and oak rose above the stony river bed, in a lost world. These were the deep and unknown forests of south-east Kosova. Then the bus stopped. At first it seemed to be a routine checkpoint, with blue-overalled MUP waiting by the roadside. But instead of boarding the bus they waved all the passengers off and we had to stand at gunpoint on the grass verge by the roadside. Three stinking oil drums filled with greyish white disinfectant fluid were behind them. A small cleansing ritual had to be performed, there was said to be foot-and-mouth disease in Kosova, we were made to wash our hands and feet in this foul stuff, while the Serb soldiers made obscene remarks about the Albanians being dirtier than their cattle. And look—here was a dirty *stranatz* (foreigner) as well. It was still the same as in 1992, Milošević had no need to bother about encouraging an ultra-right party in Kosova, he had one already: it was called the police force. Down here, even though we were only a couple of hours from Prishtina, they could do whatever they liked. They could have shot everyone in the bus and thrown us into the river and nothing would ever have happened to them. We were allowed to troop back on board the bus— like the cows on their way to be slaughtered, but our blood was still safe inside us.

The police were hunters who could not be bothered to hunt. In the old days they hunted rabbits, foxes, wild boar—these days they were getting round to thinking about hunting the Albanians, but the time for that had not arrived quite yet. Gospod Arkan and the high-ups in Belgrade would give the word when it was time to start. At that time I did not not know how much Albanian and Muslim blood had been spilt in 1945 in these obscure forest valleys in the fighting in Preshevo and south-east Kosova. The Preshevo people, led by Imam Idris Shah, had led a strong anti-communist resistance and many Albanian houses had been burnt by Tito's communist Partisans. The damp woods hung with memories, and among the creepers was old man's beard, a strange English touch—like the fact that so many of the advisers who had put Tito in power had been British. The bus lurched forward through the impoverished deep valley and past a tiny farm on a minute strip of land by a little river, then through Pasjan and Burice villages. Three kilometres away was the border near Depce. A gun sounded in the far distance, preceded by muzzle flash on top of a hill. The Yugoslav state was in action.

The time Slobodan Milošević allowed me to spend in Kosova in 1995 was within ten minutes of being over. Dimly through the trees and frozen mist the lights of the border post were coming into view, at least I thought of it as a border because it was where Kosova ended. Where the martial law system ended seemed, by comparison, to be free, but it was only another part of Serbia, Preshevo valley, which in turn was part of something called Yugoslavia, a legal state with a seat in the United Nations, what used to be called the international system. It was as if the nightmare of Yugoslavia was eternal, and someone called Milošević would be ruling for hundreds of years. Looking at the dark damp steep-sided valleys with their dripping trees and tiny farms it was impossible not to have dark thoughts. The sight of the bus waiting patiently at the border was the only consolation.

4. Arrival of the Kosova Liberation Army

The smoking gun

In May 1996 Kosova passed one of its many landmarks. Under the Sar mountains a different era began. Although the great plain in spring was as marshy as ever and still frozen in places under the melt-water, the political ice was breaking. In Belgrade the Serbian opposition made a serious attempt to end the Milošević regime. In Kosova the Kosova Liberation Army arrived on the scene and that world would never be the same again. I filed this story for the European edition of the *Wall Street Journal* on 26 May:

Prizren, Kosovo

Below the Byzantine castle walls of Prizren, it is just about possible to imagine here that the old Yugoslavia is still in existence. It is Kosovo as seen through the eyes of the Dayton negotiators. In the agreement signed last autumn in Ohio, there was nothing included about this troubled province with its 90% ethnic Albanian population, governed under emergency laws from Belgrade since 1989. With tensions rising, the local Serbs, who make up most of the rest of the population, are beginning to feel uneasy. And despite the international community's hopes, whoever wins the Albanian parliamentary elections this Sunday will probably not be able to restrain their Kosova kin if the current situation leads to more violence.

Kosovo was a multicultural, multiracial and generally peaceful place. The communities do not mix much, nor do they love one another. But they never did—it is not Slobodan Milošević's fault that mixed marriages are almost unknown. But earlier this month five Serb policemen were cut down in a hail of bullets in the village of Decani, along with two Bosnian Serb refugees. Decani is a poverty-stricken 100% Albanian rural community nestling under the mountains near the border with Albania. Responsibility was claimed by a previously unknown ethnic Albanian underground group based in Switzerland, where there is a large Albanian diapora community. It is the first retaliation of its kind from the Albanian population, who deeply resent the Serb martial law. It has changed the local political atmosphere in fundemental ways.

Serbs who have lived for generations in the Kosovo capital Prishtina were fearful last week, quiet and subdued in their little cafés and restaurants, sitting drinking slivowitz under portraits of Chetnik heroes. There is only one Serb for every nine Albanians in Kosovo now, with the largely Muslim and Catholic Albanians having over twice as many children as the average Serb. Dragan Marković is a teacher, and in his spare time he trains in a gun club. It is almost certainly linked to one of the paramilitary groups in the region run by alleged war criminals like Arkan, but he refuses to discuss that. He is more concerned about a general strategy of community defence.

'What do we do now?' he asks. 'We are so outnumbered, and how do we face a long terrorist campaign? I think it would be better to have a war if we have to. Many of the Albanians would leave and go to Albania. It would not be like the *kraijinas*, other Serbs would help us.'

That may be the case but what Albania has to offer in the way of a solution to the intractable problems of Kosovo is hard to discern. It is an awful long way from here to the capital in Tirana, with its diplomatic community and growing bustle and prosperity. Albania is in the throes of a parliamentary election campaign where the future of President Sali Berisha is on the line. He was elected in 1992, and over the last four years has followed a radical free market policy that has made him the darling of the IMF and the World Bank, but left the infrastructure of the country in difficulties and a growing gulf between the rich and poor. His critics accuse him of authoritarianism, and see his reelection as opening the way to a right-wing dictatorship. Supporters see him as having decisively broken the hold of 50 years of communism on the nation.

In the eyes of the international community he has been a restraining influence on the Kosovars, but it is hard to see now how his reelection will make much difference to events on the ground. In the formal sense, he has certainly been a moderating influence on the Kosovars, but with the beginning of an armed underground, the calculations of constitutional leaders, Serb or Albanian, will be fundamentally affected. The angry and bitter young men in the diaspora communities in Switzerland, Germany and the US who see violence as the only way forward are very unlikely to bother much with the Tirana government, any more than the provisional IRA has ever taken instructions from Dublin governments. International bodies such as IFOR in Bosnia are equally impotent to influence developments.

They see Kosovo as having been sold down the river at Dayton, and the Ohio agreements as a kick in the teeth for the moderate and responsible policy the Kosovar leadership, under Ibrahim Rugova, has followed in the last few years. The Serbian military administration in Prishtina has refused to allow the Kosovar parliament to meet in the last four years. A certain kind of Albanian patience has simply run out, inside and beyond Kosovo. Young Albanians in Kosovo itself did not bother to hide their satisfaction at the Decani shootings, although the older generation were much more circumspect, with keen memories of the efficency and ferocity of the Belgrade repression of Kosovo uprisings in the past.

The shootings and general rise in political tension have provided very unwelcome new problems for both Mr Rugova in Prishtina and Mr Milošević in Belgrade. The official Kosovo line is that the shootings were a Serb provocation, but virtually no one outside the Rugova public relations office believes that. The existence of an armed underground, run from the diaspora but using Albania as a safe base, has been rumoured for some time. In response, the Kosova Serbs are looking for action and leadership from Belgrade, at a time when the Bosnian crisis and Serbia's economic woes are taking up most of Mr Milošević's time.

Yet he cannot write off the Kosovo Serbs—as he did the Croatian Serbs—without threatening the heart of his own political identity, and that of all Serbs, who regard Kosovo as the heart of their state. The great medieval Serbian religious monuments, such as the Patriarchate at Pec and the church at Gracanica, are all in Kosovo. Taking control of the local party and exploiting the grievances of the Kosovo Serbs were central to Mr Milošević's rise to power in the late 80s. On the other side, Mr Rugova's moderation is under severe pressure from the growing radicalization of the young. Whatever the details, it looks as if Kosovo is in for a long difficult summer.

The only hope for the international community is that some sort of negotiations between the parties on the restoration of democracy in Kosovo might start and make progress and take the wind out of the radicals sails. But with attitudes hardening on both sides of the ethnic divide, it seems a distant hope.

Wall Street Journal Europe, 24 May 1996

The violent events in central Drenice when the KLA began attacking the Serbian army and police defined the heart of the struggle in the next two years. In modern history we think we know when wars begin, the salient and well-learned dates such as 4 August 1914 and the Allied declaration of war on 3 September 1939 following Hitler's invasion of Poland. There is war, which is abnormal, and there is peace, which is normal. It is hard for us to understand situations where people disagree whether there is a war or not. This is especially the case with many 'insurgency wars'. In Vietnam war had been in progress in one form or another for twenty or more years before the Tet offensive in 1968—which for most of my generation was the beginning of the real war for Vietnam. When did the struggle of the modern IRA in Ulster begin? In 1969? Many well-informed people would not agree. Kosova was the same. Journalists in Kosova then had the difficult responsibility of trying, in Martin Bell's words, to make a 'first sketch of history' when many people of a pro-Serb inclination might not agree that there was any real history to sketch.

In Kosova my war started in a real sense in the bright sunny long-grass-and-wild-flower spring days of May 1996, but the Kosova Liberation Army had been formed three years before, and some older militants in Albanian Kosova would point to the struggles of Demaci's armed groups in the 1960s and the remnants of Ballist resistance in Drenice in the '50s as signs that the war against Slavo-communism had never ceased since 1944. Demaci was an early exponent of pan-Albanianism, and caused horror in diplomatic circles in December 1991 when, after being awarded the Sakharov prize by the European Parliament, he backed a call from a group of intellectuals for an international assembly of all Albanians. Others would mention the Llap *ceta*[1] in the 1980s as an example of Albanian armed resistance. For its part the Serbian government in Belgrade never agreed, right up till March 1999, that there was a war at all; it was merely conducting an anti-terrorist campaign. The term 'organised criminals' was common, to depoliticise the nature of the people's resistance and allow police-state methods to be used against it; admitting to being at war would have added force to the Albanians' case, and given an implicit legitimacy to their view that the territory of Kosova might be genuinely subject to dispute. The Serb newspapers always used to hate Veton Surroi saying, as he liked to do, that in Kosova 'peace is war, war is peace'. In their view Kosova was 'normal' apart from the activity of 'terrorists'. Yet in the perception of the London and US media, particularly *The Times*, a few shootings did not constitute a war. When I telephoned the Desk

---

[1] An armed gang, later meaning a guerrilla group.

from Kosova on that May date, nobody was much interested in taking copy. It was still only six months after Dayton, and the prevailing view was that the problems of the Balkans had been solved there, and now that the Americans were involved there was little to worry about. The strongly pro-Berisha people on the paper tended to see me as a leftist who was interested in promoting the Albanian issue in Wapping as a way of making trouble for Berisha. On this issue they were under relentless pressure from the Foreign Office media machine.

But the *Wall Street Journal* office in Brussels, which ran everything in Europe, was dominated by bright young American talents who were not subject to the dead hand of the pro-Serb setup in London; they wanted copy, and so I filed. The story was deeply resented by the Foreign Office, and I began to realise that the depth of British complicity with the Milošević regime and Serbia went beyond the simple matters of Titoist links and historic sentiment that I had seen so far. Active work against the Kosova liberation forces was going on in the present. People clearly knew about the nascent resistance movement and were determined to let Milošević snuff it out without publicity. It was a determining moment in my working life. At the same time the Democratic Party government in Albania had been kept in power by the internationals in Tirana through the OSCE legitimation of a wickedly crooked election in May–June 1996 that should have set every alarm bell ringing. There was, in fact, a plain conspiracy between leading members of the Conservative government, the Foreign Office and the intelligence services to prop up the Belgrade government and keep Albania poor and marginal and Kosova within Serbia. Manipulation of the media was a key priority. But some people at *The Times* knew of these unpleasant machinations in Whitehall, and were helpful. Des Houghton, a Murdoch appointee from Brisbane, phoned me and said that he thought I had a real talent for analysis of Balkan matters, and should ring in with ideas for copy; I would be the *Times* 'Balkan expert'. Did newspapers have Balkan experts? I was not sure. But if being a Balkan expert meant that I could try to get more of the story into the paper, so be it. The Foreign Office and MI6 would try to suppress the truth about the looming war, and the task all journalists covering the Balkans would face over the coming period was to work out how to break these stories without being accused of trying to stir up trouble when our friend the peace partner, Slobodan Milošević, was hard at work with us in the post-Dayton 'peace process'. It was an onerous responsibility.

I met Miranda Vickers for a drink before Christmas that year at O'Riordan's by the Thames in Brentford, and she was full of bounce and energy and plonked on to the table among the Guinness glasses a copy of the *Independent* with a story she had written about the 'Pyramid crisis', a looming run on the banks in hitherto successful Albania. Perhaps the policy of the lie machine in Whitehall was not based on such secure foundations after all. Our book on Albania was in production with Hurst and Co. in Covent Garden, and there was a sense, after so many years, that the ball might be coming in our direction, out of the control of the spin doctors.

In March 1996, earlier that same year, I had been in Belgrade, speaking at an official British conference in the Sava conference centre on the future of Kosova. My friend Ivor Roberts was British ambassador in Belgrade, and it was with great difficulty that he had obtained the agreement of the Serb authorities for it to take place. Now, for the first time, there was a sense of urgency in British diplomacy over Kosova although in the flatulent and evasive world of the Tory government that had let Bosnia bleed to death, that did not necessarily mean much. Although he was also pro-Serb, Ivor Roberts had an understanding of the depth of the Kosova crisis that was unusual in London, and there were rumours before I went of new developments. He was half-Italian, a Catholic, and had been closely involved in the Vatican-brokered education agreement that Rugova and Milošević had signed the previous autumn. The conference provided no startling new insights. Most of the participants were filmed by Serbian state television, but as soon as I started to deliver my paper on the Albanian national question the cameras were switched off. It was a time when Western diplomacy was preoccupied with reforming and civilising the Milošević regime. Now this can be seen as having been a hopeless task, but then, in the post-Dayton atmosphere, Milošević was a partner in the 'peace process'. The Kosovar Albanian participants included some good people, like the key Rugova henchman Fehmi Agani, who was to be so tragically murdered in May 1999 alongside the railway track in Prishtina.

In the woods and villages of central and western Kosova—in a small, tentative way—the open war had started. On 21 April a medical student, Armend Daci, was killed in Prishtina; a Serb fired a rifle into his apartment, and the shot went into Armend's heart. The women's forum of the Kosova Democratic League organised a candle-lit vigil at the site of his murder, and then organised a demonstration of 10,000 people without asking the LDK leadership for permission. In the craven and dependent world of the LDK at that time, some elements in the leadership acted as local agents for the Milošević police state. On 22 April five Serb policemen were killed and five more wounded in attacks at Peje, Stimlje and Decani, and on the Mitrovica-Peje road Dragana Nesić was killed and Slobodan Dudić wounded in an attack on a police vehicle. The media in Kosova had given little space to the killings, but the BBC stated that an organisation calling itself the Liberation Army of Kosova—Ushtria Climitare e Kosoves (UCK)—was responsible, and that such actions were a warning to the world that support given to the Serbian aggressors while the will of the occupied people of Kosova was ignored could only lead to continuation of the armed struggle in Kosova and the conflict in the Balkans generally.

When I read in a local newspaper that in an interview with a Belgian newspaper Rugova had said the killings were a provocation by Serbian extremists, I felt a ghastly sinking feeling. If even the Serbs knew that this was the real thing—the beginning of the war for Kosova—why did Rugova deny the obvious? I remembered Miranda telling me a month before in our favourite pub that she thought Rugova would never break with Belgrade. So what was happening, and how could it be understood? I went again to see Miki Vasić, then a more or less infallible guide to Kosova Serb opinion. Prishtina was crawling with heavily-armed blue-uniformed MUP, staring at foreigners as though a look could kill. The politics of Star Wars villain Darth Vader were taking over the town. A man in an Arkan beret sat cleaning his gun in the grocer's shop opposite the house of the University rector. He took it up, aimed it at a group of random Albanian passers-by, and then began cleaning it again. It was symbolic. I felt transparent—he would see through me and see the bones underneath.

I sat with Miki Vasić in the café on the concrete slab by the University library, and considered the options for the Kosovo Serbs.

The long untended grass around our feet was full of midges—the richness of a Kosova summer was about to break. The library is one of the weirdest public buildings in the Balkans, a mess of modernist versions of Ottoman domes, lost on a Prishtina hillside. It was a crazily appropriate place to discuss the coming explosion.

'It would be better to have a war against them than live through a long terrorist campaign. The Israelis found that.'

Miki was a short and tough middle-aged man with a crew-cut who wore jeans and a leather jacket. He taught at the University, a real Kosova Serb in his presentation of himself, though rumoured to be partly of Jewish descent; he said he came from Macedonia. He loved Kosova women, whom he called his chickens, and always had a new one whom he had met dancing at the seedy El Greco restaurant frequented by sanctions-busters up from Thessaloniki, men with big stomachs and chunky gold rings. He lived with his elderly mother, who was in a permanent state of siege in her Dragodan flat and hated people even ringing up for Miki; perhaps she was jealous of all his girls. Nobody really knew where Miki stood. Most journalists ended up thinking he was in the secret police but that may not have been true. He had been with Milošević in the early days and run the Serbian Information Office, and in that position was the main point of contact for foreign journalists. When Catherine Seddon was making her Kosova film for the BBC in 1993, he was the main fixer for the Milošević people, and certainly seemed to get on with them—whoever 'them' might be. Then he fell out with Belgrade— the details were obscure. On some occasions he was astonishingly critical of the regime. Kosova was like that.

Did they wish to drive out the Albanians? In fact, yes. Milošević was reviving the 1930s theory of Vladislav Cubrilović, who wrote the first coherent plan to subject Kosova to ethnic cleansing. There would have to be a war and many would be killed or have to leave. There were too many Albanians, that was the simple fact. One of Miki's peculiarities was his obviously genuine love of Irish poetry and literature—every time I went to Kosova he would ask me to bring a new book to add to his Irish collection. Possibly he saw the Serbs as the Irish of the Balkans—perhaps not easy to deal with, but charming, full of character and lovers of the arts. In some ways he seemed too unconventional to be a Prishtina apparatchik, and I sometimes wondered if he really worked for Mossad, the Israeli government secret intelligence agency, which at that time provided the brains for Yugoslavia in all sorts of subtle ways; it was rumoured that one of its largest foreign operations was in Belgrade. The boss was supposed to go to Cyprus to help the regime sort out its finances. Milošević had been a banker and valued such people. Mrs Vućić, his financial wizard, was said to be Jewish.

At the same time Veton Surroi was more mysterious than usual. It was he who had said to me in London a little while before that it was time I came to Kosova again—it had been too long since my last visit. Personal matters, other work and visa problems had intervened. It was all too familiar, dealing with Veton, seeking his opinion. But now the war had come, and as in all wars there was the sense of the ground moving, cracks, tremors, uncertainties about what is to come. Certainly there was war in the present, Miki Vasić was right about that. But war was also emerging from the past, and I did not know what that past was and how to deal with it. But then nobody else did either. I went to see him in his office, and he insisted that we talked in the corridor. I asked the necessary, inevitable question: 'The Kosova Liberation Army. Who are they? Do they exist?'

'They do exist, yes, they are real. They are very underground and very conspiratorial.'

I had asked him if the new military force existed. It was a silly question, in retrospect. He had said all that needed to be said, for years ahead.

What was the immediate past in Kosova in 1996? How could it be understood? It took me years, seeing it only in glimpses as an outsider, to begin to get to grips with this conundrum. The world of Kosova after the Second World War was little known or understood in the outside world. There had been resistance to Tito, and fighting on a serious scale had continued till 1949. Some Albanians on the losing side had gone to Turkey, while others had stayed to fight on for the Albanian identity in Kosova. This issue had split many villages, and still does to this day; those who stayed did not always take kindly to those who had left. They had followed a quietly heroic path by refusing to adopt the Turkish identity forced on them by the Titoists; to have the pride and glory of being an Albanian, they had

opted for the poverty of the villages. The farms never had any
money to restore their great gates after a Serbocommunist police
truck had crashed into them for the tenth time. They were the front
line in the repression of the Albanians. They had made a hard
choice. What had happened to the people who had gone to Turkey? Nobody knew. Sometimes flashy Turkish coaches came from
Bursa or Istanbul loaded with people, full of black plastic sacks
stuffed with good Turkish clothes for the family.

Then the present intruded suddenly and brutally. In Prishtina I
had gone out for a meal with a colleague to the hotel outside
Prishtina on Kosova Polje, and found that the old watering-hole had
been taken over by gangsters from Bosnia, wild Bosnian Serbs with
long black pigtails held by silver rings, and staring eyes. They looked
like cocaine types, and had an entourage of thuggish local young
men in shell suits and tracksuits, the Kosova fry following the bigger
predators from the north, the barracudas, sharks and conger eels of
the dangerous Bosnian sea. It now cost over £100 a night to stay
there. Foreigners were unwelcome, particularly English-speaking
ones. In a gloomy corner of the bar a group were playing cards with
Deutschmarks stacked high on the table, enough to keep a Kosova
village fed for a week. The hotel used to have a nice garden; roses
grow well in Kosova and the old Turkish varieties are wonderfully
scented and on a warm summer night give a garden a special richness,
but these men smelt of blood, spewed guts and spent ammunition.

The area west of Prishtina towards the massive dusty lignite power
stations at Obiliq had always been doubtful at best, with the little
railway station a centre of cigarette smuggling for many years. The
presence of the Bosnian gangsters was particularly worrying; being
hardened and used to war and especially its profits, they would not
have bothered to come down to Kosova unless they thought there
were going to be some. The only consolation was that they did not
look as if they were about to volunteer to fight for Holy Serbia,
unlike the intense young men who proliferated in Kosova in 1992,
when there was still a lot of idealism about. Now we had all·got used
to war, it was very easy to relax into the routine: war for many people means business. Miranda and I were no different, our book on
Albania after communism and the world of Sali Berisha was already
exciting prepublication interest. Without the war and political struggles associated with it the book would just be another obscure aca-

demic volume, but my war was different, being against those areas of academia notoriously opposed to Balkan Studies like St Antony's College in Oxford. Under the Milošević regime gangster capitalism was gripping Kosova by the throat. Violence was spreading like a fog. In 1992 Arkan had been seen as a protector and and even a liberator, and Kosova was oddly quiet, despite the frequent prognostications in the intelligence community about an uprising. Now the war was here and there were dead bodies, but no one in Whitehall realised it. My story for the *Wall Street Journal Europe* and a piece Miranda Vickers wrote for *The European* on 20 June were attacked by the FCO media machine as exaggerated and alarmist. I sometimes felt as if we were working for Tantalus, trying to roll a great stone up a hill and finding it always rolling back down towards us.

I needed time to think, which it was impossible to do clearly in Prishtina. Dust from the Obiliq power station chimneys clogged the brain cells. Friends from the chattering classes seemed even further from reality than usual. Prishtina intellectuals sat in cold cafés smoking and talking about French films and post-Modernism and forgot what was happening in the villages. Rugova did not forget, even if he patronised his villagers and took them for granted, and had a very incomplete notion of what was happening. He thought in little Rugova myths, and knew the history of every village in Kosova and made a little myth about it. This has never changed; in the 2001 election campaign he was talking about the need for Kosova to be protected by the Sar dog—the massive, beautiful animal that guards Kosova sheep from wolves and bears. This was the myth, whereas the reality was that Kosova needed an army. When one—the KLA—was born, he was so lost in the myth that he could not see that a new Albanian army was actually there.

I took the bus to Prizren. Its light was always clearer, it was close to the freedom of Albania, there was the timeless beauty of the river flowing through it like the great stream of Balkan history that had never dried up there since the Romans built their town called Theranda. It was also a mixed town, with its large Turkish minority and relatively modest and peaceful Serbs, the oldest Serbian community in Kosova. Bumbling, elderly, washed up by history, they were worlds apart from the steelhard thugs working for Arkan in central

Prishtina. My friend Sabet Jusufi is a jeweller there, his Omega shop on a street corner near the bus station. He is rotund and genial, a qualified master watch craftsman who had lived in Switzerland for many years. A patriot who on the surface was a model of respectability and political moderation, he used his wide-ranging contacts in the Swiss Albanian dispora to perform many essential services for the national movement. He promised to take me one day to his village in the Sar mountains south of Prizren, but it was a dream; we both knew it would be illegal for him to have a foreigner in his house there overnight, and a day trip up there in the wilds of the Sar would be impossible. Sabet had a little nostalgia for the old Yugoslavia; he thought Ante Marković might have succeeded in his 1990 reform programme with more support from the West, and the total dominance of Milošević might have been avoided. Like many older Albanians, he saw things in personal terms: the personality of the leader of Yugoslavia was what mattered. This was a heritage from Titoism, and it affects the ideas of many foreign observers to this day. So unable to make this village visit, we always talked in his shop sitting on little stools, he with his eyeglass clamped firmly in his left eye or swinging on a cord from his neck. His shop temporarily became an embassy for Kosova, a tiny safe house in a hostile, dangerous and beautiful city.

In those days after the signing of the 1995 Dayton Accords there had been an effort to brush up the police image, and in less tense cities like Prizren the ubiquitous blue combat fatigues were replaced by flashy uniforms with white belts. It was very strange. A very tall man with a black moustache stood on the pavement opposite Sabet's shop in this strange outfit, with a fixed, rather weird smile on his face. He only carried a small handgun at his waist, the vicious-looking sub-machine guns normally carried by MUP personnel were not in evidence. To him we must have appeared as part of the 'good' Kosova, or at least the 'better' Kosova—a local Albanian businessman of neat, conservative appearance serving a foreign customer. Sabet was not on any black or grey list and was thought by the Serbs to be a loyal Rugova supporter who had never been in trouble with the police. The Serbs in those days always distinguished between urban Kosovars, who in their private view were on the way to some sort of civilisation (their own, run from Belgrade), and the rural Albanian

people whom they regarded as little better than wild animals. But in
the little shop we were safe, and free to talk—about survival, the
nature of Kosova life, whether Yugoslavia could ever survive,
whether Kosova might ever see the world of the 1980s return, a
paradise time for Sabet when he prospered and became an official of
the Swiss watch-repairers' association and could travel where he
liked, finances permitting. Now he had not been allowed to renew
his passport and never left Prizren, his formerly wide horizons
shrunk to the workbench in his little shop. There was nevertheless
much to be learned from him: how a town like Prizren worked, its
fierce and justified pride in its culture and traditions, the strong
Turkish thread in the culture of many inhabitants, even including
some of the Serbs who sat poor and unemployed in the café by the
Ottoman arched bridge just above the turbulent mountain river.

His views were always an index of mainstream Kosova Albanian
opinion, and I always looked forward to seeing him. I wondered if
Rugova's claims about an influx of Serb refugees were justified. In
Prizren it was doubtful. There did not seem to be many Serb refugees in the town, although I had seen a new settlement being built
close to the main road to Gjakova—rows of mini-bungalows in
open fields, with no facilities whatever. The Milošević regime was
not very generous to its own refugees, and this oddly suburban construction seemed quite deserted. It was not hard to see why. If you
had just been driven from your house by Muslims in Bosnia, you
were not likely to rush to move into a more than 90 per cent Albanian 'Muslim' community in Kosova. It was a cynical new form of
colonisation by the Belgrade government. As Rugova correctly said,
there was plenty of room for them in Serbia itself. I telephoned *The
Times* to see if they were interested in a refugee story, but post-
Bosnia the paper in common with the rest of Fleet Street was suffering from Balkan fatigue, and the Desk was not interested. This was
depressing; if the newspaper did not want any copy, I could not file
any expenses (work in Kosova was anyway run on a shoestring in
those days). There was a strong pro-American current on the Desk,
which I shared, but it was taken too far, to the extent that after the
great US achievement at Dayton the problems of the Balkans were
believed to have been solved. Unfortunately this understandable
view was partly responsible for the massive crisis over Kosova that

was to come in 1998 and 1999. With so little prior reporting published in 1996 and 1997, the nature and depth of the crisis were not
understood, even by the best educated and informed of British and
US public opinion. My old Foreign Editor at the *Independent*, Godfrey Hodgson, once compared the press to a lighthouse where the
beam swung around, briefly illuminated something, then left it in
darkness. That was how it seemed to me with Kosova. On the other
hand, readers could get Balkan fatigue too, and the experienced
Desk staff at Wapping like Denis Taylor and David Watts usually
had an accurate instinct for what was in people's minds as they
opened their newspapers in the morning.

Back in Kosova the military forces on both sides were getting organised for the war to come. Rugova's party office had a more and more
irrelevant air and was often half-empty, and not worth the struggle
to visit it through the deep mud and filth behind the football stadium. Violent incidents proliferated. On 2 August several explosions
ripped through MUP stations in Prishtina and Podujeve, and dozens
of people were beaten and detained in gaol. Podujeve was particularly tense. Rugova condemned the 'terrorist acts'. Arkan visited the
damaged police stations and demanded that the police take 'concrete measures' against the 'terrorists', and added that the police
baton had two ends 'and that the second beats better', a clear warning to the Albanians that if necessary his volunteers would be able to
help the police. It was clear what a Kosova war would be like, with
massive attacks by Serb paramilitaries on the civilian population. I
had met Arkan in Belgrade after a press conference three months
before, when he had been on model behaviour in a smart grey suit,
said good-morning politely and introduced me to his son, a nervous
youth with spiky blond hair.

Arkan had explained to me at some length how his mother came
from Kosova and I was free to visit her and talk about the problems
of the Kosova Serbs at any time. After Dayton, he was trying to
change his image to that of the respectable businessman and family
man, and there was not a single leather-jacketed heavy to be seen in
the room. His Hollywood-style house in the posh diplomatic suburb
of Dedinje was only guarded by a single black-suited security man.
Diplomats' wives shopped at his bakery, said to have the best bread in

Belgrade, and he appeared to be becoming a model citizen. In the Dedinje pecking order, his Hollywood mansion was becoming over-shadowed by the vast crenellated mansion being built for Bogoljub Karić, the stupendously rich denizen of the Karić banking family and one-time Milošević associate. In the press conference Arkan had neatly fielded a question from a Canadian CNN correspondent, and went out of his way to be nice to CNN. We were told that the main reason why he was holding the event was to dispel rumours that his political party was planning to stand against Milošević in the coming Serbian elections. In the odd world of Belgrade then, this was thought to be a major news event. There were always elections in Serbia; if measured by the number of elections, the country would have been numbered among the most democratic in the world. In Belgrade, European normality was the name of the game. I left Arkan wondering if the Tigers would soon be learning to play cricket, such was the admiration he had for Britain.

On the other side, I had also met Ibrahim Rugova in May when he was uncommunicative. We were part of the same world, but at war. However, the war did not touch most of Kosova, which was at 'peace'. Both leaders condemned 'terrorism'. The story was moving, but in a way that made working out how to report it in a balanced or truthful way almost impossible. If I had filed something for *The Times* which started off by saying that Arkan and Rugova had said the same things about attacks on Kosova police stations (which in any case I had not seen), it would understandably have been impaled on the sharpest spike in the newsroom in record time. In late 1993 Arkan had been a discredited figure in Kosovo Serb circles, and now he was active again, bright, cheerful, aspirational. The view in the British intelligence scene was that he was no more than a puppet of Milošević, a rational view at one level, but one that begged many questions. The central political question for the future was how far Rugova and the LDK were also becoming part of the Kosova past, and that was not material for a news story either. It was a difficult time.

It was also a difficult time for reporting in Belgrade. In December I visited Ivor and Elizabeth Roberts at the British embassy and found the city dominated by huge demonstrations against the government which were addressed by fiery speakers who denounced the Milošević regime. In the Dedinje diplomatic quarter there was little confidence that they would succeed, and Zoran Djinjić, the main protest leader and after October 2000 the Serbian Prime Minister, was still tainted in British eyes by his associations with the Bosnian Serbs. He was also seen as a protégé of the Germans and the Americans, the *bêtes noires* in Balkan terms of the Major government in London and much of the officer corps of the British army in Bosnia. There was still a firm commitment in London to the Milošević regime, and little wish for a change of government. The emphasis was on making Dayton work, with vague and unspecified 'reforms' and little else. Over the Sava bridges, the old battered city was dark and cavernous and full of secret and open policemen, but sullen and menacing rather than seriously dangerous. Life can be very cheap in Belgrade, but this was not one of those times. I wanted to write something on the demonstrations and spent the afternoon of 12 December following the hundreds of thousands of people trooping through the damp cold streets, with doctors in white coats, nurses in their uniforms and every possible variety of ordinary workers, many of whom had not been paid for months. The mood was serious and angry but there was little sign of any revolutionary fervour or a real willingness to confront the regime, let alone with violence. When the protesters were asked by the police to leave the key Dedinje political quarter alone, they did so.

The Times asked for copy, and later in the day I tried to file from the old Hotel Beograd, in a downtown street near the beautiful old railway station. The phone was hopeless and many other downtown lines I tried seemed to have been cut by the police. Reluctantly, therefore, I went back to the embassy residence, where I was staying, and filed from there. I wrote that 'a great human snake is passing through Belgrade, bringing the city to a halt', but that 'the police have more than adequate resources', and 'without support from the industrial workers or foreign governments, or both, Mr Milošević can sit out protests more or less indefinitely.' And I quoted a waiter who told me that 'the Americans would not know what to do without Milošević to hate', and that Bill Clinton was only making verbal threats about reintroducing sanctions. Little was happening on the key industrial front; some factories were holding short strikes, but 'the trades unions have yet to show that they are able to organise a national protest.'

It was all standard commonsense material in my opinion, with plenty of voices from the Belgrade street, but there was a furious reaction in official London, particularly to a section of the story which described anti-British drawings on a banner condemning the alleged association of the British embassy with the Milošević regime. The story was removed, for whatever reason, from later editions of the paper on 13 December, after it had run as more or less uncut copy in the first international edition. I discussed this with Ivor Roberts, who apart from his other qualities is one of the few senior British diplomats who actually understands foreign journalism and its problems. He was sympathetic but conveyed the impression of a large authoritarian machine operating above us that was quite indifferent to the rights of news organisations. I gathered that I was regarded by some in the FCO security scene and MI6 as an Albanian spy in the embassy residence. Only five months before I had been an official British speaker at the Sava Centre Kosova conference.

Once again there was incontrovertible evidence of the extraordinary hold the Milošević machine had in London under the Conservative government, and that little could be expected from diplomacy for democratising Serbia, let alone Kosova. A British propaganda machine had been set up to 'defend Dayton', and Serbian democracy, human rights and Kosova were expendable. Now British readers of *The Times* on the London underground train or in the farm kitchens of Worcestershire would not know how unpopular the pro-Milošević policy of the Major government was in many liberal and opposition quarters in Serbia; and would not know that they did not know.

Leaving Belgrade a few days later to return home for Christmas, I was sure 1997 would bring renewed violence to the region, because in this coercive and totalitarian atmosphere, where Western governments were hand-in-glove with Milošević, even the most pacific Kosovar Albanians would see that they had little to lose by taking up arms against Serbia. Democracy in Belgrade had been sacrificed to 'protect Bosnia', as a friend on the train said to me. When I took up the issue with the Desk on my return, I was told that 'important news' had come in from America, which displaced my Belgrade opposition story from the later editions.

Guns for hire

The road from Kosova to Albania is hard, like many other things in northern Albanian life. In those days no warm and sociable buses travelled in that dangerous territory, only isolated cars. The rutted and potholed asphalt winds across the windy, cold and austere dry limestone highlands under the looming peak of Mount Koritnik before dropping into the White Drin valley and winding down to Kukes. But despite the potholes, it is the only hard-surfaced road for miles around. Kukes used to be Ottoman Kukush, a little mountain town where the White Drin meets the Black Drin and the rivers merge to start their long journey across some of the lonelinest and wildest country in Europe before running into the Adriatic across the wide gravel delta near Shkodra. In the old days you could occasionally meet Kosovars travelling this road, and in 1993 I had a lift from a wealthy flour merchant with a business in Switzerland that brought him a superb Mercedes coupé. He was a strong critic of the Rugova leadership and I had the feeling he was on a political assignment of some kind. But in those days you did not ask questions about such things, but merely listened and were grateful if people told you something. Sometimes, as in a Pinter play, the silences meant more than the words. He fiddled with the radio and drove with one hand on the wheel.

'Kosova cannot carry on as it is,' he said.

There was a long pause and he found a station with Shkodra music, a piercing hard *lauta* tune—in my mind's eye I could see the great lake and the cormorants quiet and studious on their rocks. Their eyes would glint down at the fishy water, a rich feast in the poor Great Mountain Country.

'Kosova will change, we will make it change. In time.'

Up here in the mountains hundreds of miles east, the vast cloud formations hung over the surging White Drin. As we drove down, the occasional flock and soaking wet shepherd in a cape were the only signs of human life. This was Ismail Kadare's Great Northern Plateau, with its Homeric scale and intensity. The battle to come for Kosova would be extraordinary, as we knew in our hearts, but no one could foretell how it would have to be fought, from the sacrifices ordinary families would have to make to free themselves from Serbian rule, to the precision of the cruise missile launched from a ship in the Adriatic that destroyed Prishtina post office. The drama would stretch across continents, from the esoteric technology of USAF Strategic Air Command in Omaha, Nebraska, to the little hand-dug trenches in the woods on Mount Pashtrik—such as a Roman centurion might have ordered his men to dig. The Yugoslav army would lay wires through the undergrowth, a little hook at the end of the wire would explode the booby-trap, you would become human meat, bits of flesh hanging in the oak scrub. A wandering fox might come along and eat you. But that was five years ahead. The Drin was sending a warning in that lonely drive, a sense of the inadequacy of the individual to face and take part in such a struggle. The vastness and majesty of the Drin valley was a warning to us, the northern landscape as an oracle. The quartz veins in the limestone glittered in the sun, the car bumped its way through the muddy rutted road. It was far from its Stuttgart origins, my benefactor's wonderful solid Mercedes, the nearest approach the motor industry has yet made to creating immortality in metal. It was our little black train, as in the Woodie Guthrie song—we were on it, not on the way to a million-dollar fortune but to a war. If it was your final ride, you would die in the war, get whacked, as the British army prefers to say. At the moment its most important job was to take us safely across the border into Albania. At the border were a few tired and shivering officials, trying to be helpful for a payment of ten dollars. A hungry dog looked at us from the passport office steps.

This year the struggle for Kosova was to move here, to Albania. Dr Berisha's government would be overthrown, and this would have a fundamental effect on Kosova. In the view of the numerous purveyors of received ideas in the international community, 1997 was the year when the Albanians lunatics would finally seize control of their bleak and mountainous asylum, and the Albanian Question in the Balkans would move on to the international stage. In their view this began the chain of events leading to disaster for the 'Balkan peace process' that had triumphed at Dayton, Ohio, in October 1995. Others saw in it a more positive side. The end of Sali Berisha's time in power enabled the Albanian people to grasp more fully their Balkan destiny, and broke the main control mechanism of the internationals over the Albanian national question. Thus the flood of freedom and genuine political struggle for Albanian human rights and national freedom would develop fully. The Kosovars were to owe a great deal to the impoverished workers and their families in places like the Albanian Adriatic coast town of Vlora which most of them had never seen.

In the dry and windy streets of Tirana in January there was no way of knowing the scale of the storm to come that would put Albania on the front pages of newspapers, and transform the atmosphere in Kosova. A cold blast came down from the snow on Mount Daiti to the east of the turbulent, poor but wonderful little city that has been the Albanian capital since 1912. Tirana is a long way from the northern plateau, oranges hang in the winter sun in chaotic old Ottoman house gardens with whitewashed walls. The wind from the Adriatic an hour away stirs the dust. This winter wind often chills and dampens the streets, and brings cheap anoraks and leather gloves on to the stalls of the street vendors. Then it blew where angry depositors had lost all their savings in the collapse of the Sudja pyramid banking scheme. Hard-won money from work on Greek building sites had disappeared into thin air. Interest rates of fifty or sixty per cent had produced a bubble that eventually had to burst.

The angry creditors were besieging the Sudja offices in central Tirana (actually the little old house of Mrs Sudja, the bank proprietor), smoking, jostling, shouting insults, thin women with babies out for revenge, burly leather-jacketed men who ate too much *burek*, children shelling sunflower seeds to chew for a while before spitting them out. The star of the show or villian of the piece soon appeared, with all that sense of weird melodrama that has always affected the politics of the city. Mrs Sudja was a large and wonderfully self-confident Roma lady who suddenly swept on to her balcony holding a well-charged chamber-pot, which she emptied over the crowd. The TV cameras and press pack whirled. The Tirana streets were alive again, for the first time since the overthrow of communism in 1991, when the same people had toppled the huge gilded statue of Enver Hoxha and the power of Europe's most severe regime. Nobody in the crowd had any doubt she had just pissed into it, and perhaps her friends had as well, to ceremonially anoint the people she had de-frauded. A picture by William Hogarth of eighteenth-century London street life had suddenly moved to Albania. The depositors were in a rage, and someone threw half a brick up at the balcony that crashed through a plate-glass window. Slivers of glass covered the front row of the crowd. The series of events that was to last five months and destroy the Democratic Party government and later play a vital part in ending Serb power in Kosova was beginning. The bar was about to open, the saloon would never shut, however many bad or good guys came into town. The guests were arriving, hidden in huge old cars with smoked glass windows from different parts of Albania, those that the government had swindled and betrayed, like the thickset chain-smoking army officers in the south, the miserably poor from the Cole district in Vlora, the farmers and grape-growers of Shkrapar. The army officers had told their hapless conscripts that there were only beans to eat in the barracks and then one day the beans ran out. The waiters were filling all their glasses; nobody knew what was in the bottle. The only certainty was the old Enverist idea that in Albania the people were sovereign, and Berisha was bringing in more and more foreigners who were directing the country and stealing all the money. They drove four-wheel-drive monsters with names like Land Rover and Toyota and sometimes killed your sheep or goats as they tried to cross the road in the way they had always done.

In the bottle was a lethal heady brew that nobody had drunk before, a poison for the neo-communists whom the internationals had bankrolled and called Democrats. The crowd shouted to Mrs Sudja that she should go back to the gypsy quarter where she had started off as a local moneylender. Before that she was supposed to have taken in washing to make a living, and her problems now gave a new meaning to the term money laundering. But it was a sign that Tirana politics were moving back towards the street—which, in the opinion of many good judges, was always their epicentre. The power of the government was vapourising.

The police watched from a distance and plotted small deals among themselves, indifferent to Mrs Şudja and her grubby fate. Tirana had an unredeemed nineteenth-century quality after the fall of communism, there was a driving sense of the revolutionary crowd and its power that Walter Benjamin would have recognised writing about the Paris Commune in 1871. It is very different from the dull suburbanite individualism, the sad geranium-watering and dog-walking concerns of post-1989 Hungary and Poland where the most exciting thing in life was to visit the foreign-owned supermarket. There was nothing in Tirana to compare with the ruination of Prague by commercialism. It was about to become an important place in Europe. The foreign policy establishments hated the fact that they would not be able to control and manipulate events in this small, strange, difficult country. The chatterers in Prishtina were always complaining how cultured they were and how uncouth and rude Tirana was, but as events later in the year were to show, in Ronald Reagan's famous phrase, they hadn't seen nothing yet. The people in the Albanian streets were to liberate the weapons that would help change life in Kosova for ever, and start the process that would destroy the traditional world of bureaucratic communism and Slobodan Milošević hundreds of miles away to the northeast across so many wooded hilltops and savage mountains. What was this weapon?

A short history of a legendary weapon: the Automat Kalashnikov (AK-47)

There is something unique about the sound of a Kalashnikov AK-47, a pneumatic repetitive phut-a-phut, rat-a tat, that once heard is never forgotten. An AK fired into the air sends a magic chill down the arm that holds it, the six hundred rounds a minute spinning straight up two miles into the air before turning round and making the long fast journey back to earth. It can kill on the way up, it can kill on the way down. It is a gun that will turn the most pacific and unmilitary of human beings into potential street warriors, just as those least interested in cars can be moved by the sight of a 1930s Bugatti or a Mercedes Benz Cabriolet. In its own way the AK has an equivalent mystique: the cold metal speaks. It is best fired with a straight and extended arm with the body well balanced and the knees bent and a little more weight on the foot further away from the weapon. Then there is not merely the chill of the first recoil, but a long shuddering echo of vibration coming back up from the earth where you stand. This is not just the adrenalin rush similar to that of a foot on a 300SL accelerator pedal, although that element is there; the earth is sending a message back that history can be changed and the powerful are not always as powerful as they may seem to be.

There was once a Soviet army officer called Mikhail Kalashnikov, whose personal history was the stuff of legend. Born in 1919, he had the Russian equivalent of a high school degree and worked for the Turkestan-Siberian railroad system until he was drafted into the Red Army in 1938. In the army he became fascinated with the operations of firearms and a latent genius for mechanical inventions was awakened in him. One of his superiors noted this interest and enrolled him in an armourers' training course.

In addition to gaining basic armourer skills, Kalashnikov became a tank driver, and soon invented several devices for use in tanks. These inventions helped him gain a number of military promotions as well as a job as technical supervisor in the factory making the inventions he had created for Soviet tanks. Given his interest in firearms, the experience of seeing modern machining operations probably influenced the later design of his AK rifles.

In 1941 Kalashnikov was called to active duty and fought in the battle for Bryansk. His tank was hit by a shell and he found himself in hospital with a wounded arm. While convalescing he made good use of his time by studying all the firearms books he could lay hands on. Because of the seriousness of his wound, Kalashnikov was allowed six months' leave after being released from hospital. He spent the time in his home town Alma-Ata designing a sub-machine gun which a machinist friend, Zhenya Kravchenko, helped him fabricate. Once Kalashnikov had a model of the sub-machine gun, he took it to various communist officials in Alma-Ata until he found one who was interested in sponsoring him to continue work on the new firearm. This official got Kalashnikov a job in the model shops of the Moskovsky Aviasionniy Institut, which had luckily just been transferred to Alma-Ata.

After the war, from 1946 to 1948, work progressed on the Kalashnikov rifle. As with other modern weapons, progress was slow, with changes having to be made every step of the way. But the final result was extraordinary, a gun that still worked more or less whatever you did to it, like the Nikon F3 cameras the Vietnam war photographers would hide in a bucket of water when the secret police came for the film. The F3 and its film would come out of the bucket as good as it went in.[2]

---

[2] I am indebted for this information on the history of the AK-47 Kalashnikov to Duncan Long, and his authoritative work *The Complete Kalashnikov Family of Assault Rifles* (Boulder, CO, 1988).

Although the birth of the AK-47 was slow, in Albania it speeded history up. Out of 70 million Kalashnikovs that have been produced world-wide, Albania stored about 600,000 in local magazines in March 1997. They were not fated to remain in store for long. They were the product of Enver Hoxha's defence doctrine, where an armed people, imbued with the magic of his ideas, would be able to defeat a Warsaw Pact or Western invasion. It was a highly optimistic view, and the best known and still visible product of the defence plan resulting from it has been the hundreds of thousands of little concrete bunkers that litter the Albanian countryside. The general derision these little boxes have understandably produced among foreign and diplomatic visitors to Albania perhaps blinded them to other, less obvious and more effective elements in communist defence strategy. The local magazines, little grey stone sheds near police stations stored with a good supply of AK-47s, were to have much more tangible results. Although by 1997 six years had passed since the one-party state had collapsed, little had changed in the Albanian military world except that Sali Berisha had sacked most of the more competent officers in the army and replaced them with friends from northern Albania who may have been anti-communist politically but had no useful or relevant military experience. The Defence Minister Safet Zuhali was a former teacher of maths in high school.

Although in January 1997 the outside world did not know it, the Albanian army was on the point of collapse. Some years later on a cold winter night in Kosova my friend Denny Lane, then an outstanding United Nations administrator in Kosova but once Colonel C. Dennison Lane, Green Beret in Vietnam and sometime Defence Adviser to the Albanian government, told me that in 1996 the army was 'doomed'.[3] It was not what his masters in the Pentagon and NATO wanted to hear, and like many messengers in time of war and conflict since Cassandra, Denny lost his job, four months before the 1997 uprising. In the traditional context of loyal US satrap rulers, the Tirana Democrats were ideal, and some in the Pentagon did not wish to hear about any problems. I first heard this from Denny in 2001 and it was reassuring to know how the grip of the Serbs and the Berisha myth on mainstream political and diplomatic thinking

[3] See 'Once upon an army' by C. Dennison Lane, CSRC G-114, September 2002, www.csrc.ac.uk.

could ruin the jobs of a mainstream and distinguished military man such as Denny, and of academics and writers like Miranda Vickers and myself. But in the months to come the dance of the Kalashnikovs would begin, and the people who had them would become the new Sultans, a popular uprising would come to the streets, and the government would fall, in the first successful armed uprising in mainland Europe since the Second World War.

I had filed to *The Times* on Mrs Sudja and her business problems, and all was well with the Foreign Desk, but three or four weeks later the uprising began in southern Albania, first in the Greek-minority areas, and it was clear that a big story was going to break where many journalistic skills would be needed. Millions of dollars were being lost every day as the main pyramid banks in the big towns collapsed, including VEFA, the biggest of them all. It was difficult to know what to do, there would certainly be a big demand from the networks like CNN and the BBC World Service for expert comment, and the last thing I wanted was for the media in Britain to be dominated by the pro-Democratic Party acolytes of the Oxford Helsinki Human Rights Group, an advocacy organisation of the hard right. Miranda, Sir Reginald Hibbert and I had already crossed swords with them over their defence of the Berisha government's behaviour in the May 1996 election manipulation.

On the other hand, it was vital to get back to Albania as soon as possible to see at first hand what was happening. *The Times* seemed to have been advised by intelligence service contacts in the regular FCO news briefings for journalists that this was a serious event and an Albanian civil war was possible between the Tosk south and the Gheg north. This crude formulation was to dominate many official perceptions for the next two months, although it did contain an element of truth. The Berisha government was a very northern affair. Rapid decisions were made by the Wapping management. The war reporter Antony Loyd had come into southern Albania, and Richard Owen, a distinguished figure, had travelled to Tirana from Rome. I was still technically a freelance but as I wrote most of my material for *The Times* and was sometimes billed on CNN and elsewhere as a *Times* journalist, I was regarded as such in the outside world. This caused problems in Wapping that were never satisfactorily resolved. I think Graham Patterson, the foreign editor, and Peter Stothard, the editor, felt that I might be getting a little close to the story and that fresh eyes were needed. But nobody actually tried to stop me returning, as it seemed to me essential to do.

The first TV pictures showed the people of the small town of Sarande near the Greek border taking over the streets, and Berisha was moving troops into the region. He sent a MiG to try to bomb the little town of Delvina, near Sarande—a farce which only strengthened opposition to the government. I knew the area fairly well, and it was clear to me that the nearby city of Gjirokastra held the military key to the whole situation. I had also heard on the grapevine in Greece about plots and plans by disaffected nationalist army officers loyal to the ideas of Enver Hoxha who were said to be working with the Greek secret intelligence service against Berisha. Relations with between Greece and Berisha were poor in those years, and these people were likely to be the leaders of the people's committees that were taking over the southern towns and villages. Gjirokastra, dominating the main road north from Greece to Tirana, had a fierce and uncompromising quality with its craggy citadel and dramatic mountain fastness above the Vjoses river which had fascinated Byron and his friends in 1809. It was a frontier town with magnificent houses with grey drystone walls a metre thick. Enver Hoxha himself had grown up there and it was also the home town of the novelist and storyteller Ismail Kadare. If Gjirokastra joined the opposition every household in Albania would know that this was a serious attempt to overthrow the government.

On 9 March the city changed hands and the uprising spread across the south, having begun in Gjirokastra. At eleven o'clock in the morning I had been drinking coffee sitting on a sweetly patterened old Ottoman rug in the Bektashi *tekke*, listening to the Baba expounding Shi'ite doctrine as it developed among the Albanian Sufi mystics. This *tekke* was founded in the nineteenth century by missionaries from Gjakova in Kosova, so there was a distant link. At mid-day the last members of Berisha's party still in Gjirokastra fled from the town hall in wildly driven black Mercedes heading north towards Tirana. As they went they slewed from one side of the road to the other and kicked up clouds of dust and stones. Soon afterwards, the sound of helicopters filled the valley as Berisha's Special Forces landed and tried to storm the town. But the people broke open the magazine and distributed the weapons to all and sundry. Girls as small as eight wielded AK-47s and the intruders were driven back to their helicopters parked in a field near the river by very unfriendly fire.

In the chaos of the fighting I did not know if Antony Loyd was even in the town, since he was somewhere down in the river valley near the magazine. Our street, about half way up the mountainside above the town centre, was taking fire from the opposite side of the valley—people loyal to Berisha, someone said. The occasional round dropped on to the rocky paths between the houses after hitting the high walls yards above our heads. But the fog of war does not take long to descend; it is a terrible but accurate cliché that once the fighting starts nobody knows what is going on except where one is, and possibly not even there. The BBC had nobody in Gjirokastra that day; Paul Wood was in Delvina, so I phoned in and was on all the main BBC news bulletins reporting that the town had changed hands, that this was no longer a minor disturbance but a major national event. The only telephone that worked was in the Greek consulate, and the wonderful generous consul, Nicholas Kanellos, organised a rota to use it and threw open his doors to all whom he could help. The natural caution and conservatism of the Greek minority in the south had been overcome by their loathing of Berisha—this even extended to Greek officialdom. By seven in the evening the town had become an armed camp and the ancient cita-del that had seen so many wars—Roman, Byzantine, Ottoman, twentieth-century—was again having artillery pieces set up under its walls. Lines of tracer fire ripped up into the clouds as the amateur gunmen swigged raki until they were scarcely steady enough to carry the ammunition across the road. A wild crowd from some-where up in the mountains came to the consulate door, announcing that they were '*Sigurimi*', and let off hundreds of rounds into the air. The air was heavy with gunsmoke, and splats of red fire from the AK-47s burst out across the alleyways between the large beys' houses. Spent brass bullet cases lay on the paved streets. A tall tough man in a leather jacket shot hundreds of rounds into the air. Nicho-las, an urban Athenian and a true man of peace, shook in his shoes but was not browbeaten, and quietly asked them to go away. You were not alive in Gjirokastra that night without an AK-47 at hand;

even little boys of kindergarten age ran around with plastic bags full of bullets. Albania was an armed society again. The great taboo Titoism had imposed—the disarming of the Albanians—was about to be broken, and it had started in the south, about as far in Albania from Kosova as you can be. It was very ironic.

President Berisha appeared on television, and called for this 'Partisan' activity to cease. All the journalists were crowded around a little black and white television in the Kotoni household, and a gentlemanly man from *Le Figaro* offered packets of Gauloises from his vast supply. The French journalists and cameramen were very brave and got some of the best coverage of the day. An Agence France-Presse cameraman lay flat on the roof inches from an artillery piece and he filmed it starting to lay down fire on the pro-Berisha positions across the valley. The television broadcast was very revealing. Berisha looked tired and nervous, and far from being master of the situation. He knew what the fall of Gjirokastra meant. The town was set in a swathe of mountains and crags, south of the Logara pass and west of the deep ravines above Sarquinishta and Glina, and the castle of Ali Pasha in Tepelena. Here all was lost for the foreigners' favourite Balkan President. His choice of words was interesting, the Partisan tradition (derived from popular national resistance to Fascist occupation in the Second World War) was the central tenet of Hoxhaist doctrine; it was how the country should be defended against foreign attack. It was not surprising he was afraid, he knew the force of Partisan warfare in the traditions and education of the people.

I was sharing a room with my friend Tim Judah, then working for the *Sunday Telegraph*. We bedded down in the grand old Kotoni house, not far from Enver Hoxha's birthplace, as the endless rat-a-tat of the dance of the Kalashnikovs echoed across the miles of fields below the towering snowy peaks of the Buret mountains. These bare mountains on the opposite side of the valley were covered in dry limestone scree. Gjirokastra, a hard uncompromising city of stone walls and forbidding stone houses, has seen much military drama and conflict in its long history, but it is doubtful whether it had seen a single day that was more dramatic and important than this. If Berisha's forces had been able to crush the people the uprising would have died, but as events turned out they did not, and the whole of southern Albania was there for the taking.

At dawn the next day, the occasional dark bird of prey drifted high above the River Vjoses, while the donkeys near the bus stop in the lower town were being loaded with weapons to take across the Aoos narrows to the waiting insurgents in Permet, about thirty miles to the north-east. This was the next strategically important town as the rising spread towards Tirana, the capital. In the north and in Kosova, the KLA was not slow to act upon the unexpected and unprecedented opportunity to buy weapons. Kosovars had nothing to do with the uprising but were among the first beneficiaries. Within two days, Kosovar arms traders would be in Gjirokastra with old pick-up trucks and wads of Deutschmarks, tall serious men speaking in thick northern accents, and with the driving energy and ruthless practicality that the Kosovars can muster in defence of their land. Two years earlier I had stood with Miranda Vickers on a hill near Sarande, twenty miles from Gjirokastra on the coast, observing a family of poverty-stricken Kosovars who had moved south trying to cultivate a rocky patch of poor land. Researching our book, we were trying to understand something of the effect of the Berisha government on migration from the north down to southern Albania. The man was sweating profusely as he dug in the sun. A line of pathetically old and faded clothes hung on a washing line against a dramatic and beautiful blue Adriatic seascape. It could have been pioneer Montana or Idaho in 1880, man against virgin soil, heroic workers' effort.

Then a Kosovar in southern Albania was an isolated, poverty-stricken curiosity, but the new KLA visitors were from a very different background, serious well-educated young men with a purpose. Some could speak German, often with a Swiss accent. They were superb organisers. The first Albanian diaspora forces were entering the fray, something new was coming to the Balkans from the rich streets of Geneva and Zurich, an ironic revenge of the poorest people in Europe, nurtured by little newspapers with names like *Zeri I Kosoves* that kept hopes of freedom alive.

I saw the same thing on the quayside at Durres a few weeks later and filed a fairly routine story about the small arms sales there that *The Times* ran in the paper the next day. Hundreds of AK-47s were being loaded into Kosovar car boots from an open-air arms market in the port. Thanks largely to David Watts, Denis Taylor and Des Houghton on the Foreign Desk I had written a number of analysis pieces about the causes of the crisis that had validated anti-Berisha positions. There was suddenly real interest in the fate of Albania. In Britain people went to car boot sales to buy books and china and spanners, in Gjirokastra and Durres you bought more lethal goods. Everyone knew what was coming, the least educated elderly southern peasant as much as the Swiss Kosovar intellectual working in the political underground with a degree in engineering from Zurich University. I walked along a narrow alleyway in Gjirokastra and saw a great commotion as a tiny old lady in black with broken spectacles seemed to be driving her chickens out of her henhouse, waving her arms madly and shouting at them. They squawked and flapped with their ginger-brown wings up a foot or two above the cobbles. When I looked in, the henhouse was stacked from floor to ceiling with munitions, mostly AK-47s. The chickens would have to lay their eggs for her in new surroundings, with military furnishings. In the Balkans everybody knows what to do when war approaches, knowledge is handed from generation to generation, even among poultry-keeping old ladies.

When I returned to London I ran into Joanna Hansen, a Foreign Office Research Department official I knew who was an expert in Balkan matters. The Research Department was nothing to do with MI6 (although many foreigners think it is), and had good links with some journalists. Although we were on good terms personally, Joanna was hostile and criticised the story. Even with the good people in the system, the spin machine was becoming increasingly dominant. The necessary myth that the Kosovars would never turn to armed resistance was under threat, but that would not prevent the Serbs and their numerous sympathisers in the Foreign Office from trying to maintain it in the difficult years ahead. People of great personal integrity and independent judgement like Joanna and her colleague the Russia expert Janet Gunn on the Russian Desk worked under intellectual siege in Whitehall, where all that mattered under the Conservative government was the security of the Serbs—the 'big people' of the Balkans, as one smarmy official once described them to me.

These events took place in the full glare of media attention in the spring sun glittering on the Ionian sea. The magnificent natural theatre of the Vjoses valley in southern Albania was ruled by armed men and women in insurrectionary mood. What was happening in the damp and mist of the endless oak and beech forests of Kosova hundreds of miles to the northeast? The Kosovar establishment in Rugova's Democratic League in London were all strong and often dogmatic Berisha supporters, and a crisis was to begin in their world-view. They thrived on the absence of accurate reporting about the reality of Kosova—as did that of the Foreign Office. Something needed to be done about it. There were acute problems of access to the story. Milošević had declared Kosova 'closed'.

After the appearance of my *Wall Street Journal* story on the arrival of the armed struggle in Kosova in May 1996, Yugoslav visas were 'delayed', as the official at the London embassy put it. The Milošević people had also not been pleased with my contribution at the March 1996 conference organised by the British embassy at the Sava Centre, and they liked news of the reality of Kosova even less. A warrant for Thaci's arrest was issued on 11 July 1997, and he was tried *in absentia* that year and sentenced to ten years' imprisonment. The MUP claimed that he opened fire on a police vehicle, 'together with the Drenik terrorist group', on 25 May 1996 at a railway crossing near Glagovac. The Ambassador, Ivor Roberts, told me that Milošević did not like journalists going to Kosova. So much was obvious. There was also a technical news problem. Although news filtered through to London of further attacks on the Serb police, they were clearly small and isolated incidents, and did not seem like the actions of a nascent army to foreign desks; the story did not 'move'. But Kosova did, although I was not there to see it.

Milošević and his allies in the West were fearful of the Albanian uprising contagion spreading to Kosova. Intelligence links between the Yugoslavs and the British had been close for many years, and in his history of the Kosova conflict Tim Judah notes that most bugging devices found by the KLA in the mid-1990s were of British manufacture. It is not surprising that with the same local intelligence sources, and formal and informal interchanges of material, the British and Serbian governments thought in much the same way about Kosova. One popular although wild scenario was that a civil war would develop in Albania and the northern 'tribes' would instigate a rising in Kosova to help Berisha fight the south. Most diplomats knew little about Albania, but they did know that Sali Berisha's wife came from Montenegro. The Serbs took advantage of Berisha's difficulties. A crackdown on the nascent KLA was started, in the obscurity of the remote forest villages of northeast Kosova. In media terms Kosova was forgotten by most people, but it was not forgotten by the military planners in Belgrade: Milošević, the master tactician, saw an opportunity to break the KLA when the attention of the international community was on Albania. Fear spread through Kosova like a bacillus, and nowhere more than in the farms north of Podujeve. In the received wisdom the armed underground were dependent on the proximity of Albania to Kosova, and regions like Dukagjini and Drenice, near the Albanian border, were meant to be the centre of the armed resistance. International community gurus like Carl Bildt repeated endlessly in 1998 the mantra that the key to controlling the KLA was to close the Albanian border, or have it patrolled by an international military force. This depended on a perspective which failed to understand the nature of the KLA and saw it as an import from Albania. But the roots of the movement were deep and nowhere in Kosova was tougher or more committed than the northeast villages. On my first visit to Adem Demaci in 1992, the people of little Pollate had given two of their sons for Kosova, and when Demaci commented on it at the time, his diminutive, fearless face showed little emotion. After his release from gaol in April 1990 he had moved out into the larger prison of Kosova itself. In the struggle to escape that prison people sometimes died.

The Llap valley is one of the most remote and least known regions in a little-known country. A dark slash of forested valley running north from the town of Podujeve, it is only a few miles from the border with Serbia. Every village is peopled by Albanians, mostly millers who use the fast-flowing streams that break out of the rocky valley slopes to grind flour that has given Kosova good bread for generations. In Ottoman times the Llap people were great traders, and bought wheat from as far north as Niš in Serbia to grind between their heavy granite millstones and feed the burgeoning mining town of Mitrovica, home of the workers in the lead and silver mine at Trepce. The villages are hidden in the beech woods, self-contained, with little white mosques and solid grey stone farms with huge carved double doors. When visiting, even after 1999, you would enter the enclosed farmyard slowly, and if you walked in fast you might be mistaken for a Serb intruder and be shot on sight. Llap was the front line as much as a trench in the battle of the Somme. Tito had stolen the Kosovars' arms in 1956 and for years they were defenceless against the Interior Ministry police. In the chaos after 1945 some Llap people abandoned their Albanian identity under pressure from the regime and went as exiles to Turkey. Others stayed, and saw themselves as standard-bearers in the struggle against communism. Here Albanian nationalism was something conservative, and life in a village like Pollate was lived under siege. There had always been small secret groups of underground conspirators against Titoism who met in the back rooms of cafés and in the summer sat on the straw bales discussing freedom, and avoiding those who had always been the curse of the nation—the informers and collaborators with Titoism who would bend to the overwhelming pressure of the Titoist regime and welsh on them to the police. The informers usually won. Pollate was so close to Serbia.

The force of the illegal struggle was consistent, and had never let up since 1945. The name of Adem Demaci is best known in connection with it, but in the Llap valley another name is famous—that of Ahmet Haxhiu, a burly dark-eyed man whose family had resisted the attempts of the Serb colonisers to move people into Llap after 1912. Haxhiu himself had joined an illegal organisation in 1963, when Demaci was serving a five-year prison sentence. Demaci's organisation, called Levizja Revolucionare per Bashkimin e Shqipteve, the Revolutionary League for the Unification of the Albanians, organised clandestine activity for the freedom of Kosova. In April 1964 the open struggle began, with the coordinated flying of the illegal black and red Albanian flag throughout Kosova. The flag means a great deal to ordinary Albanians—not for nothing is the national day in November each year known as Flag Day. It was a declaration of war. The Yugoslav secret police, UDBA, were not slow to react, and when Kosova became too dangerous Haxhiu moved to Zagreb in Croatia to continue the illegal struggle from there. But UDBA had a long arm and later that year he was arrested and moved to the prison in Prishtina. In the Kosova prisons torture by the police was routine, but the little groups continued their work as best they could, and along with the student leaders like Bajram

Kosumi and Hydajet Hyseni and elder statesmen like Rexhep Qosja laid the foundations for the major strikes of 1989. Messages and political texts in the newspaper _Rruga e Llirise_ (roads to freedom) were smuggled in and out, and groups of supporters met and discussed them in the safety of the Kosova woods, protected by the green oak scrub from the eyes of the secret police. It is not widely understood nowadays how far the Titoist regime repressed basic human rights such as the right to strike. The words of the Doors song 'They have the Guns but We have the Numbers' applied, but the numbers were still small and the police had almost all the guns, all the tanks, all the artillery pieces, all the grenade-launchers, all the torture houses, all the money and the computers, and all the telephone-tapping machines and the files on suspected activists. Belgrade had a mighty repressive machine that functioned with international assistance and approval—Britain and Israel had supplied the bugging equipment, and in 1989 British diplomats watched as the tanks rolled into Trepce. The little Llap _ceta_ was an inspiration to the young but it could not withstand the forces ranged against it. Ahmet Haxhiu moved to Swiss exile after leaving prison. The little groups had failed, and the mass organisation of the Kosova Democratic League grew out of their defeat. Far away in Gjirokastra we might as well have been on the moon as we knew nothing of what was happening in Kosova. But the diplomats and Western governments did, through their intercepts of Milošević's military communications, and did nothing to stop the gaolings and shootings, or ambushes of militants like Zahir Pazarditi, mown down in a car by a bridge on the Vustri road.

The next morning in Gjirokastra was a Sunday and I telephoned in, with great difficulty, from the Kotoni house telephone to _The Times_ Foreign Desk staff in Wapping. David Watts was a tiny echoing voice in the far distance. He seemed less interested in what was happening in Gjirokastra, with the steady thump of an artillery piece in the distance and answering small arms fire from the pro-Berisha forces on the east side of the valley, than in whether I had read the _Sunday Telegraph_ that morning. What did he mean? I had no way of buying or reading a British paper stuck in the middle of an armed insurrection in the southern Balkans, and its correspondent, Tim Judah, had been no more than a yard away from me fast asleep the previous night. He was now hunched in conclave with the *Figaro* correspondent over a great pile of bullets the little boy of the house was trying to sell him. The kids in the town said that everyone else was armed and the journalists were missing out. But David was emphatic: 'It's pretty strong stuff. They have put the knife into you and Miranda Vickers. The Oxford Helsinki people.'

He started to read something out and then the line was cut. David was a rock of personal and professional integrity who had been a distinguished *Times* correspondent in Southeast Asia. He retained his extraordinary inner calm, even during the most frantic moments on the desk. If he said something was serious, it was. After a few minutes of frantic dialling I managed to get through to my wife Sue in Bath and asked her to get the paper. Speaking again, later in the morning, she said I would have a libel case on my hands. It was a brilliant sunny morning in Gjirokastra. Even the dogs and cats seemed exhausted by the turmoil of the day before, and lay stretched out asleep on the stone shingle roofs.

I went for a walk and looked at the post office. From here, six years before, I had filed the story for the London *Independent* that recorded the demolition of the last statue of Enver Hoxha left standing in Albania. Then I had to wait in the kiosk while a single line was connected by an elderly dragon-like female operator who clearly worked for the secret police and thought Enver was wonderful. The story had to be shouted to the *Independent* copytakers, a word at a time. But I managed to file somehow. Yet now the *Sunday Telegraph* was claiming I was a collaborator and sympathiser of Enver Hoxha. This was throwing down the gauntlet. When I got back to London, it seemed time to show our opponents that there were some limits to their attempts to shut us up and suppress the truth about Albania and Kosova. Antony Daniels, a doctor in Oxford and prominent member of the Helsinki Human Rights group, had written in an article that I shared Enver Hoxha's views on religion. He also tarred my colleague Miranda Vickers with the Enverist brush. We sued and won a good financial settlement, and a mountain of articles which gave us very good publicity, helped discredit the Democratic Party machine in London and the people in MI6 and the Foreign Office who were behind it, and squash any ideas they might have had of international or NATO intervention to save his government. It was sweet revenge, after many years of difficulty. The FCO spin machine had failed in this round of the battle, but I had no illusions that it would be back for another contest before long. This was true, but it never recovered its power after 1997, and in a key development there was always American sympathy and sometimes quiet unofficial help for our work from that time onwards. The Americans knew the FCO machine only too well, and in Bosnia had finally overcome it. American intelligence officers had been important in London in exposing British MI6 officers posing as journalists in the Bosnian war. I gathered that it was largely a result of American encouragement that led to my appointment as the *Times* 'Balkan expert'. In the United States they had no wish to repeat the Bosnian experience in Kosova. I had always thought the phrase 'God Bless America' a sugary cliché, but now in a modest way I began to understand why it meant so much to so many ordinary people.

5. Development of the War

The summer of 1997 passed in a flurry of controversy, writs, personal attacks and good stories. The acrimonious disputes with the Oxford Helsinki Human Rights Group and favourable libel settlement with the *Sunday Telegraph* had improved my standing in Wapping considerably, and as a result I had a more or less free hand to cover whatever I wished in the region. In Skopje in July when fighting broke out in the west of FYROM, I had a small scoop as the only foreign journalist around. It was clear that the ice was cracking there as in Kosova. Up on the beautiful Alpine meadows of the Sar mountains carpeted with wild flowers the crested larks were singing. In the towns below, particularly Tetovo and Gostivar, weapons were being purchased and stored.

On 12 July my copy ran in *The Times* under the headline 'FLAME OF ALBANIAN UNREST THREATENS MACEDONIAN TINDERBOX'. I had rushed across from Skopje to find the ethnic Albanian towns of Tetovo and Gostivar under armed occupation by the heavy mob of the Macedonian Interior Ministry paramilitary police, and the centre of Gostivar, a tidy conservative town with some fine Ottoman monuments, a chaotic mess of broken glass, ransacked shops, angry young men at street corners and spent brass cartridge cases everywhere. The Macedonian security people wore flak jackets, metal helmets, leg-protectors and steel-covered boots. As they sweated in the heat, they were jumpy and hostile. After I had hidden my notebook and camera behind a hedge and told one of them that I was an aid worker, they eventually let me into town. After an outbreak of violence which left two young ethnic Albanians dead and forty people with serious gunshot wounds, tension had gripped everywhere in western Macedonia with frequent roadblocks and a heavy special forces presence. More than 200 people had been taken to hospital after a dispute over the right to fly the Albanian flag over Gostivar town hall escalated into violence. The Macedonian special forces had taken over and gaoled the mayor, Rufi Osmani; then five hours later an angry Albanian crowd gathered and tried to eject them from the building. Scuffles broke out, followed by bursts of gunfire. Then the 'security forces' took the town apart, breaking into and wrecking the jewellery shops and stealing the gold chains and Swiss watches. It was a Macedonian dress rehearsal for what was to come in Kosova. Many of the 'Macedonian' soldiers were actually ethnic Serbs who lived in a Serb enclave in FYROM near the northern town of Kumanovo, and there was extensive Serbian secret intelligence activity in the Macedonian army. The soldiers were badly paid, and resented the growing freedom from communist period restraints that the Albanian businessmen enjoyed. For them smashing and looting the shops combined politics and economics. The two armies were united in vehemently anti-Albanian attitudes.

I hid in a café and watched from the loo window as two Macedonian soldiers walked down the street and smashed every car windscreen with pickaxe handles taken from a hardware shop opposite. If there had been any Albanian or foreign heads nearby, they would have smashed those too. The Macedonian army had some strange methods of peacekeeping. There was nothing new about all this. I remembered on a previous visit to Gostivar seeing a monument down by the river to various Partisans from the Second World War period. They all had Slav names, and stood strangely isolated in the brilliant early morning sunlight in the frozen park, with lumps of ice hanging from the plants above the rushing river. Gostivar had wanted to be part of Albania after 1944, and the Titoists had taken the town apart then. Punishment for Gostivar came from every generation of slavocommunists, and it was a miracle that so many fine Ottoman and Islamic buildings had survived.

I was unable to file from Gostivar because the authorities had cut all the telephones, and I found a helpful Swiss-based Albanian who drove me back to Tetovo thirty miles north at over a hundred miles an hour in his BMW. The phone in the Hotel Macedonia there worked, unusually, and I just managed to get through to one of the wonderful East End ladies who took copy at Wapping in time to make the first edition. First a cheerful greeting, then the sacred ritual word 'Catch', the few letters so that the Wapping mega-computer could ID the story, 'byline?', where you were, then the floodgate opened on the word 'copy?'. I tried to make the violence in the street smell off the page. This was Balkan journalism like Tintin used to do it, all that was missing was Snowy the Dog. I checked into the Hotel Macedonia in Tetovo intending to have a shower and a few drinks, but was so exhausted that I slept for nine hours fully dressed on the bed, and woke up thinking I was getting too old for Balkan newsgathering. A summer holiday beckoned, on the beach at Zakinthos, but even there work intruded, with a big ecology story about the Greeks' scandalous neglect of the turtle nesting beaches there. There was not generally much love for Greece among *The Times* Foreign Desk staff; Michael Binyon liked to say, correctly, that 'hysteria' and 'paranoia' were good Greek words, and Greece was seen as the main obstacle to Turkish EU membership, a popular cause on *The Times* Desk at the time. The story didn't have to fight its way on to the page, but found an open door. It got half a page with a big photograph, with some excellent additional material from John Carr in Athens. From the point of view of work for *The Times*, it was summer *mirabilis*. After the £10,000 libel settlement from the *Sunday Telegraph*, I went to the Oddbins over the road from Stalag Wapping, filled my rucksack with as many bottles of Veuve Cliquot as it would hold, and distributed them round the office. A particularly sweet smile spread across foreign editor Graham Patterson's face with his white curls bouncing over his brow as his bottle arrived on his desk. Revenge on the ever-plotting diplomats and the Oxford Helsinki Group was sweet, even if not as long delayed as the *Kanun* recommends.[1] I knew newspapers well enough to know that these good days often do not last long.

As autumn approached, news began to seep out of Kosova of a major acceleration in the Kosova Liberation Army campaign, with attacks on Serb military and police installations. I applied repeatedly for a visa to go in, but nothing happened. I began to wonder if I would ever see Kosova again. Instead I saw a great deal of the interior of the Yugoslav embassy visa office in Lexham Gardens, Kensington, with notices on the wall offering flights that did not fly to places that were no longer in Yugoslavia. The officials were helpful, but authorisation

---

[1] The *Kanun* of Lek Dukagjini is a traditional legal code used in Kosova and northern Albania to regulate family and land disputes.

from Belgrade was needed before a visa could be issued, and it had not come. At ground level the absurdity of the fiction of 'Yugoslavia' as a functioning state with a future was obvious, but it did not stop the relentless dedication of Western governments to the old ideal. Then the *Guardian* reported that the KLA was now a functioning guerrilla force in central Kosova. Someone had got in and obtained precious access to the story. The Serbs had presumably decided that it would be useful for them to have observers and journalists around, for what they saw as an anti-terrorist campaign. *The Times* had carried nothing about it, and after a Wapping lunch with David Watts and Denis Taylor, who were positive and interested, it was time to make a major effort to go. I put in another visa application at the grim and gloomy Yugoslav embassy in London, for the period of the Orthodox Christmas in January 1998. To my surprise and relief it came through.

I was anxious about the story, having been down this road before; it was very unclear from what I could discover in London how strong the KLA had really become. The central question was whether it was capable of conducting a real war rather than isolated attacks on Serb security personnel. I flew into Thessaloniki on an old Olympic plane, which just managed to land on a cleared strip of runway. On either side of it was deep snow, and the temperature on the train up to Skopje was Arctic, with even the wealthy cocaine and cannabis dealers huddled shivering in vast leather overcoats. It was the Journey to a War yet again, the journey where myth fades and you encounter new history. Or was it? The Kosova Liberation Army was an ever-elusive phenomenon, Ibrahim Rugova was continuing to maintain that it was a fiction, controlled by the Serb secret police; the story would have to be handled very carefully, to try for the first time to sketch the history that was really evolving. War reporting is usually about the fate of the victims, and at the beginning of a conflict there are never many of them. In the grim arithmetic of war reporting, single figure numbers of dead bodies are never going to make the KLA news, double figures are necessary or, as one Milošević aide put it later in the conflict, referring to Serb army activity against the KLA, 'a village a day keeps NATO away'.

I flew in to Belgrade and planned to travel down to Kosova by train—journalists were supposed to clock in at the Press Ministry and secure full accreditation before doing any work. The old city seemed desolate and grey in the rain. Little old ladies sat by the roadside with a few pairs of socks or bottles of washing-up liquid for sale. All Milošević was giving to his supporters was unconcealed grinding poverty. Serbia was bleeding. Ivor Roberts had left his old post, and my friend from the New Democratic Party, Tahir Hasanovic, said that he had a poor successor who was always criticising Ivor in public at functions for being away during vital crises. This seemed like empty and malicious gossip, although it did feel as though the British 'special relationship' with Milošević was dying. Whatever criticisms might be made of his approach to Milošević, Ivor was carrying out policy decided in London, and he was a cheerful and exemplary representative; his wife Elizabeth became a great expert on the history of Montenegro. His critics in London claimed that he ran the embassy like an inn, but in reality his approach at least kept open a dialogue with many sections of Serbian society at a time when communication was difficult. The policies of the Major government often caused savage personal tensions in his life since he knew perfectly well what the regime was doing, but had to keep on acceptable terms with Milošević personally in order to preserve the unique British access to him. He has written a book about his experiences, 'Dialogues with Slobodan Milošević' which the British government has yet to allow him to publish.

I slept on an uncomfortable bed in a box-like room in the Hotel Belgrade, but there was hot water. The streets were plastered with blue and white posters for Milan Milutinović, Milošević's candidate for Prime Minister, and for his electoral opponent Vuk Drasković. Seeing his picture brought home images of Wapping, where Dessa Trevisan, the ex-*Times* resident in Belgrade expelled by Milošević, still had some influence. Dessa was a strong admirer of Drasković and close to the famous *Times* columnist and former editor Simon Jenkins, and both were said to be pro-Serb, or at least instinctively anti-KLA. I had never met Jenkins but had heard that Dessa was very critical of my work. She was declared *persona non grata* in Yugoslavia in the early 1990s and so could not get a visa from the regime; this had brought her practical writing life to a standstill.

At one level everything in Belgrade seemed exactly as in 1970 when I had first seen it, the little rows of old fashioned shops below the Hotel Moscow—places where you bought an old-fashioned party member's pork-pie hat and the leather shop that made a holster for your side-arm with your initials on it. I wasted a day with the bureaucracy and then got up at five the following morning to take the 6.15 train down to Kosova Polje station. It took about ten hours and I had four burly men for company, going to service Obiliq power station, they said. The fields were white with frost, and the puddles in the cart-tracks were frozen. The train rapidly filled up with Serbs, for in the old Yugoslav travel hierarchy Serbs took trains, Albanians took buses and Roma had a horse and cart or walked. We drifted down through the endless small towns and cabbage fields and orchards of central Serbia, with tidy whitewashed modern houses, the heartland of the Milošević regime, outwardly decent and hard-working but inwardly resentful and angry at their poverty and isolation. The line south from Rasca, at the heart of the original Serbian state into Sandjak, the old Sandjak of Novi Pazar, veered southeast and then southwest towards the Ibar river valley and Kosova. The Sandjak is as remote as it was in the 1930s when Rebecca West travelled there—poor, small fields brown with dead maize stalks, beige soil, brim-full fast streams, low limestone crags with dwarf beech clinging to the rock. Classic little *zadruga* settlements (groups of small farmhouses, usually occupied by related families) were surrounded by grazing fields and thin hungry-looking horses and cows. The roads were empty, with almost no cars. We then crossed the Kosova border, just north of Janinje. Hills about 1,000 metres high fade into higher mountains in the distant grey mist of the Ibar river valley. Conical haystacks, lovingly built on wooden frames, punctuate the fields; chickens peck at the edge of a wood; white smoke floats from a chimney. The hewn wood of the farms is beautiful, this is a deeply human society, the buildings speak of the sweat and labour that built it. A policeman cycles home in his blue uniform looking like a prosperous alien from Belgrade as an elderly couple follow a wooden plough pulled by an ox. Here the Milošević world was medieval in its technology and poverty. An old Ottoman fortress towers above the road, with smooth stone hexagonal walls, there is a mine, and then the vast modern metallurgical plant at Zvecan near the huge Trepce base metal mine with its towering chimney belching dangerous pollutants. In the midst of this backwardness and poverty, the Belgrade machine was stealing

100 million dollars a year from the bowels of the earth, the annual profits of Trepce. Prishtina lay a few miles to the south. I had reached the war, the front line spread over the whole of Kosova.

Prishtina, the dead city and city of the dead, was deserted and cold, with dark and gleaming ice on the streets. It seemed as if life was carrying on in a tomb, and one day Belgrade would close the lid with a heavy stone and no one would ever see the light again. Hundreds of starlings huddled in the city center, roosting in the lime trees for warmth. They had left the Arctic wasteland of the Great Plain for Prishtina. The open snowfields were empty and still. Melting and freezing snow from the roofs made icicles often two meters or more long pointing down at you. It would be ironic to be killed on assignment by an huge icicle but it was clearly not impossible. There were so many routine ways of getting killed in Kosova in those days that an unusual way was an interesting thought. Kosova Albanians then were obsessed with the problem of poisoned school radiators, although ever since I have been going to Kosova some weird disease that most people have never heard of was in the news. According to the 1990s urban myth, the Serbs had put something behind the school radiators that poisoned the classroom air and made the Albanian children mortally ill or left than with a tendency to epilepsy later in life. I had had an argument with a friend about the implausibility of it all on a previous visit, but it was still a subject of serious comment in *Bujku*, the only Albanian-language newspaper Milošević allowed. It also seemed bad politics to peddle this sort of thing to visiting foreign journalists and academics when there were so many undeniable and real threats to Albanian lives and dignity, but that did not stop a few of the sillier LDK intellectuals doing so.

Most of the street lighting had been turned off to save scarce electricity, so as one walked in the evening to Spaghetti Toni's restaurant there were only glimmers of light from the windows of apartments where whole families huddled around their stoves and slept in a single room against the cold. I visited some friends, and the teenage daughter was gloomy. 'One day soon the Serbs are going to come and kill us,' she said, staring at the fire. The meal we had felt like the Last Supper, although no one in that family would ever betray the nation.

Most of the town was in total darkness, inhabited by thousands of Rip van Winkles who seemed to be sleeping for thousands of years. The enemy were more animated, the MUP police stood at street corners and nursed their machine pistols in clouds of freezing breath wearing sinister black balaclavas. Some people were taking the slow way to oblivion. The management of the Grand Hotel were all blind drunk when I arrived there, swigging from litre bottles of wine. There were new faces, including a stunningly beautiful dark girl with long legs who was more or less paralytic and kept collapsing behind the bar. New faces in the Grand were always disturbing: new people joined Arkan's entourage only when profits were expected to rise, which usually meant dead Albanians in some form or another.

If this girl was Beauty, the other newcomer was the Beast. A man said to be connected with Ratko Mladić's nephew had also joined the group of smugglers, gunmen and Serb nationalist idealists known as the management team. He was a distant young Bosnian Serb, immensely tall and thin, who sat with his long legs stretched out like a stick insect. He looked very Russian, elegant, lethal, in a Hugo Boss black suit; in the Grand it had to be black. Over his high cheekbones and narrow forehead the skin was tight and pallid, his eyes were cold. I wondered if it was related to drugs—a lot of heroin and cocaine was around then in Prishtina, mostly on its way to Italy and France—but maybe he didn't need white powder and Serbian nationalism was enough. His presence did not aid a relaxed approach to living in the Grand, or to my story. I could not sleep that night, unable to empty my head of images of Srebenica and mass graves. The hotel guests and staff were like people on a beach looking out to sea, and waiting for the *tsunami* wave of death to break over them and carry them all away. Life in the Grand (if the daily nightmare could be called life) was always in touch with the next world, the still body in the corridor, the bullet through the head at the edge of a frozen field, the blade drawn across the throat before the body goes into the ditch for the foxes.

As well as death at the Grand, there was sex. As it took place in this very weird hotel, there was also an atmosphere of danger and conspiracy. The back stairs ran down to a locked and chained steel door that was rumoured to open on to an underground passage linking the hotel to the nearby Yugoslav army provincial headquarters across the road—the entrance to the Underworld, literally and metaphorically, a place of forbidden knowledge if this was true. But the officers and NCOs need not have feared walking across the street. Prishtina was and is always full of urban myths of various kinds, mostly with a sinister flavour. According to the chambermaid the steel door was never used, but this was not true—I had once taken the back stairs when the lift was broken and found it open. It didn't seem a good idea to wander into the passage, an Albanian who had gone too near even the front entrance to the HQ in the street had been shot dead in broad daylight. Heaven knows what the JNA would do to anyone caught snooping around their cellars. The officers would come through from the army HQ, pick up a hefty Romanian or Roma girl from the nightclub, take her upstairs and shag her on one of the narrow Grand beds. The girls were supposed to take on all comers, but as they cost so little they were usually adopted by one or two officers. I was curious about the arrangements and asked a waiter. He discovered that the cost of a woman was twenty DM, but thirty for one who would take it up the backside. This apparently meant one of the older ones. The whole odd system was designed to stop any risk of fraternisation with the Albanian *untermensch*. Roma and Romanians were the lower orders but acceptable as sex partners for a Yugoslav officer. If a girl was lucky, their patron would find them a job as a waitress or something in Belgrade.

Despite, or because of its gnawing sense of death and decay, the Grand had a hold on you, however interesting the work in the outer world of Kosova society where the future was what mattered. The hotel represented the past, the dark and deep sub-conscious mind and memory of Yugoslav Kosova, a place where you sat in the black lounge chairs and were held by the tangled chains of history. The myth from the past could freeze you, adding to the fears of the present and the terrors of the future war that was surely to come. It was time to go to work, leave this place of tribal myths and encounters to do a day's work in the bright and sunny but very frozen fields and oak woods of Drenice. At least in the open fields and heathland the fear was definable and concrete, a man pointing his gun.

I located my favourite taxi driver, Mr Bajramović, who called himself a Serb for security and economic reasons although his family was from a mixed Bosnian background, and began negotiations about getting to the alleged 'liberated areas' in central Kosova. It would be a difficult and dangerous journey and I wanted to go with someone I knew and had worked with before. Mr Bajramović had first entered my life three years earlier on a story about diesel smuggling from Albania into Kosova during the time of United Nations sanctions against Serbia. I remembered staring with him at a row of cans of diesel and admiring his skill at identifying the pinky red evil-smelling Albanian variety. He was rough, poor, strong and cheerful, with brown broken teeth and stinking breath, and had a Smith and Wesson handgun in his glove pocket.. As a driver he absolutely loved looking after his journalists, and also no doubt made extra money from telling the secret police what everybody had been doing. And he loved his side-arm. After a day or two working together, it was customary to leave him some extra money towards his ammunition costs, since imported Smith and Wesson bullets were expensive compared to Yugo-manufactured material. It was a high status weapon, and Mr Bajramović saw himself as an aristocrat among the Prishtina drivers.

The car would have to travel west from Prishtina, then turn north from the main Peje road towards the Kline/Llaushe villages which the KLA were supposed to control. He was surprisingly calm, and said that it would be safe to go as long as we were sure to be back in Prishtina before dark. In fact, it was a very easy story to do, as it was soon clear that the Serbs had abandoned a significant area of central Kosova to the KLA rebels, and much of the Drenice countryside was deserted. The Yugoslav army had not yet got to the landmine-laying stage which a year later would have made the journey very difficult and dangerous. My waiter contact said that the war was being supplied from Prishtina, in trucks which left at night to take food to the insurgent soldiers there. If this was true, it would be a sensation; the KLA was thought by many analysts in the West to be a group of rural, Maoist insurgents and Prishtina was known as a civilised LDK town of the educated 'moderates'.

We drove out in the old Honda from Prishtina in the direction of the film studio, a relic of the relative degree of liberalisation in Tito-land twenty years before, past chilly fields with a dusting of fresh snow. On the left was the massive barracks and logistics centre of the army's Prishtina Corps, sheds and parade grounds stretching as far as you could see, with artillery pieces and tanks in lines under the lime trees. It was probably also the site of an Ottoman barracks—the lime tree in Kosova is nearly always a sign of a place of Turkish occupation. The Serbian proverb runs that 'where the Turkish foot had trodden no grass will grow', but lime trees often do; they are often found in mosque courtyards. In front of us was the vast bulk of the steaming lignite power stations at Obiliq, which churned out electricity for all of Kosova and much of southern Serbia. Rubber conveyor belts looped across the lunar landscape, bringing the smelly brown coal from huge opencast pits where the natural wealth of Kosova was despoiled to bring more or less free electricity to the ruling circles in Belgrade. A pillar of dense grey smoke rose hundreds of feet into the air above Obiliq B generating station. The giant Westinghouse turbines churned in the building below. The dust of Obiliq permeated the Prishtina air, and turned to a fine sticky mud in wet weather. The chattering classes of Prishtina did not have to go far out of their city to be reminded that Kosova is above all else a mining area, where the people have drawn metal and energy from the earth for thousands of years.

The old car navigated across central Kosova towards Peje, with the occasional flock of starlings for company. It was a bright sunny morning. Mr Bajramović played one of his favourite Bosnian tapes, a long slow lament remembering some Christian defeat at the hands of the Turks. The name of the 1389 battlefield, the Field of Blackbirds, is one of the few non-mythical elements from that time, the flocks still fly everywhere on the central Kosova plain, sometimes starlings, sometimes jackdaws, sometimes rooks, but always black, in a world of their own outside the turmoil of human history but symbolic of it. Some see them as sinister, but to me they are always as much Kosovar birds as the people, sociable, self-reliant, sometimes quarrelsome, tied to their sacred soil for their food, working endlessly and hard in the wild flowers and mud. They would soon be foraging in wartime Kosova.

Across the plain and the flat neatly grazed fields the Serb security road-blocks had gone, near Gllogoec some boys had lit a fire on top of a sandbagged roadside post and were letting off a catapult at something. The feared and seemingly invincible Milošević machine was collapsing in Drenice, or had already collapsed. This left a vac-

uum over central Kosova in the daytime, but at night it was filled by
the Kosova Liberation Army, without doubt, pacing across the huge
fields cultivated—as in the Middle Ages—with maize and others
crops in strips. It was unbelievable after experiencing the seeming
invincibility of the Milošević machine for so many years. Change
had come to Kosova, even if the clear pools of water in the fields
and patches of weeds and brambles were unchanging. We turned
north off the main road north towards Skenderaj, Red Drenice as it
is called. Mr Bajramović gently released the catch of the old
Honda's glove pocket, so his Smith and Wesson would be handy.
He knew he was going, in Serb terms, into the deepest heart of
darkness. In an uncompromising land Skenderaj was the hardest of
Albanian hard towns and districts, the heartland of the Ballist rising
against the communists after 1944, and a byword for rebellious
patriots ever since. The communists had built an ammunition factory there, near Prekaz village. The word in Prishtina had been that
the village of Llaushe nearby was at the centre of the rebellion and
the ammunition factory was under heavy guard. The tidy white-
painted farmhouses slipped by, with their high walls and massive
fifteen-feet-high wooden gates. The domestic fortresses of the Albanian farming families would soon be needed.

On the outskirts of Llaushe there was an abandoned blue police
armoured car. Young men openly carrying arms patrolled the streets,
and the cows stared out from their wooden byres into land without a
Serb to be seen. There had been a quiet revolution. This is some of
what ran in *The Times* a day or so later, on 8 January 1998.

KOSOVO GUNMEN FORCE SERB POLICE TO BEAT RETREAT

Albanian rebels in the central Kosovo hills of southwestern Serbia have
scored their first important success against the security apparatus of President Milošević of Yugoslavia with the withdrawal of hundreds of police. In
an area from Titova Mitrovica in the east, to Pec, near the Albanian border
police patrols are nowhere to be seen and cannot operate in the countryside because of the threat of attack.

There have been at least 20 deaths in gunfights in the area over the past
year between security forces and Albanian rebels. Driving from Prishtina
through the area this week, there were no police visible during an 80-mile
trip. A year ago it was normal to be stopped every few miles.

The little towns west of Titova Mitrovica, such as Klina, Llaushe and
Rakos, have become centres of support for the KLA, and over the past three

months there have been regular armed clashes between Albanians and the police, The Serb security apparatus is gradually giving way, and only the military can venture into the hills.

In Llaushe, guarded by a blue armoured car, the family of Halit Geci, a teacher shot by accident in a melée several weeks ago, continues to mourn. His cousin Istref Geci is pessimistic about the future. 'I think more violence will come. There is no political solution to see now, in Belgrade or Prishtina,' he said. Elections for the Government of the self-styled Kosovo-Albanian Republic are due on March 22, and Dr Rugova is looking increasingly irrelevant and beleaguered amid the deepening crisis.

The uprising in Albania last year produced a seemingly unlimited supply of weapons and ammunition for the KLA. Serb control of the border is breaking down in some places, particularly west of the key town of Djakovica, where Serb and Albanian villagers have been preyed on by paramilitary gangs who seem to be based in Albania.

The army base in Titova Mitrovica has tanks and armoured cars at the ready, but it is far from clear what use they will be against such a shadowy enemy.

Local Serbs fear a lengthy breakdown of law and order but see little help coming from Belgrade. An obvious danger being aired in the Serb bars of Prishtina is that Arkan, the paramilitary leader and alleged war criminal who comes from Kosova and has extensive business interests here, may enter the fray.

The copy included other background material but the bare bones set the agenda for the struggle that was to come in the media, as on the ground. When a new conflict is going to start, journalists have to assume that readers know nothing about it; as time goes on and they get to know more, the job gets easier. This story was in essence an exercise to make clear what the military agenda of each side would be. It turned out to be reasonably accurate except that I implied the KLA had, or soon could have, many weapons from Albania, which was not the case. Although some Serbs, including Milošević's people in Belgrade, contested the details, saying it was the Orthodox Christmas and the police were all having a day off, and the usual gaggle of diplomats repeated every Serb distortion and lie, it was unarguable that Milošević had lost control of at least parts of central Kosova, although naturally people might have different opinions about what constituted 'control' of such a traditionally rebellious area. The police might enter an area one day and find they soon had to leave it. Such was insurgency warfare, anywhere, after all, and in Kosova it was always notoriously difficult to tell when war started and peace ended.

The Drenice region of central Kosova stretching from villages like Prekaz in the north to Malisheve and Rahevec in the south was a byword for the values of war. Intellectuals call it the Albanian Sparta, and the young men of Drenice 'those who do not know fear'. Much of the terrain is windswept upland with poor soil and none of the comfortable post-Ottoman urban culture of towns like Prizren or Vushtri. Many north-facing slopes cannot be farmed at all and are oak scrub and forest. People ate what they grew and if you did not work hard on your little farm you did not eat. Many villages on the uplands were in food deficit, and deficiency diseases like tuberculosis were still found. Families depended heavily on income from sons and daughters in the diaspora. Government officials and tax-collectors were hated figures.

In the nineteenth century Drenice had been at the forefront of the struggle against the Ottomans, and in the twentieth it had produced many brave soldiers who fought the Anglo-French imposition of royalist Yugoslavia in 1921 after the Versailles Treaty and the Axis occupation after 1941. But the most important Drenice rebellion in the twentieth century was after the Second World War, an uprising and guerrilla campaign against the Titoist communists that lasted until February 1949. The people fought the imposition of communism, but with no help from the West. Tito's regime, with its British backing, was allowed to do much as it liked and over 1,000 people were killed and many others went into exile, mostly to Turkey. Forty-seven villages were burnt out by the Titoists, and thousands of cattle and other livestock were plundered. The grandfather of Hashim Thaci, Sinan Idriz Thaci, was centrally involved in this resistance movement, and a close associate of Sadik Rama, the nationalist leader.

Some knowledge of this history of struggle and war did not help much in understanding the present. Interviewing the Geci family was a grim task. The aura of recent violent death hung over the farmhouse, with its minature-sized farm outbuildings made of lovingly crafted wood. It would have been the perfect setting for a film of a Thomas Hardy novel. The first work I had ever done on a newspaper was writing up a shopkeeper's death for the *Evesham Journal* in Worcestershire on a school holiday job, and that was no easier.

Widows' rooms always look very empty, however they are furnished. It all looked pathetically vulnerable. I took my shoes off, and was shown into the austere and bare white painted men's room, with some rugs, a picture or two, and very long low sofas running round the walls covered in sheepskins. The male relatives of the murdered Mr Geci, a local teacher, were surprisingly relaxed and welcoming, but the women looked pale and drawn. A single metal wood-burning stove stood in the middle of the room, with a chimney going up through the roof. There were fresh white lace curtains, as in Turkey. There was a quiet palpable tension. A daughter of the family appeared with coffee, and she agreed to be interviewed as her mother was still too upset. She said that in the gun battle in the village a day or two before, the police had fired indiscriminately at civilians who had then been driven away. This was certainly true. But by whom? I asked her if the KLA were in the village, at which she shrugged. Outside in the farmyard a small brown Jersey cow stared at us, equally trapped in its dumbness. I asked more routine questions, and then the girl fell silent. It was time to go. On the way out I visited the cow, calm in its wooden shed. Unlike the inhabitants, it had no idea what was coming; a month or two later the shed would be taking artillery fire, and the innocent animal would be dead.

When I returned to the car, Mr Bajramović was in agitated state. As a Kosova 'Serb' he was nervous in such a militant Albanian village, although as a journalist's driver he had a protected position. He was munching on an apple someone had given him. As a Prishtinaite, he was treated with added suspicion, whatever his ethnic group. An elderly man stood by the car with a white *pliss* and folded arms, his minder. He viewed him carefully, but not with outright hostility, they knew a local Serb when they saw one, and knew he was as poor as they were. He was disliked, and would not have been safe there on his own, but he was not subject to the bitter and uncompromising hatred reserved for the police and the army. But the irrepressible Mr Bajramović had been working on my behalf, even in this hostile and dangerous place.

'Down to the school, the school', he said.

He more or less shoved me into the car, and we drove down to the lower village where the KLA, in a manner of speaking, was in action. Three or four young men were guarding the school, one with an old gun, the others with what appeared to be wooden staves, or pickaxe handles. It was a homely scene, that could have easily have been dropped into an episode of the British television series 'Dad's Army' about the Home Guard in the Second World War. On a dirt road above us one or two other young men were engaged in military drill. So far, this was no more than an improvised village defence force. There were some weapons around—there were always weapons in Balkan villages—but a year earlier it would have been inconceivable: they would have been quickly arrested or shot by the MUP. The wooden staves and old rifles had a simple message: we are going to fight for our Kosova. We then drove out of Llaushe, having seen the new army, such as it was, and went to look at a nearby cross-roads. This was where the May 1996 attack that I had reported for the *Wall Street Journal* had taken place. I now knew it had been led by Hashim Thaci and wanted to see where the fabled underground leader had cut his military teeth. There was not much to see, only a cluster of street stalls by a rebuilt but empty police post, and then we took a turn towards the giant ferro-nickel plant at Gllogoec.

Here fear of the KLA was in full flood and determined the new security policy. The plant was surrounded by heavily-armed MUP paramilitaries, and new concrete protection enclosures were being built. We were not allowed very near, but with a Serb driver it was possible to talk to one or two of them, and one told Mr Bajramović that they were afraid of the KLA, which came out at night and took over the villages. This was not surprising: if the MUP and army had been completely withdrawn to guard military installations, there was no one left to stop them dominating the countryside. It would be only a short time before they emerged fully in the light of day and took full control of all of Drenice, apart from a few heavily protected installations such as the ferro-nickel plant. The Serbs had clearly given up on trying to control the roads. The war in the north of Yugoslavia had sometimes been a war about infrastructure, and it looked as if this might also be the case in Kosova. Thinking this, a terrible physical fear ran through me on the way back towards Prishtina. What on earth would the battle for Trepce be like? Or the battle for the Obiliq power stations?

Back in the Grand Hotel, miraculously, the telephone worked, and I had just managed to file to Wapping when a gypsy band burst into the lobby. There was a burst of bright-coloured shirts, swarthy men in old jackets with battered brass instruments. They played strange jazz versions of old Serbian songs and military ditties, very fast, as if on borrowed time. When a war is starting, small actions of daily life suddenly become frenetic. The Grand was happy; many of the Kosova Roma were more patriotic than the Serbs, and wrapped their babies in a Serbian flag for their baptism. The beauty behind the bar was still drunk, moving like a witch on this Prishtina *Walpurgisnacht*, with shimmering long arms, bejewelled fingers, rolling black liquid eyes, a perfect sense of rhythm. Every man in the bar was watching transfixed and would have given anything to take her to bed. Then the senior receptionist arrived in his new suit (new suits had arrived from Serbia to make the staff look smart for Christmas) and threw the Roma out. Communist habits continued in odd ways in Milošević's and Arkan's Prishtina. Beauty slumped on a stool again and looked for her wine bottle.

Three months before, at a British Kosova crisis conference at Wilton Park, Veton Surroi had told the astonished delegates that the price of donkeys was rising in western Kosova and northern Albania. This tubby crop-bearded old friend was at his most abstruse, staring at the assembled delegates; the favoured Kosovar in London had mystified them. His beard was turning the same colour as mine. As we are also the same shape, we agreed over a few drinks that if he ever became President of Kosova, I could be his double, although there are safer jobs in the Balkans than being double of a head of state. At a more serious level, although Veton frequently and rightly criticised Rugova for his mythical approach to Kosova and its problems, he was not above making a myth or two of his own. He meant, clearly, that donkeys were being bought as a means of transporting arms from Albania to Kosova, but this escaped most of those attending the conference. The illuminati of the diplomatic world there had no concept of a human society in Europe where donkey power could be important, let alone affect a war. It was a measure of the extreme sensitivity of the possibility of war in Kosova that even a star leader and commentator like Veton in a prestigious private conference needed to have recourse to these polite evasions.

Sitting in the bar of the Grand that night and minding a vodka, I thought back to what he had said. There would need to be an awful lot of donkeys to supply weapons to all who would want them. At some point, perhaps quite soon, the centre of gravity of the story would move across from Kosova to the bleak high plateau of northern Albania and the Dead Man's Gulch towns such as Bajram Curri. I believed that the Albanian government no longer controlled Bajram Curri and Tropoja after the spring uprising, but if they did not, who did? How much help would they, or could they, give to the Kosovars? I had no idea, and no particular wish to go there and find out. It was going to be a tough summer, but nobody could have foreseen the bitter, mighty struggle ahead for all participants—the KLA, the Serbs, the journalists, the diplomats, the ordinary people of Kosova. One of the few common factors that all involved in Kosova usually share is the depth of emotion that any involvement brings, the sense of meeting the central dilemmas in human life and history, but no one could have anticipated the agonies ahead. The Kosovars were and are the toughest and most resourceful people I have ever met, but even their exceptional powers of endurance and rank-and-file organisation were to be sorely tried by the end of the year.

Diplomacy was unlikely to help. The following morning I was having a cup of coffee in the offices of Veton's newspaper *Koha Ditore*, and Julian Braithwaite from the British embassy in Belgrade rang up. He was the son of a former ambassador to Moscow, Sir Roderick Braithwaite, and although very young had been put in charge of Kosova matters. The British embassy partly financed *Koha Ditore*, just as it paid for the New Democracy party in Serbia, both of which facts Milošević presumably knew, and although a vital and exemplary journalistic enterprise, *Koha Ditore* was also used by the Embassy as an intelligence sounding-board. Julian Braithwaite wanted information on Drenice, and grilled the acting editor Baton Haxhiu and me for some time about it. His questions were interesting, because although he knew Drenice was poor, that was all he knew. I told him a little about the history of Drenice region before he started asking awkward questions with no place on an open telephone line in a Milošević-ruled state. Every phone in Kosova was tapped, and anything anyone said went straight to UDBA (the Serbian secret police). A cynical view would be that the Embassy and FCO did not mind sharing information with Milošević who was still officially in the category of someone who was part of the solu-

tion, not the problem, or putting my security or credibility at risk.
British diplomats were extraordinary; when anyone before a conflict tried to tell them any Balkan history other than the received
pro-Serb orthodoxy they were not interested, and when a conflict
started, and it was too late, they became interested. Julian was an
energetic and open-minded young man, without the blinkered
arrogance of many of his colleagues. The episode made me feel it
was not surprising that the Kosovars were taking to their guns and
buying donkeys; otherwise, for all the efforts that the European diplomats were going to make to give Kosova independence, we would
be attending Ibrahim Rugova's press conferences for the next thousand years. Even knowing the diplomatic scene fairly well, it was
difficult to connect it with the developing conflict on the ground, a
problem that quickly became more acute in the next few weeks.
The war would develop in the villages, as Balkan wars always do,
and the diplomacy in the towns; or, in the case of the real top players like Richard Holbrooke, the Clinton administration's Balkan
envoy and architect of Dayton, in the media and cyberspace. The
sense of the Homeric world was overwhelming, as the Holbrooke
god would eventually have to visit earth and meet the Kosova Liberation Army. Perhaps he should wrap himself in a cloud of invisi-
bility while he did so, since it would not be a popular event with
many people.

The first offensive

Cyberspace is a long way from the winter mud of a Kosova village.
Sometimes in history, as on 8 March 1997 in Gjirokastra, or in
Kosova in early March 1998, a single day can possess more significance than a whole year. As winter retreated and the spring barley
began to poke up in the fields through the melting snow, the pace of
the war accelerated. The improving weather meant that the heavy
vehicles and armoured equipment of the Yugoslav army could be
mobile much more easily. In the depths of late December and early
January most of rural Kosova was reduced to frozen stasis, and even
tracked vehicles were immobilised in the sticky brown mud and
deep pools of icy water. This was ideal weather for the tough Albanians who had been brought up in these villages. With their intimate

knowledge of the local terrain they followed little paths through the scrub, whereas the Serbs depended on asphalt roads. The Serb conscripts were often town boys who, though well-equipped in a technical infantry sense, had limited anti-insurgency training and an overwhelming fear of operating in the totally hostile Albanian communities. They were unable to break up the close and ruthless networks the KLA had created in its heartlands. Some commentators have wondered why the Milošević machine resorted to mass ethnic cleansing of Kosova in the summer and autumn of 1998 and the spring of 1999, rather than run an efficient counter-insurgency campaign. The answer is that they had tried to do this in the first offensive in the spring of 1998, and largely failed.

Albanian power in the form of small and mobile KLA units was spreading over most of central, western and north-eastern Kosova, but they had not yet met much serious opposition. It was equally clear that Belgrade was planning its own spring offensive. Both sides wanted to avoid taking many casualties, the Albanians because they had so few trained soldiers and the Serbs because it was important to conceal from Serbian public opinion the extent to which another decimating war for Yugoslavia might be in the offing. As a result of Dayton Milošević had been able to prolong his rule and force the people to put up with poverty and decline in exchange for peace of a sort. Most intelligent Serbs had no wish to see the country plunged into yet another period of war. The Serb authorities in Prishtina and elsewhere were clearly making a security assessment and pumping any journalist or visitor they could find for information about what the KLA were doing. The London Yugoslav embassy traded visas for information. Belgrade had a major problem, in that it generally preferred to work with Rugova and deny that the KLA ever existed as a proper military force, merely referring to it as 'bandits' and 'criminals', but if a major counter-insurgency operation started this fiction would disappear; there would be a real war in which the Serb army was supposed to abide by the Geneva rules. The media dimension would increase dramatically, and Kosova Albanian collaborators in the LDK and elsewhere, a vital part of the Serb system of rule, would be undermined. This risk now had to be taken, and the seasonal factors affecting Balkan conflicts were becoming important.

The summer would be crucial, with the gentle swirls of scythe-cut hay drying in the fields, the stalks always making a contour line as if on a map. If the fighting was fierce, it would still be lying there, brown, damp and rotting, when the last wild flowers came out in September. Then the autumn rain and hailstorms begin, the hills turning a soft Irish green, and the more distant mountain peaks are lost in blue and purple. The tractor-drawn carts fill the roads, the unique long thin Kosova vehicle only about a metre wide but ten metres long, laden with ten or twenty young oaks ready to be cut for the winter log pile. September is the log-cutting and pepper-drying month in Kosova. A family fills its cellar with staple foods to survive the winter. Old ladies hump bags of flour. Cattle sheds and sheep-folds are mended with freshly cut new beechwood to protect the animals from the coming gales and blizzards. The autumn rain suddenly turns to snow as the fierce north Bora wind blows down from Bosnia. Somehow the Albanians had to find a way to survive the turmoil of war in the summer until the autumn and winter provided less favourable conditions for their opponents. It was a dilemma their political and military leaders faced too, the dilemmas of Thaci, Haradinaj, Remi and Haliti reproducing, hundreds of years later, the dilemmas that Skanderbeg and his generals faced during the Ottoman invasion of the Albanian lands. In those days, around 1440, there was a formal campaigning season and the Ottoman army went home for the winter. Nowadays the Serbs returned to barracks and watched Red Star and Partisan play football on television.

All of us—Serb soldiers, KLA soldiers, journalists, police, spies, the Red Cross, diplomats, aid workers, commentators, interpreters, television crews, drivers, media fixers, doctors, secret policemen—would need to draw upon our deepest reserves of experience and knowledge to survive and do our jobs, little cogs in the great engine of the developing war that would only stop when NATO entered Kosova on 11 June 1999, in the unimaginably distant future. Before then 10,000 who were alive that night would be dead, hundreds of thousands would have been made refugees, and the most advanced military technology in the world forced the retreat of the Serb forces from Kosova. But nobody knew what was to come the next day then in the spring of 1998, let alone next week, next month or next year.

When I had returned to London from Kosova in January after my visa ran out, there was no sure way of knowing what was to develop

there either. It was not long since the controversy over the fall of
Berisha in which I had been deeply involved, and there was every
prospect of the same people in England playing the same negative
role over Kosova. Human rights would be the critical issue. It was
not a matter of being 'right' or 'left' over the Balkans but whether
human rights and human dignity mattered. Even having just been in
Kosova, and knowing the pent-up forces determined on war, it was
difficult to convey to people in London the extent to which the
KLA was a military reality, and the severity of the crackdown that
was coming. Milošević was going to risk a very bad press in exchange for a quick end to the KLA insurgency. Serb analysts in Belgrade had seen one of their most consistent and primitive fears
realised in the people-power aspect of the Albanian uprising in
1997, and were busy answering queries from their political masters
on whether the same process might overtake Kosova. In classic
counterinsurgency theory the best way to end a movement is to
snuff it out before it grows too large to control, and this was the
route Belgrade would take, no doubt privately advised by some
Euroid ambassadors in Belgrade, and possibly even assisted with
intelligence data.

After a week in London it was easier to see the direction events
were going to take. I had some contacts among Yugoslav diplomats
and officials, and good ones in the intellectual community in Belgrade. They generally thought that Milošević would try to break the
'terrorists' before the spring came, and in general they were correct.
He would clearly not want reporters around. I and many others
stood no chance of getting another visa quickly. Access to the story
was becoming a key problem. *The Times* had been able to obtain a
visa for Tom Walker, a young journalist who owed much of his reputation to his coverage of the Albanian uprising in 1997. He was a
good writer and was unusual among journalists who specialised in
the region in being on good terms with the Foreign Office. The
British and the Serbs were seen as having a 'special relationship', just
as Germany and Austria did with the Croats, and Serbia often got a
sympathetic press in Britain in the early 1990s as a result. This did
not take place in the United States or on independent US television
channels such as CNN, much to the Serbs' discomfort.

The story moved on to the leader pages in the next two weeks,
with the *Guardian* writing on 16 January that Milošević must be told

that Kosova was not an internal Serbian matter, and that conflict there could soon set the southern Balkans alight. This was a perceptive forecast; the military movement that was intended to do this had begun, with movement of Yugoslav heavy armour into Kosova from the big barracks at Vranje and Niš, and the operational redeployment of existing Prishtina Corps forces. If you lived in a village in central Kosova or the western mountains where the KLA was also stirring, this meant one terrible and simple truth, that an artillery shell might come straight through the wall or roof and blow you, your family and your farm animals to pieces. It was not long before artillery fire was directed in this way, as it had been at Sarajevo and Vukovar in the Bosnian and Croatian wars. Militarily the tactics were archaic, an inheritance of the Yugoslav army from early communist years of dependence on Russian military doctrine, where peacekeeping meant reducing rebellious rural insurgents villages to rubble in a way a Roman general might have admired in the first century AD. In the time-honoured phrase of Livy, they made a desert and called it peace.

I remember how miserable I felt walking around Wapping one afternoon on the way to a meeting, knowing that this was going to happen. The dust from Virginia Street and the Mile End road blew round the huge trucks delivering rolls of paper. It was always 'the plant', a news monster that ate raw material and produced millions upon millions of newspapers a year. Soon the papers would be filled with pictures of burning Kosova and dead people including, possibly, people I knew well. Albanian women would be raped, young Serbs would roast in upturned APVs. I did not relish the next six months. It was good to know Wapping was there with its eternally tough, sensible and realistic staff and I felt fortunate to be able to write for News International papers. The loneliness that affects all foreign correspondents is much easier when you know there is something solid back at the London ranch. Peter Stothard, the learned and scholarly editor, had recently written in the paper, apropos something else entirely, that journalism deals with the bad news and often the darker side of life, and that was true. But in the East End rain I thought how much easier it was when the story was of sudden death—perhaps an earthquake that reduced a city to ruins, a gas explosion or a train disaster, rather than a war that could have been prevented years ago and was now inexorably unfolding.

In Kosova the next phase of the war was born in Prekaz village, a few miles from Llaushe where I had been the month before. Prekaz was an agricultural community in a grassy valley three miles south of an ammunition factory, and the Jashari family were small and moderately prosperous farmers and well-known community leaders. They had inherited the Kacak tradition of rural Albanian rebellion, and had attacked the police in the past for intruding on their property.[2] They lived in a large complex of farm buildings that was first attacked in January, and finally destroyed by intensive shelling and an infantry assault on 5 March With one exception, the entire Jashari family of fifty-two people was killed, some bodies being charred beyond recognition. The Jashari brothers were involved with the KLA, and Adem Jashari had been arrested and gaoled in Albania as long ago as 1993, an illustration of the real relationship of the Democratic Party government to the national movement. A botched attempt to kill the family by the MUP on 22 January had intensified local feelings. The Serbs were driven off by a group of KLA fighters. Then in March the farm, a stout old wooden construction, was taken apart by artillery and small arms fire in an hour or two. The battle was as if choreographed, with the entire Jashari male clan making a last stand inside. A Kosova house is difficult to defend. Timber is nearly always the main construction material, and Kosova villages, particularly in Drenice, often stand on the open plain with little cover and easy visibility for artillery or rocket fire. A single rocket can start the fire that destroys a home where a family has lived for hundreds of years.

My friend Tim Judah wrote of this: 'The deaths of the Jasharis left Kosovo reeling. Years of accumulated frustration boiled over and demonstrations were held across the province. Within weeks everything began to change, the status quo that had held since 1990 began to collapse and everyone was shocked by what was happening.'[3] But not everyone reacted in the same way. Milošević humiliated Robin Cook, the British Foreign Secretary, when he visited Belgrade and tried to point the Serbian leader in a more reasonable direction. Absent from the Prishtina street demonstrations were Rugova and

---

[2] The Kacaks fought for Kosova in the 1920s against Yugoslavia and Tirana government repression.

[3] See *Kosovo War and Revenge* (Yale University Press, 2000).

the LDK leadership—in my own opinion, then and now, the biggest and worst single mistake and betrayal of Kosova by a leadership that has so often been accused of betraying the trust of its loyal followers. The Jashari massacre was a massive and open human rights crime that would have engaged the sympathy of the world for the Kosovar cause if it the leadership had reacted in the right way. Instead Rugova sat in his house, the LDK issued wordy statements, and the initiative on the ground passed irrevocably to the KLA and the militants. There are times when a good argument can be made, or not made, for saying that the war started on a particular day, but there was only one date when a central political error was made that ensured, that the tide of blood and violence would become a flood: 5 March 1999. Some diplomats and journalists are struck by the ferocity of the hatred shown towards Rugova by other Albanian leaders, even the most reasonable and 'moderate' such as Arben Xhaferi in Skopje, but the total organisational incapacity of the LDK after 5 March has affected the collective memory deeply.

The destruction of an entire family is a matter of the utmost gravity in Kosova Albanian society. Unnatural death is not uncommon there, for political or other reasons, and individuals are lost in the ceaseless struggle against Serbia, but the *fis*, the family root, the stem, must carry on. Sometimes the death of an individual is compared to the loss of a branch from the central tree trunk. The destruction and massacre at Prekaz was meant to send a message to the Serbian public that Milošević had the Kosova crisis under control, and that, as in 1945–9, brute force would succeed in crushing Albanian aspirations. The opposite was the case, and the misjudgement at Prekaz set the war in motion in a quite fundamentally different way, and support began to mobilise for the KLA within the often divided and factionalised Albanian world in a way few people had believed possible. While the feared SAJ anti-terrorist units were in action in Likoshane village a few days later, Hashim Thaci and his colleagues were active building the military framework in Drenice. Adem Demaci was in talks that were to lead to him becoming the KLA political spokesman. In Prishtina the events at Prekaz caused a fundamental change in the atmosphere. In Kosova terms they had the same symbolic and media impact as the Bloody Sunday shootings in Derry in 1972 had on relations between the British Army and the IRA and its Catholic supporters. In the Kosova Albanian mind the war, in terms of a mass struggle involving the whole of Kosova, began in that first week of March. It was all hands on deck, from the Albanian cafés in Chicago, New York and Paterson, New Jersey, to the *Kneipers* (drinking dens) of Hamburg, the shops of Lucerne and the bars of Geneva and Zurich.

Like most other Western newspapers, *The Times* had nobody with a current visa in Kosova at the time of the Jashari massacre and the barbarity at first went almost unreported. No doubt the authorities in Belgrade had studied the media situation before deciding on the decisive crackdown. When the story was broken by the Albanian media, it was subject to the usual suspicions of exaggeration and spin from the pro-Serb elements in the British and American press. Only a few frontline people like Philip Schmuker, a gifted American journalist filing for the *Daily Telegraph*, got to the heart of the story. Milošević's strategy was clear, in that he had been happy to allow the media in to break the story of the KLA in Drenice, but then wanted them out while his initial 'anti-terrorism' operation was going on. In Wapping the *Times* Desk was prompt in understanding the significance of the events, and I was given almost a whole page of the paper to myself on 6 March to set out the historical background, write a colour picture portrait of Rugova and a chronology of the main recent events. I also had room to do an early analysis piece headlined 'Unrest ignites fuse to Kosovo timebomb', in which it was possible to say both what was obvious—that Kosova was a Balkan timebomb that had never gone off for ten years but was now doing so—and more important contemporary observations that the Foreign Office did not want to hear, for example that I thought the vast majority of inhabitants did not want to live in any form of united Yugoslavia, and that many people were becoming increasingly radical and sympathetic to the KLA. It seemed necessary to put forward some sort of policy suggestion, so I said that Kosova needed its own independent United Nations rapporteur to try to bring the parties together.

The realities of diplomacy were fairly depressing. At the same time the British ambassador to Belgrade, Brian Donnelly, was visiting Prishtina, and diplomatic activity accelerated. I had crossed swords with Donnelly many years before, when I had written a long feature for the *Independent* about violence among British tourists in

Greece, and did not have high expectations in that quarter. Apart from personal issues, the diplomats were paying the price for long years of exclusive contact with Rugova and his entourage, and there was nobody in the KLA for them to talk to, even if they wished to do so. In the towns people began preparing for the war they had long feared, with panic-buying of essentials in local stores. Cellars were stacked high with bags of flour, beans and rice.

After the success of the Dayton agreement in Bosnia, and the limits of European diplomacy, eyes naturally turned towards the United States for a solution to the crisis. Yet its activity inadvertently accelerated the slide into war. The US envoy to Yugoslavia, Robert Gelbard, had arrived in Prishtina on 22 Febuary for a one-day visit and held a disastrous press conference. It was not really his fault. Robert Gelbard is a cheerful as well as an intelligent man, who had the freedom of Kosova at heart but had been given an impossible brief by the State Department, which was still clearly in the frame of mind that Milošević was a 'partner for peace', and was appeasing the Serb position. It lacked the clarity of the CIA and many of the Pentagon people about what was involved. In his statement Gelbard observed that further economic sanctions might be imposed upon the Belgrade government, and that the US government believed the Kosova crisis should be resolved within the Yugoslav borders. Both sides should refrain from the use of force, and he condemned the 'terrorist actions' of the Kosova Liberation Army. This remark caused uproar in Prishtina, since it seemed to suggest a moral equivalence between the state terror of the Yugoslav army and police against families like the Jasharis, and the poorly-armed village self-defence mechanism which the KLA essentially was at this stage in most places. A *carte blanche* was given to Milošević to do what he liked, and 'anti-terrorist' operations accelerated, in the form of relentless shelling of villages where the KLA was alleged to be. It meant that the old *status quo* was decisively ended. Kosovar Albanians had seen the Dayton process reward the Bosnian Serbs' aggression with a mini-state of their own, and understood that the international community only moves when there is a threat of force.

After Dayton a key correspondence had been formed in Britain between the Foreign Office spin machine wishing to promote

Dayton as the answer to the problems of the whole region, and intelligence interests, principally in MI6 and their French equivalents, which had believed that the Serbs would (and should) always rule Kosova. Some British embassies in the region were particularly hardline exponents of this view, particularly that in Athens which always had a distinct atmosphere of its own—élitist, arrogant and profoundly anti-Albanian. The Athens embassy was a prestige operation for the British, who claimed that because Greece was the only EU member in the region it had a special role to play in deciding policy. In practice this meant laying down an ill-informed but prescriptive policy position (few Athens diplomats had ever been north of the Greek border) that usually reflected the obselete and often bizarre nostrums of the Greek right. Its central objective was to build a neo-Titoist Yugoslavia, using Milošević as a 'reformist' communist, to protect wider Greek interests in the region. The notion that Greece might be better served by a policy that balanced Serb and Albanian claims in Kosova does not seem ever to have entered its thinking, then or since.

The key issue in these months was the effort to break down this consensus based on ignorance, ill-remembered history dating back to the Greek civil war, and vehement anti-Islamic feeling which only gave the Yugoslav army an excuse to do as it liked in Kosova. Robert Gelbard clearly had no idea of the serious consequences that would flow from his words, and the State Department backtracked soon afterwards and gave a strong message to Milošević that he must stop the repression and violence. But Milošević knew the Europeans were on his side, and the United States still had the Dayton albatross (in Kosova terms) tied around its neck, and the Serb leader gave his military commanders a free hand in the field. Many of them had fewer moral qualms about killing Albanians than an English countryman would have about shooting a pheasant, and they were not slow to intensify the campaign of military repression.

The Serbian dictator thought he could play the British card as he had done in Bosnia under the Major government, a process of appeasement that has been exposed in Brendan Simms's book *Unfinest Hour—Britain and the Destruction of Bosnia* (London: Penguin, 2002). He did not seem to realise that the advent of the Blair government would lead to a major policy reorientation in London, although at first the process was slow. As long as the crisis could be confined to Foreign Office 'management' this was probably a reasonable assumption, with the Foreign Secretary Robin Cook showing distinctly pro-Serb tendencies after a more independent start in office. His statement on 3 March also made the KLA an equivalent negative force to Milošević's terror squads, despite the obvious fact that if there had not been Yugoslav terror for so many years the KLA would never have come into existence to defend homes and families. Milošević had no understanding of the nature of the new Blair government, with a foreign policy team of a new, strongly pro-American orientation being built up which would take a different view of events. But in the meantime traditional chancery diplomacy had to be given its time, and the worst agonies for the people would begin. The chanceries would fail, as for so long they had failed Croatia and Bosnia. Milošević moved more and more men and equipment into Kosova. In the Albanian diaspora more support moved towards the KLA.

In villages across Kosova, but mainly in the west and centre of the country, old weapons carefully hidden for years were removed from their hiding places, and night-time patrolling of neighbourhoods developed further. The KLA was less of an army in any traditional sense than a spontaneous people's movement. The best picture of the developing war in this area is to be found in the Decani KLA commander Ramush Haradinaj's brilliant little book published simultaneously in Albanian and English, *A Narrative about War and Freedom*.[4] Hundreds of men wished to join the KLA but could not because of the chronic weapons shortage. Some of the limited number fortunate enough to have weapons had little or no ammunition. There was an organised group of fighters, maybe no more than 2–300, and a large number of supporters and people trying to do what they could in their own towns and villages. In different and varied localities, the people had seen what could be achieved by popular insurgent action in Albania, and the early growth of the resistance owed much to the Albanian people at a symbolic level. At this stage in the war, this was its greatest strength, for the Milošević forces had no intelligence on where the KLA might be developing, and no doctrine on how to oppose it. Serbian intelligence had long concentrated on

[4] By Zeri, Prishtina, 2000.

the leading figures in the early underground organisations such as Xharvit Haliti and Hashim Thaci, who were seen as classic conspirators, and as a result it had little sense of how the KLA would develop as a popular movement. Yet the KLA's initial lack of organisation was also a great weakness, for without a formal military structure the supply of weapons was totally inadequate. The emphasis that Thaci placed on security considerations and political reliability in deciding whom to recruit as KLA 'sleepers' in the early 1990s was essential to avoid Serb infiltration, but it made some vital logistics and organisation activities very difficult once the spread of the war was rapid. Another key weakness was the attitude to the Kosova issue of the Tirana governments, both Democratic Party and Socialist, between 1992 and 1998. Although the northern border guards could be bribed to let material through, collusion from the Albanian government was essential to import the large quantities of small arms and other material needed for a war. Under both Berisha and Nano this was never properly forthcoming, and foreign agencies traded information with the Albanian secret intelligence service—this led, directly and indirectly, to the arrest and even death of some KLA members. Perhaps the most notorious arrest was that of the KLA founding father and Llap mountain hero Zahir Pajaziti, who was imprisoned by the Berisha government for a border arms smuggling offence in 1995. There were some outstanding patriots among the Albanian army leadership and recently retired officers such as Colonel Shaip Zeneli. They organised assistance, but by doing so continually risked arrest.

The reaction of the Serb security apparatus after Prekaz had an inexorable logic that led to the targeting of the entire population. An important question for future historians will be the degree of British complicity in this process. According to Tim Judah (as already mentioned), the bugging devices the KLA leaders found in premises were often of British manufacture—possibly they were bought by the Serbs on the open market, but such deals are difficult without government consent. Some KLA leaders such as Shaban Shala, for a long time head of the KLA in Drenice, had authorised contacts with US, Swiss and British intelligence officials as long ago as 1992 in Switzerland. Leakage of information within these organisations to Milošević's secret police was always possible, either by accident or as a result of deliberate policy. The information about the pro-Serb inclination of most MI6 officers revealed in the renegade spy Richard Tomlinson's book *The Big Breach*, coupled with the political orientation of the Major government, makes such a possibility real.

Tom Walker wrote a good story from Prishtina saying that he had met a Serb policeman at a roadblock who had reacted to the news of Adem Jashari's death by saying 'Public Enemy Number one is dead, the bastard. Only two million to go'. In the minds of the Serbs was the old plan first put forward by Vojislav Cubrilovic in the 1930s, to drive the Albanians finally out of Kosovo and reclaim their land. Slobodan Milošević was taking up this mantle, but it was important for him to disguise his true intentions from the international community. The rhetoric of anti-terrorism provided such an opportunity, and that of anti-Islam enabled the Serbs to claim that the KLA was a 'Mujahidin resistance' organisation. Walker reported in *The Times* that the 'Albanians are falling into the trap of a media war and desperate for attention, have pushed forward witnesses to the police terror.' This was a strange judgement. The hundreds of thousands of refugees were to prove the most potent weapon in the Albanian armoury later in the summer when they dominated the television screens.

In Prishtina 30,000 people marched for freedom and fought a pitched battle with police. The Serbs used water-cannon and baton charges to break up the demonstration, after sixteen Albanians had been killed by Serb forces over the previous weekend. They chanted 'We will give up our lives, but we won't give up Kosova'. A reporter broke his leg when he jumped out of a first-floor window in the *Koha Ditore* building to escape the police. Veton Surroi was beaten up in a separate incident near the radio station. The police put out a statement that the demonstrators were supporters of 'terrorism'. The Tirana socialist government, with its collaborationist Greek links, was silent, but Sali Berisha, as Opposition leader, put out a statement calling for the EU and America to intervene. A Kosova marker in Tirana politics had been put down that was to have serious consequences in the months ahead, and lead to assassinations of individuals and an attempted coup by September 1998.[5]

The Serbs thought they knew where their most determined opponents lived—in the villages in the hills nearest Albania, communities

[5] See Vickers and Pettifer, *The Albanian Question*, London: I. B. Tauris, 2005.

far from the eyes and ears of the international community. They were also far from the knowledge or experience of all Western journalists and media people. The epic battle for the Kosare corridor that Ramush Haradinaj and his unit fought to keep the arms transfer route open to Albania was in a place where it was more or less impossible for foreigners to go, a few miles from Albania up a precipitous mountain track in deep forest. It would have been necessary to leave Prishtina, cross most of Kosova (assuming the police would let you through roadblocks, which they would not), and then shake off security surveillance to enter the vast and empty forests with the Albanian border beyond, high in the mountains. The only way to do this was on foot. There was no local transport that could be hired, and local people were terrified of illegal association with foreigners. The rule of law, even the Yugoslav communist version, was non-existent. The police could shoot or arrest anyone they liked, without consequences. In some places within the border security zone the police and army would shoot to kill as a matter of normal military procedure. The theatre of war in the west was *terra incognita*, even to the most experienced and knowledgeable, and in the spring of 1998 this was one of Milošević's greatest assets. The only type of reporter able to cover the story would have been one with experience in the Special Forces, which no one had.

The Serb army and security apparatus still had unchallenged control of the roads so that, for instance, they were able to prevent thousands of mourners converging on Prekaz for the Jashari family funeral. The local media were in a better position, and as a result some photographs of the funerals found their way into the international press. On 4 March a huge crowd of over 40,000 people gathered on the Likoshane hillside to bury their dead there. This was covered, with some Western reporters simply walking over the border from Albania into Kosova to get there, and for some people the Kosova story almost seemed to merge into the Albanian story that had taken so many pages of copy in 1997 only a few months before. This had some effect on the tone and atmosphere of the reporting, with the media instinctively seeing the rank and file of the Kosova Albanians as the same sort of people as those who made a justified stand against the pyramid sharks in Albania the year before. Also, a significant number of media people had worked in Bosnia and had strong anti-

Serb inclinations. Here, in media terms, attempts at media manipulation by the Tory government and MI6 in Bosnia sowed dragon's teeth that benefited the Kosova Albanians.

In London there was intense interest within the media in establishing the identity of the KLA. The movement did not have a named leader, or anybody who could be interviewed, although there had been a representative in London for some time: Pleurat Seidiu, a young doctor. At that point he was still operating incognito from a garage in Finchley. The Serbs had issued background intelligence briefings to their friends in the media and the Foreign Office and other government ministries, based on intelligence about the activities of people in the diaspora like Thaci. The organisations like the LKCK (the National League for the Liberation of Kosova) and the LPK (the Kosova People's Movement) to which he and others belonged were characterised as 'Marxist' or 'Enverist' and were often alleged to be funded by crime or drug money. Although little or no concrete evidence was ever produced to support these claims, they had some effect in predictable quarters. Belgrade has considerable backstairs influence in Interpol, and was able to stereotype the KLA as a 'narcoterrorist' operation, a ridiculous claim given the situation on the ground.

The radicals of the LKCK were then, in my experience, mainly a Prishtina and central Kosova party, whereas the LPK had more strength in the diaspora, particularly in Switzerland. Some commentators have speculated that ideological differences between them were less important than leadership personalities. It was a time when the political appeal of Albania as a state-model was waning, and the United States was the only international partner in which the Kosova Albanians could have any faith. Perhaps this was so, and certainly a leader like Hashim Thaci was involved because these organisations provided a strong and secure underground system of organisation which the Serbs could not penetrate, rather than 'Enverist' ideology. Thaci has had little or no interest in radical social or political theories since his student days, and has Blairite views on most subjects. However, there was a basic difference between them: the LPK was more élitist and saw the need for an army as central, while the LKCK focussed more on the possibility of a popular uprising against the Serbs.

Despite the limited influence of left-wing political ideology, the success of the KLA in this period owed more to Marxist *military* models than its leaders have generally wanted to admit. On 8 April 1998 Kurt Schork had reported for Reuters that KLA guerrillas were 'freely roaming the countryside', and that 'if you don't find the KLA, they will soon find you.' He added: 'KLA members refuse to discuss tactics or strategy. Military analysts say their future, if any, is as a hit and run force...but the sight of men digging trenches in the hills suggests the KLA may want to hold isolated patches of territory while harassing the Serbian police. That seems a suicidal plan for a foe capable of dealing a devastating blow with helicopters and heavy weapons against individual locations.'[6] The liberated zones in the countryside were a classic derivative of the theorists of revolutionary war, but in some senses they were misleading. Although they obtained media focus that spring, the war was always alive in Prishtina and in the key Vushtri-Podujeve-Llap liberated area, as far from Tirana or Tetovo as it is possible to be in the Albanian lands. In the view of Commander Remi, all significant Serb police activity had been stopped in the Llap and Podujeve area as early as the autumn of 1996, a factor that had helped precipitate the crackdown and run of arrests in the north-east in January 1997.[7]

The mass media arrived in the spring of 1998, and since all Prishtina KLA activity took place in the illegal underground, in conditions of considerable danger and stress, the Albanians took care not to advertise the urban presence of the KLA to the media. Those hundreds of early morning journeys that the TV trucks took out of Prishtina to Malisheve, Likoshane and the first Drenice refugee camps perhaps illustrate more about the way television redefines the agenda of a modern war once it gets involved than anything specific about Kosova. The war was going on almost everywhere in Kosova except places like Gjilan, where the KLA was weak, but the outside world was told little about it. An interview with a key underground leader in Prishtina like Valon Murati would have been a story for a print journalist, but nothing for television. The mass of apparently leaderless refugees living under plastic sheets provided perfect television to show the lives of the victims of the conflict, and unanswer-

---

[6] See Vickers/Pettifer, op. cit.
[7] See 'War for Kosova', Remi, 'Zeri', Prishtina, 2000.

able footage in the cause of humanitarian intervention, but almost nothing of value about what was at stake politically. The instinctive media—savvyness of the peasants effectively conveyed their own appalling experiences at the hands of the Serbs. In turn this redefined the diplomatic agenda, since a clear priority was to get people back to their homes and off the television screens, rather than examine the roots of the war, which were in Belgrade.

In retrospect this probably helped the Kosova Albanian cause somewhat. However carefully conducted, interviews with the KLA leadership could have fallen into the trap of seeming to expose small groups of intense and obviously politically motivated individuals to the glare of their opponents' spin machines. Even someone as articulate and skilled with the foreign media as Hashim Thaci or as brave as Ramush Haradinaj might have had difficulty convincing a hostile interviewer that people had only joined these little groups when they were new for practical survival reasons and not because they wanted a 'Greater Albania' or a communist revolution as prescribed by Enver Hoxha. Those who had chosen to stay within the LDK for a long time, like Remi, would have been characterised as 'entryists' or 'subversives' in an otherwise 'moderate' movement. The seriousness and mild austerity that the military culture of the KLA encouraged would have been seen as unattractive to foreign eyes, which were used to seeing Balkan paramilitaries as hard-drinking, gun-toting successors to Lord Byron's klephts. The profound family links and kinship between young men would have been classed as characteristic of a mafia, and the heroic willingness to die for a free Kosova could have been seen as 'fanaticism' compared to the urbane coffee-table intellectualism of Rugova. Sometimes silence is golden, as the old proverb says, and for the KLA underground that spring it certainly was. Apparently ordinary and innocuous young men and women in the Prishtina streets watched the media in action and made their evaluation, while the media may have looked back and occasionally filmed them without having the least idea who they really were.

At the Ministry of Defence in Belgrade the military planners were deliberating over maps and charts of Kosova. They had a good formal military education, which the Albanian soldiers did not. The philosopher Geoffrey Best has written that the way in which a society chooses to wage war is not only tied to concepts about the actual practice of war, but also mirrors how that society sees itself, and implies a specific set of understandings about the nature of war. The Serb generals had a major problem. Wars are usually fought to defend some existing society that seems to the protagonist worth defending; but Kosovo Serb society was so deeply dysfunctional, as it had been for many years, that Serbs had been leaving more and more rapidly. What was actually being defended in Kosova? The society defended in practice was ever more narrowly based on the army itself, the police (controlled by Milošević in Belgrade) and the security apparatus. Although the media sometimes sought Serb views, and a fine British television documentary, 'The Valley', depicted the problems of the Kosova Polje Serbs, television in 1998–9 mostly showed Kosova as an exclusively Albanian society, with the Serbs more or less exclusively seen as part of a repressive foreign military apparatus.

Thaci and his military planners thus had a much easier task; they saw this Milošević-controlled machine as illegitimate and colonial, and it could therefore be attacked on a moral basis. They were able, in time, to transfer this understanding of reality to NATO, so that not only Kosova would be covered in the NATO bombing campaign, but the whole of Yugoslavia. This was why the KLA was able to win key Western support, where so many previous Balkan popular movements had not. The Serb army was a more unified and better functioning organisation than the KLA, but it was very resistant to change, whereas the KLA was constantly changing—not as efficient, but flexible and able to survive adverse circumstances. It combined the characteristics of a popular movement with those of an army. In a certain sense it 'was' Kosova. Among other things, the Kosova campaign in the spring of 1998 was a test of the capacity of a traditional Clausewitzian army when it came to repressing an insurgency in modern Europe. The Yugoslav forces did not fare well in the end, a fact that has since given many conservative diplomats, soldiers and internationals pause for thought before committing themselves to support for Kosova. How would the Romanian army, say, conduct itself if faced with trouble from the country's Hungarian minority? Would the Belgian army be of any value in a conflict between Flemings and Walloons? Might the Spanish army sometime be forced into the Basque country in a crisis? These are problems from the dark subconscious of the European military and diplomatic mind, but however remote, they could not inconceivably become reality one day. Soldiers from the British army involved in Kosova had spent many years before arriving in Prishtina in 1999 in an unsatisfactory, ultimately inconclusive campaign against the Irish Republican Army. The French army is said to have scenarios for intervention in French cities if inter-ethnic violence between the Arab and Muslim minorities and local people should break out and get beyond police control. The current 'peace process' in Ireland originated, at least in part, because British governments felt a military victory was unattainable.

Kosova independence, when it comes, will rest in part on a successful insurgency war, if not a general uprising, and it is not a precedent the rulers of the European Union states would wish to see followed elsewhere in Europe. The apparently unjust and irrational support that Slobodan Milošević has received from some of these quarters arose not from any particular admiration for him or for the Serbs as such, but from a sense that one of the methods of state control—the last resort of 'sending the troops in'—might not work in a modern society with modern mass media and concepts of legality in peacekeeping. Kosova in February and March 1998 was becoming a laboratory for the testing of these theories, something that was unknown then to all participants in the struggle on the ground.

The struggle was not only being conducted on the ground. Just as this was the first war where the international mobile telephone network was to play a decisive part, so it was also the first war which spread to the Internet with a new front being formed in cyberspace. In Croatia and Bosnia the Internet had played a part but with power cuts and lack of access to computers it had had a limited role. In the Kosova conflict the Internet developed as a fully-fledged weapon, particularly in the hands of the Albanian diaspora who were able to circulate sympathetic media stories with great rapidity in their own scattered communities, and mobilise financial and material support for the war in way that made it very hard for Milošević's counter-insurgency operation to succeed. Observers in the outside world and even well-informed writers and diplomats involved were often unaware of the full dimension of this aspect of the conflict until well after it had finished.

The centralised nature of the war coverage in and around Prishtina was important, with almost all reporters returning to sleep in the city most nights, and the Media Centre circulating each morning copies of all stories that had appeared in the world press about Kosova. So governments and policy-making agencies tried to by-pass the independent reporters and communicate their information directly to the world via the Internet. This led to further fragmentation of official viewpoints, and just as the *modus operandi* of the KLA was new, with its loose decentralised structures, so the flow of information about the Kosova war was asymmetrical, unpredictable and ultimately beyond the capacity of any élite group or the government to control.

A Way

According to the material that was beginning to appear on the Internet about the First Offensive, the Kosova war 'posed new challenges for journalists'. In essence this meant that the problem of finding the action in the war meant either confronting the Serb army and police checkpoints or finding ways round them. Back in the Prishtina Media Centre the government spread disinformation— and some information. The war was in the depths of the woods. Check-points still existed on all the major roads, which sometimes worked and sometimes did not. And because the Serbs knew that journalists could take the by-roads and dirt roads, they began to mine them. Work became much more dangerous.

One night it had rained heavily and the street (since 1999 renamed after Mother Theresa) along which one walked home from the theatre bar was a river of brown water inches deep, with every drain blocked. The stream ran down towards the communists concrete pinnacle celebrating Unity and Brotherhood, over the top of the post office's concrete steps, and down towards the post office. This was the post office that in May 1999 was to experience perhaps the finest technical achievement of the United States Navy in the war, an inch-perfect hit by a cruise missile from a ship out in the Adriatic hundreds of miles away that fired the top of the building and by an electromagnetic shock took out all the electrical equipment in Milošević's phone lines but did not damage the historic buildings nearby. Tonight the water was running down the post office's pale grey concrete like a river. Below the main street the stream took a quick right, and rushed down further steps into the street which winds round towards the jewellers' shops where silver filigree was worked and the one selling the great Kosovska sheepskin bed underlays, and finally found some obscure way to cascade over the old railway track into oblivion.

The same water in the countryside would be soaking the refugees under plastic sheeting. In the morning, venturing into Drenice, it had completed its course and disappeared into the ground leaving a sea of mud. Somewhere a village or two would be being shelled, but to discover where was impossible. The best one could do to get to it was to try a promising road. The truck-mounted artillery pieces left the barracks early in the morning; it was possible to follow them, until after a while they would become aware of you and then you would be stopped and turned back. Shelling started around lunch time, and often lasted only a few minutes, and the first guide to the location of the chosen village was a column of smoke in the distance. The nearby roads would be closed for a time, and as the light started to fade, the army would go home to barracks. For the soldiers involved it was, in its way, not very different from a day's work in the office, or a training exercise. They had no clear idea of the havoc they had created, and never saw any of the people who were being killed or maimed, or the farm animals that were turning into blackened carcasses. In their armoured vehicles they were safe from the KLA and more or less indifferent to journalists. They sat around drinking slivowitz and relaxed after a period of shelling. It was as if the once great and dignified Yugoslav federal army with its origins in the heroic wartime Partisan movement that had defeated Hitler had become a cheap police state machine. As if to defy world opinion, Slobodan Milošević actually went on an election campaign tour to Kosova. It was a hurried affair, a few rushed photo-opportunities, and a rally in central Prishtina where he said 'The word Kosova is frequently being used in pressure against our country.... There are no pressures under which we will yield an inch of Kosova or Metohija.' It was the last speech he would make in Kosova.

The summer of illusions

When another visa eventually came through at the end of May, central Prishtina had been transformed into a media city. In the evenings cicadas were noisy in the trees above the dusty streets. The city that had been menacing, dark and lonely the previous winter was a cheerful, sunny and gregarious place where old friends and colleagues met and drank coffee or something stronger. The full panoply of the international media had arrived. The car park in front of the Grand was full of white armoured Land Rovers and Toyotas with 'TV' written in thick black adhesive tape on the roofs and doors. Whether this would deter or encourage Serb gunners was a matter of opinion. A large white satellite dish had been set up on the grass, with cables trailing down to it from a fourth floor window. An upper floor of the hotel had been emptied of guests to make a media centre. A service company based in Cyprus had moved in to look after the vehicles, and its crew swapped stories about wars in Afghanistan and Beirut, and what the Hizbollah interpreter did the first time he drank alcohol. Kosova had hit the big time; the days of coverage by reporters with biro and notebook were over for ever, or so it seemed.

Green and inexperienced journalistic newcomers asked the way to the 'front', and seemed disappointed when anyone who knew anything at all about the Kosova war told them that there wasn't one. They were standing on an invisible front line in the middle of Prishtina. Some of the greatest war coverage has always been generated by correspondents following in the dust thrown up by an advancing army, from the time of Julius Caesar to the beach landings in Italy in the Second World War where Ernie Pyle followed the GIs into the breaking waves and over the sand. His work is honoured by a plaque in the Pentagon near the press gallery, and for good reason. For straightforward action reporting the reporter finds the front, gets in behind whoever is winning or seems to be winning, and lets the infantry do the rest. It is even reasonably safe while your side is advancing, but rapidly becomes less so as an advance slows down and Desks demand more and more dangerous 'action' of close infantry encounters. In Vietnam many photographers were killed in these circumstances. This close combat in the Kosova war was not reached until the reorganisation of the KLA in the spring of 1999.

All this was ahead in June 1998, when all that mattered was that the 'CNN effect' was in full flow, and it remained to be seen what results it would have. It was certain that the arrival of the television heavy battalions would alter the agenda. In the disparaging language of British army commanders in Bosnia, the 'media circus' had arrived, although those with a less jaundiced view (I believed the jaundice originated in Ulster) might regard the media as a vital part of the apparatus of democracy. By early June a whole series of international ultimatums to Belgrade had expired, Richard Holbrooke's well-meaning diplomacy was going nowhere, and star names such as CNN's Christiane Amanpour had arrived to cover the NATO 'flyover' on June 15 which was the first real warning of military action. Nobody knew exactly what NATO was planning, except that the operation had been designated a 'live fire exercise' called 'Operation Determined Falcon'. Because, understandably, NATO had no press office in Kosova, there was no way local journalists could find out more. Foreign crews relied on the local staff of Veton Surroi and other newspaper owners for basic information, which meant that the day of the NATO overfly was awaited in a fog of universal ignorance. The name 'Determined Falcon' turned out to be the only determined thing about it. NATO's General Secretary Javier Solana said in a statement that it was designed to show Milošević that NATO had the ability to project power rapidly into the region. Six Royal Air Force Jaguar fighters were going to take part.

In Prishtina there was an atmosphere of great expectation. The results of NATO's absent airshow were dismal. It was beautiful Kosova spring weather, the wild flowers were out and the social scene in Prishtina was being transformed, with new restaurants opening to meet the demands of the journalists and television crews. Suddenly there was a sense of energy and direction, and Albanians were quietly jubilant, the intellectuals because they knew what the political effect of the media might be, the shopkeepers because of the amount of money the media were bringing into the local economy. People worked very hard, and then, in the memorable phrase of the late Peter Thompson, the original Athens correspondent of the *Independent*, they got thirsty. The presence of the big TV news-gathering organisations changed the political atmosphere in more subtle ways. Everyone there had worked in Bosnia, and the vast majority were instinctively sympathetic to the Albanians after enduring the years of official military and UN apologies for Serb aggression against the Bosnian people, and endless attempts to fake up and re-position stories. Many producers were also critical and suspicious of official diplomatic media people after the lies and distortions that had accompanied the Bosnian conflict, and had open ears for the Albanian case. The Serbs did not really understand this for some time, and thought that the formal press handouts from the Grand Hotel official media centre detailing the activity of the JNA in some distant village would content the correspondents. It took me a little time to realise how much the Serbs in Bosnia had relied on sympathetic British and other Western intelligence officers, who planted soft pro-Serb stories, but this would not work in Kosova. Apart from the professional nous of people who had discovered the extent of their deception over such stories as the Sarajevo market bombing, at this stage there were almost no diplomats or international community people in Prishtina since the Serbs did not allow them into Kosova. As a result the media had a free run to make up its own mind about what was happening, something that in retrospect did more to save the Albanian cause in the summer of 1998 than any other factor. The Media Centre was quite well run by a British-oriented Serb called Radovan Urosevac, who after July 1999 became an adviser in the British embassy in Belgrade, but it never succeeded in influencing the journalistic agenda much. It could hardly encourage journalists to go and watch hapless villagers being shot at and forced to flee their homes.

Work at this stage of the war fell into a regular pattern, with very early morning starts for the TV trucks which lumbered out of the Grand car park towards Drenice hoping to find some action. This was often difficult; the Serbs followed arbitary patterns of activity in their shelling of villages and knew the terrain well, which the crews did not. It had been quite a wet spring; the normally appalling state of rural Kosova tracks was worse than usual, and the heavily armoured TV vehicles were sinking into the deep mud, to the Serbs' amusement. Some of their military assaults took place at night anyway, particularly the dark affairs of the SAJ anti-terrorist units. Footage or print reports of firefights were rare, and the Bosnian-trained crews and producers were initially at a loss to know what to do, having come from covering a more set-piece war of encounters between formal armies. Film of a burnt-out shed or a shellhole in a house wall has limited interest without military actors—as T. S. Eliot wrote, passive suffering is not a subject for drama, and drama is what news crews need. As a result attention was focussed on the growing refugee crisis in central Drenice, which offered easy stories with lots of human interest in the form of whole families (sometimes minus the young men if they had gone to join the KLA) who had left their shattered homes to live in the forests. This was something Milošević had not anticipated; the Serbs regarded Albanian villagers in Drenice as little more than particularly warlike subhumans, and the thought that Western public opinion might be affected by the sight of the chaotic and emotional exodus of their suffering families apparently did not cross their minds. It was not as if the KLA had much idea about journalism either—sometimes you came across the guerrilla soldiers, scruffy and intense young men with AKs who were navigating offroad in ancient saloon cars. They were cheerful but deeply secretive and unhelpful and clearly did not have much idea of how to deal with the press. As an Albanian speaker I was assumed to be a British or American spy. It was a strange war, with none of the intense focus on the revolutionary crowd of the Albanian upheaval the year before, not was it a major running setpiece story such as the siege of Sarajevo.

Although much vaunted at the time, the 15 June NATO air exercise was seen in Kosova as a limp farce. The CNN battlebus with Christine Amanpour on board had left Prishtina at four in the morning and driven up to the top of the Sar mountains in order to get some good live footage, only to find no NATO plane in sight; most of them were alleged to have done something impressive in Albania but been careful not to stray anywhere near the border of 'Yugoslavia' or make any impression on Kosova airspace at all. It illustrated how far things had to go to produce real action by the international community against Milošević, who must have been laughing into his whisky in Belgrade. Jon Swain of the *Sunday Times* and Robert Fisk of the *Independent*, distinguished senior figures who were sharing a vehicle, went off to look at the Trepce mines to do a story there and get away from the vacuity of it all. The atmosphere in the offices of *Koha Ditore* newspaper was gloomy. The international press relied heavily on Surroi's local correspondents for news from the rural areas where access was still difficult, given VJ and MUP control of the roads. Veton had set aside a wall for people to sign their names, and it was soon covered with some of the most distinguished journalistic signatures in the business. However, many of them could not find much to file about. CNN left a permanent skeleton team in its rooms in the Grand, and clearly expected the story to develop, but Christine soon left town after the NATO aeronautics in early June. The BBC had a lower profile throughout and at this stage the story was not being covered by any big name people, let alone luminaries such as John Simpson. He had not yet dignified Kosova with his august and generous presence. The Albanian journalists with contacts in the BBC Albanian Service at Bush House in London were relieved, even glad, at this since his personal outlook was reputed to be strongly pro-Serb. I felt at the time, and since, that this was an over-simplification. The problem the BBC had was that it was subject to endless institutional pressure from the spin machines in the usual quarters. Most people felt that Foreign Office influence over the BBC was a factor in this, along with the alleged pro-Serb orientation of some senior White City figures, based on the usual ill-informed sentiment about Tito, a leftist corporate culture, and memories of nice student holidays in Yugoslavia. Other networks had slightly different perspectives.

Bill Neely was a regular visitor, and his network, ITN, clearly took it all very seriously, but there was a sense that the BBC was still under some external FCO influence, and one cameraman I met told me that it was the received wisdom in their White City headquarters that the whole rebellion would die out by the autumn and Milošević would win this one, just as he had won Dayton. I felt depressed to be British, and profoundly grateful for the presence of American colleagues like Philip Schmucker and of CNN who did understand what was at stake. If Milošević won in Kosova, as he wished, and drove out the Albanians, he would be in power in Belgrade for the next fifty years or, as Ivor Roberts once observed, five hundred years if he lived that long.

The largest concentration of refugees both near Prishtina and in a relatively accessible place was at Kerzhareke, a tiny place in the Cerralaves hills about five miles south of Gllogoec. I first went there with an ITN crew, hitching a lift in their armoured Land Rover and sitting crammed in the back with a mountain of equipment. Fighting in and around Gllogoec had been continuing on and off all the time since I had seen the Serbs fortifying the ferro-nickel plant in

January, and savage ethnic cleansing had happened in many of the villages. We drove out of Prishtina towards Peje and took the usual road south from Gllogoec, through a deserted no-man's-land where rows of shops in villages had every window broken and the shelves stripped, and where the great farmhouse walls had round shellholes a metre across. Dead animals were everywhere, some of them burnt after being set on fire by the Serbs, with blackened legs sticking out from their bodies. Carved entrance gates hung at crazy angles and looked as if Genghis Khan and his horde had passed through. Small columns of people filed along the roadside, usually following a tractor loaded with their miscellaneous belongings, like footage of displaced persons in the Second World War. Turning west into the hills, we followed a narrow valley up to Kerzhareke, and soon hit a traffic jam where another TV truck had stuck in the foot-deep beige mud, blocking the road, and there was a melée of little carts and a tractor and cart stuck behind it.

Nothing could prepare you for the agglomeration of human misery beyond. About 5,000 people were camping out on slightly higher land by a stream, and living under plastic sheeting. The great majority were women and children, trying to preserve some semblance of human dignity and health in the wet and mud. Traumatised elderly women in their flower-patterned baggy trousers sat hunched on the damp earth floor of improvised plastic tents, staring fixedly into the distance. If war reporting is about creating pictures of the victims, here was a huge supply, and the whole chaotic medieval scene of course made wonderful television. Milošević had made a serious error in launching his First Offensive when he did, in early spring. Kosova people are very tough and could live like this all summer and autumn. In winter the deaths of the vulnerable little infants would begin. The effect of these scenes on world opinion would be dramatic. I interviewed a little man who was cooking meat over an open fire. He said: 'We were driven out at night. Now we live here. What are we going to do?' I had no answer but said I would write down what he said for a newspaper or magazine. Others told the same story. A group of young lads were carving the initials 'UCK', Ushtria Climitare e Kosoves (the KLA), on a big beech tree. They were having the time of their lives, it was a great adventure. More adolescents were carefully cutting an old oildrum in half to make a drinking trough for their animals, who were tied up in an enclosure hacked out of the oak scrub. The younger you were in this war the better the older the worse. Many of the older people still seemed to support Rugova. This was a young person's war—there was a massive generation gap in the Kosova community. The house was everything to the village women, and some of them rarely went out except to market once a week. Most older people thought they would never see their houses and land again. Nothing could convince them that they could ever win against the Serbs, or that real international support would come from NATO or anyone else. Their outlook was based on a mixture of Muslim fatalism, lack of confidence in the KLA, and ignorance of the political skills of Thaci, Demaci, Haliti and the leadership. In a narrow military sense their fears were understandable. The village militias, of which the KLA mostly consisted at that stage, could not defend them effectively against long-distance artillery shelling. Having seen the token and fatuous NATO fly-past the day before, you could understand their lack of confidence in foreign help. The great victory the internationals had allowed Milošević at Trepce in 1989 was still at the back of many older minds. The residual support for Rugova among the older generation was concealed from the foreign media, possibly because I was the only writer around who spoke Albanian and the others were dependent on interpreters, mostly young and radical and anxious to impress on their foreign employers that the KLA had overwhelming support. Interviewees who supported the KLA were indeed often chosen, since the only young people who spoke any English had lived in the diaspora, and they were far more likely to be KLA supporters. This was not a conspiracy, but a natural conjuncture of events, but it did transform the status of the story in world newsrooms within weeks. On television in distant places it seemed that most of the Albanians had abandoned Rugova and 'pacifism' to embrace the KLA, and that the war would develop into some sort of mass uprising similar to the Albanian events the year before.

In fact this was a false antithesis: many people, perhaps the majority, supported both Rugova and the KLA, wishing the KLA to fight and defend them, and Rugova to speak for them. Few internationals understood much recent Kosova history, and most did not know that most Albanians, even those closely involved with the KLA and the war, saw Rugova as a legally elected 'President' who had been forcibly displaced in 1991. A minority of Albanians were still not sure who the KLA were, and the foreign journalists who went down to Jakup Krasniqi's little KLA media centre in the hills near Malisheve were much better informed than some Kosovars. Albanians who had been in exile in Tirana and elsewhere in Albania in recent months recounted stories of the reservations concerning the Kosova cause among ministers in the Greek-influenced Nano government like Pascal Milo. Again, many reporters did not know that there had been no Albanian-language newspapers at all in Kosova in any real sense for nearly ten years, and in the villages people depended for news on Milošević's state television. Many had heard rumours of activity by Rugova's 'government' aimed at forming its own army in Albania, and expected a new defence force to emerge from there. The forests were a scene of massive practical chaos and confusion, but this was parallelled by the confusion over the politics of the war. Yet the Albanians reset the media agenda in a few weeks, in an astonishing way that no one could have foreseen.

There was virtually no KLA organisation as such in these improvised camps, but even the most uneducated people who had never met a Western journalist before soon began to understand what the media needed, and kept a remarkable simplicity and dignity in providing it. People stated what they thought to the cameras and reporters with perfect directness. TV producers who had arrived in Drenice forests expecting to shoot a few minutes of 'colour' found themselves recording hours of deeply moving interviews. Like magic the whole history of the violent repression of the last decades was coming out into the open. Illiterate elderly women explained the terror of village life in Kosova, not only under Milošević but ever since the origins of Yugoslavia in 1921. In their way of thinking the best Serb—in fact the only good Serb—was a dead one, whether of the royalist, Titoist or Milošević persuasion. By contrast the Serbs were either not willing to meet the media at all or, if they were, relied on prepared statements from the Media Centre. Local Serbs who were beginning to form paramilitary organisations to protect their areas appeared as bellicose and belligerent Milošević supporters. Between the middle of March and the middle of June 1998 the Albanians won the essentials of the media war, and although coverage would wax and wane with events, the Serbs were never able to recapture the basic agenda. The Western spin-doctors had often served the Serbian side quite well in Bosnia, dealing with set-piece issues, often in an urban setting, between organised military forces, but they were not there to spin in Drenice in the spring of 1998.

There was also, despite all the turmoil and what to an outsider seemed a terminal crisis for Yugoslav Kosovo, an astonishing degree of faith by some older people in the continuation of the Yugoslav state and the communist system. Driving across Drenice a day or two later, I came upon one of the oddest scenes I ever witnessed in ten years of covering Balkan turmoil. At the edge of Gllogoec village was the post office, a fiercely ugly Yugoslav building protected by barred windows and two policemen with sub-machine-guns. About fifty elderly men, most wearing the white *pliss*, were angrily banging on the windows and trying to break in. I stopped and asked one of them what on earth they were doing. Inside I could see a little Serb official who was clearly hoping that someone would come and rescue him from these strange elderly militants. One old man said 'Our pensions. It is pension day, and the government has no money.' There was something so Kosovska about it. Only here could we be at the beginning of a major war, and the old people of the insurgent side expecting the state controlled by the other side to pay their pensions. These were almost certainly the same old people who had faith in Rugova. That at least had some rationality, however misplaced, in that Rugova was their legally elected leader and had tried to construct a legal and peaceful government for Kosova. But to expect Milošević's Social Security Ministry to pay their pensions? It was very strange. Older people in the Kosova Albanian world can be some of the most culturally conservative in the world.

Kosova Serbs could be equally conservative. I wanted to go to Obiliq, site of the big power stations, having been told that this was where the KLA would attempt to carry the war out of its Drenice stronghold and take a major industrial unit. I had successfully made contact with the KLA underground in Prishtina and because I was seen as more or less unique among the media present in knowing anything about Kosova at all, I started to be leaked various useful information. The war was already in the villages on Kosova Polje beyond the big power plants, and the mayor of Obiliq, a Mr Dushan Dutina, was sitting in his gloomy office under a brand-new portrait photograph of Slobodan Milošević, his skin bright pink in the photo like a baby. He said there were already 700 Kosova Serb refugees in the little town. There was no way of verifying Mr Dutina's numbers, since he also said that the families concerned would not talk to the press out of fear for their lives. He grumbled that it was difficult for them to get US or Canadian visas to leave, and that the Red Cross food aid directed to those who had come originally from Croatia was only enough for a breakfast. Ljubisa Ivanisević, the head of the local Red Cross, disagreed and was clearly on bad terms with the mayor. Seven local Serb families from a village called Sibiki felt unsafe and refused to stay in their homes. No, Belgrade did nothing to help, and after eight or nine o'clock at night people did not go out. 'Kosova Serbs want dialogue. But the police have to fight back,' he said firmly, as he showed me out of his office. Walking to the other end of the village, it was not hard to see why they were afraid. In the distance across the plain towards Drenice a column of smoke was rising from a burning farmhouse. The KLA were said to have killed a policeman at the end of the village, shooting him with a sniper rifle from a minaret. Maybe they had. In practice there was an invisible front line about one kilometre east of the lignite mine.

If the police fought back, as Dutina wanted them to do, the only result for the few Serbs there would have been more and more burnt houses and dead and displaced and angry people. Yet he wanted frontline action, while the international community wanted Kosova to be 'normal' and 'dialogue' to resume. But he knew there was a front line and he did not wish to admit it. I thought back to Miki Vasić's comment in May 1996—that the right choice for the Kosova Serbs would be all-out war rather than enduring a long terror campaign. This was a Homeric struggle involving every human being, every soldier and every refugee on both sides; Serb and Albanian had a lot to quarrel about with the gods, the diplomats and the negotiators. The fact that daily life continued, with people growing tomatoes and pickling peppers, did not mean that this was not a bloody front line, as much as any in Sarajevo. Kosova Serbs and Kosova Albanians shared a terrible media handicap—both were poor rural people compared to the urban people of Sarajevo.

After the excitement of the first Kosova venture by NATO had died down, I went across the border to Albania. It was a wrench leaving dear Prishtina, but the story was unlikely to move until some fresh atrocity by the Serb forces produced larger refugee movements. The balance of power on the ground did not make this likely, with many Serb security people clearly happy to play for time and rely on international unwillingness to help the Albanians and the approach of winter to scatter the refugees out of Kosova, preferably to Western Europe. Robert Fisk had been in the foyer at the Grand, and was the last person I spoke to before leaving: very much the English expat in externals, but self-absorbed in a Middle Eastern way, stressing his distance from the *Independent*, which he thought would survive now that the Heinz billionaire Tony O'Reilly had bought it. He asked me whom I was talking to over the road. In fact I had just had coffee with Jonathan Steele from the *Guardian*, but a British diplomat had also been lurking there and Fisk had seen us. He said he loathed British diplomats, all diplomats in fact, and they should be avoided. I agreed, particularly concerning this individual, who had been one of the leading supporters of Sali Berisha in the Foreign Office. But there was no time to talk about it.

The speed with which the conflict was developing would become a major issue. If Milošević was clever, he would do his ethnic cleansing slowly. As the phrase went at a later stage in the war, 'A village a day keeps NATO away.' In Albania there was a possible story in the new Kosova-Albanian army, if such existed. A new force, the FARK, was rumoured to be forming, under the control of Bujar Bukoshi, a former ally of Rugova. This turned out to be a red herring: towns such as Bajram Curri and Kukes were becoming open-air arms markets, but there was no new army in sight, and every wall was covered with pro-KLA slogans. The KLA actually had a barracks and logistics depot in Kukes with piles of neatly-folded uniforms that were being made at a factory in Tirana, and the KLA was clearly the only show in town. I felt that FARK was assisted or sponsored by foreign outsiders, as duly turned out to be the case, but there was no story in trying to find out the details. As so often happens in wartime, while the obvious story collapse into dust, another reality springs into life: in that way journalism in the Balkans is endlessly fertile although sometimes difficult for more formal and agenda-minded Desk staff to understand.

I was astonished to discover that staying at the hotel in Kukes, a windswept and poor little town commanding the White Drin valley

near the Albanian border, were a top-level American team of elec-
tronics experts. They were friendly and open, and living in a different world from the security paranoia of the British equivalents who
were later to arrive in Albania. They explained that they were making a survey of the remote and mountainous terrain along the border between Albania and Kosova, and planning to install electronic
surveillance systems to protect Albania's borders and assist any future
NATO ground troops. They anticipated that it would take a long
time, which in view of the lack of reliable local electricity and water
supplies and terrible or non-existent roads was not surprising, nor
was it their fault. It was very important material; there had been
widespread rumours about Pentagon or NASA or CIA teams operating in the region, but as far as I knew nobody had met any. I filed
for *The Times* immediately, and my copy was superbly handled by
Michael Binyon, then the diplomatic correspondent, and went out
under a joint byline the next day. He added some fascinating material, writing that the US Defense Secretary William Cohen had told
a meeting of Nordic defence ministers in Copenhagen earlier that
day that NATO did not need new United Nations authorisation to
take action to protect the Kosova Albanians, but that Britain and
other European Union partners disagreed, believing a UN mandate
authorising force was essential. We were back to the Bosnian paradigm, of clear and principled US thinking, and British and European
muddle, vacillation and appeasement of Milošević. *The Times* had
done very well, opening up the new political story that would dominate the rest of the year, namely how far the Europeans were going
to submit to Russian blackmail through the Contact Group and
allow Milošević to conduct his offensive against the Albanians, but
in the general turmoil created by the big set-piece refugee stories
nobody gave our piece much attention. Foreign reporting has many
frustrations, but one of the commonest is that the stories which
mean most in later history as symbols of a wider political or military
reality, often have least impact at the time. I did, however, deeply
appreciate the Wapping world; with its instinctive orientation
towards US activity, it would probably have been difficult if not
impossible for many British colleagues to file in the same way and
break the story.

The Kukes Americans had very short hair, did not smoke, and
grumbled about the vast majority of the local population who

drank (a lot). The sons of Uncle Sam drank Diet Coke, and jogged around Kukes football pitch in spotless white shorts and singlets under armed guard. They were clearly very professional and serious and well informed about Albania and Kosova. They had a realistic view of the citizens (if that is the right word) of Kukes, who are legendary throughout Albania for rough and primitive behaviour. Many Kukes people were ex-minor criminals from the communist period who, if they had appropriate skills, were let out of gaol early to work on the big hydro-electric schemes nearby. It was not a background or a place to encourage polite, moderate behaviour or discreet attitudes. 'The men are all drunks, the women are all irritable. Kukes is the northern badlands,' a Mr Schwab told me. Notwithstanding this, they were there for the duration, and saw Bosnia as an American success that needed to be repeated in Kosova. Uncle Sam was coming and putting in his unique asset, the massive technological expertise and practical capacity of the US intelligence and military machines. If Kukes Bad Guys stole some of their equipment, Uncle Sam just flew in some more. I had no reason to doubt that what they said they were doing was the truth, but it was also an obvious sub-text to the conversation that they were setting up a watchtower and base that could be used to provide whatever help the KLA needed if a policy decision on that issue was to be taken at a later stage. It was also clear from talking to them that they had a wildly different political conception of the Kosova issue from the British officers I had come across on a previous visit to Tirana, whom I believed to be SAS undercover men from Hereford whose main job was to guard the British embassy. They were without exception very pro-Serb. They saw the KLA as a major terrorist threat, and were seeking any news they could find about them. So did a British embassy official, Patrick Wright, a gloomy ex-naval man. The Americans in Kukes were apparently not in the least bothered that the town was full of weapons, although not totally out of government control like nearby Bajram Curri, which had no functioning local government or police at all. I had written in my notebook for that day 'Kukes—a bomb-site with UCK slogans'. But the Americans were interested in what was beyond the bomb-site. They saw Serbia as a neo-communist state propped up by Europe, and the Kosovar Albanians as our guys who were totally pro-American, pro-market and pro the modern world. In this difficult neck of the woods it needed just a little help to free itself from communism, that was all. Or maybe it reminded them in some subliminal way of their own Wild West a hundred years earlier, a chaotic and violent but productive era in American history. Or maybe they were thinking of future oil pipeline routes, or a mixture of all of these ideas.

If the British soldiers went through the same thought-processes their minds arrived at a very different destination, the wet green and mossy fields of south Armagh where Irish terrorists would try to kill them, and had already killed many of their friends and colleagues. A few weeks later in the bar of a hotel in Tirana I was grilled by a bright and fresh young military intelligence officer about whether the KLA had modelled itself on the IRA. It seemed a foolish and irrelevant question, but it was to provide the background for much official British thinking in the next two years. It was also obvious that there was going to be a big, probably British-led European operation to clamp down on the KLA in Albania. After visiting Kukes I felt this would be futile, and that the right way to stabilise the situation was to work with and strengthen the KLA, force a Serb army withdrawal from Kosova, and put a negotiated end to its misery. However, this was not a popular view in Tirana. European diplomats were still obsessed with the last battle rather than the present one, and thought, perhaps hoped, that northern Albanians Ghegs would fight southern Tosks before they helped Kosovars. This false perspective illustrated the harmful effects of vulgarised anthropology in Balkan studies, where some study of Kosova's actual history would have been much more useful for them. Counter-insurgency plans were being drawn up in secret in Paris and London to try to split the Albanian political leaders away from support for Kosova. I remembered the man in Kukes who told me, according to my June 1998 notebook, about the huge profits to be made out of gunrunning, and that 'when we have sorted out Kosova, we shall come down to Tirana and sort out the communists there.' His AK-47s bought for $50 in Dibra were fetching over $200 each out of the boot of his Mercedes. The distance between the Euroid diplomatic mentality of Tirana and the reality of the Balkans was, as ever, great.

The other dimension of the rapidly developing crisis was back in Macedonia. I had heard on the grapevine in Kosova that the government was planning to imprison Aladjin Demiri, the mayor of Tetovo. This could lead to big trouble, which would be a good story, and I wanted to see him anyway, because he was a graduate of Sarajevo University, one of the best guides to what was happening in politics on the Albanian side, and a civilised and intelligent man who spoke perfect French. Getting to Tetovo from Kukes was a major problem; my Kosova visa had run out, and the only way was to take a car down the 100 kilometres or so of dirt roads through Albania to Peshkopi, and then east into Macedonia from there. There was no visa requirement for EU citizens on the Albanian-Macedonian border at Blace, although it could be a dangerous and uncomfortable crossing in winter, with floods, landslides, blizzards and generally appalling weather in the Dibra highlands. I had not travelled this road before, and it would be useful background material for my *Blue Guide* to Albania.[8] It was also the location of many important Partisan battles in the Second World War in which our friend and mentor Sir Reginald Hibbert had participated, and I wanted to see it for that reason.[9] Although the views over the Black Drin valley were magnificent, it was excruciatingly uncomfortable being shaken like a child's toy as the old four-wheel-drive hit endless deep stony ruts and potholes. You were thrown foot or more out of the seat, hitting your head hard against the roof of the vehicle—then you did the same a minute later, for hours on end.

Within half an hour of leaving Kukes, we were high in mountains where the occasional shepherd and his flock were the only inhabitants in a magnificent and vast landscape. Thousands of feet below the car in the deep limestone gorges, the river Drin rushed north on its long journey towards the Adriatic. In the West commentators such as Carl Bildt were always calling for a border control force to master and close down the KLA; and it was clear up here that to do so would need a force of tens of thousands of men capable of living in severe conditions. Although this was a sunny June day, there was a chill in the wind coming down from the high mountains on the Macedonian border to the northern plateau. As a result of meeting the Americans and seeing where the KLA was operating in northern Albania, I was convinced for the first time that it could possibly

[8] *Blue Guide to Albania and Kosova*, London: A. and C. Black, 2001.
[9] Reginald Hibbert, *Albania's National Liberation*, London: Pinter, 1991.

win. It was an awe-inspiring moment, coupled with a terrible twist of fear in the stomach at what still had to be endured in the war. In time, perhaps soon, the Serbs would realise that they could not win easily, and then they would be at their most savage and barbarous against the civilian population. In military terms the Serbs are good winners, generous, gallant and professional, the sort of officers who so ingratiated themselves socially with many Western soldiers in Bosnia. But they are bad losers, angry, vengeful and savagely violent, and in the summer of 1998, the idea that they might come to grief in Kosova was quite beyond their comprehension.

Tetovo had been transformed by the war, although not yet as dramatically as Prishtina. The sleepy, poetic and deeply Muslim town with its magnificent Dervish shrines and Painted Mosque was busy. The first refugees were appearing, mostly old women and young children who were being taken down to relatives in Macedonia from the combat zone in Kosova in Drenice. Until the end of Yugoslavia in 1991 and Macedonian independence, there was no international border here at all. Many Tetovo families were linked by marriage to Prishtina families, and their sons and daughters studied in the Albanian language at Prishtina University. In international community terms Tetovo was very much a German town, its military base with 700 Bundeswehr soldiers being the first German commitment abroad since the end of the Second World War. On the whole they did a good job and were not unpopular locally.

I was on good professional terms with Arben Xhaferi, the leader of the Tetovo Albanians, a charming and intelligent man who had started to suffer from Parkinson's disease. I went to drink coffee with him, and it was clear as much from the nods and silences as from what he said that the Macedonian Albanians were now working fully with the KLA. Some KLA leaders like Bardhyl Mahmuti actually came from Tetovo families, and there was a long and bitter shared history of Titoist oppression in the region. On my last night in Prishtina I had had dinner with Tom Walker from the *Sunday Times* and Tim Butcher, the defence correspondent of the *Daily Telegraph*. Tim was very interesting on the subject of the KLA supply routes, where trucks left Prishtina at about two in the morning and went north towards Vushtri where they were met by tractors who took the rations and distributed them to the soldiers. In the day it was a warm Kosova spring with blue vetches and red poppies carpeting the fields; by night the same vetches would be trampled by men supplying a war. All present saw this supply route as a key to the fortunes of war; if the Serbs could cut it, the KLA would run out of food. I thought after talking with Xhaferi that the people in Tetovo were well aware of this and were setting up a southern support operation from over the border with Macedonia. Xhaferi's deputy Menduh Thaci (no relation of Hashim Thaci in Kosova) had excellent contacts in the business world on both sides of the border and was in charge of this war and humanitarian support operation.

May–June 1998 was a period of great anger and radicalisation among the more moderate Albanian leaders outside Kosova, such as Xhaferi who, like Veton Surroi, disliked Rugova personally and saw the direction of international diplomacy under the US Balkan negotiator Richard Holbrooke as strongly pro-Serb. Xhaferi thought that Rugova and the LDK could not be trusted to protect Kosova under this sort of pressure, and the best thing to do was help build up the KLA. This viewpoint was shared by all non-LDK Albanian leaders. Even in Tirana there was increasing resistance to Prime Minister Fatos Nano's policy of stopping arms transfers to the KLA. The diplomats were still lost in the Dayton myth, and thought of the Albanian leaders as pygmies from the Balkan forest on the international stage who could be easily browbeaten. They also still seemed to be thinking of the KLA as a 'Muslim' organisation—testimony to the success of Serbian progaganda in influencing their policymakers rather than to serious intelligence work in the region. They were very wrong. Arben Xhaferi is as astute, tough and artful a politician as I have met in any country, a firm atheist who never goes near a mosque. The Muslim slur was a diversion, originating also from the clever way the Serbs knew how to work with some ill-informed Jewish intellectuals in the United States and in Israel, who feared a new 'Muslim' state in the Balkans. It was a difficult issue for journalists to handle, and the Israeli role in the region was one of the great unwritten stories of the early 1990s Balkan war period. The background was unpleasant, as Albania had a good record in the Holocaust period helping their Jews escape the Germans—there is a monument to this fact in modern Israel. Almost everybody had met Mossad people on occasion but no sane journalist or writer wants to fall foul of that organisation, which in that sense depends on the fear it inspires as much as the IRA. Some Israelis were widely thought in US intelligence circles to have given substantial covert assistance to the money-laundering operations that helped Milošević survive. The Mossad set-up in Belgrade was said to be one of its largest foreign operations. This affected perceptions of Richard Holbrooke's diplomacy in a complex way that was often unfair on him as an individual. He was Jewish, and in a radio interview he gave that year on a US radio programme he referred to Kosova as the Serb Jerusalem. This led to many personal slurs on him in private conversations. I felt on the whole, particularly after reading his book about Bosnia, that his problem in this context was not that he was Jewish as much as that he suffered from a sentimental nostalgia for the old Yugoslavia. Many individual Jewish people had done (and still do) a lot for Kosova, but Israel was strongly pro-Serb and pro-Yugoslav, and Milošević was known to have contacts with Israeli leaders such as Ariel Sharon. According to some British intelligence sources, Sharon strongly disapproved of the overthrow of Milošević in the autumn of 2000.

I had informed Veton Surroi of a secret visit Holbrooke had made a few weeks before to London, where my sources said that there had been a private agreement to let Milošević destroy the KLA and then force a Dayton-type deal through on Kosova between Milošević and Rugova with Holbrooke in charge of 'proximity negotiations'. I did not file to *The Times* about this because the story would have been seen there as anti-American, but it was not widely realised how close Holbrooke had been made to come to the British Foreign Office in the latter stages of the Dayton process. The reward given at Dayton to the Bosnian Serbs for their aggression in Bosnia was in essence the result of Anglo-French pressure on the Americans. The hitherto moderate Albanians like Xhaferi saw that a deal would be a bad deal for Kosova, and that if necessary the war on the ground would have to be accelerated and spread to prevent negotiations starting. I repeated to Xhaferi my view that NATO would not move in any decisive way for Kosova unless the conflict threatened the stability of Macedonia. The same logic was to reappear in the autumn of 2000, when the spectre of imposed negotiations using Rugova reappeared after the downfall of Milošević and the bogus October 2000 'revolution' in Belgrade. The Preshevo valley conflict in 2000 and the subsequent war in Macedonia itself in 2001 were directly inspired by these fears of a sell-out over Kosova independence.

Rugova might well have handled a Dayton on Kosova—if it had been held in 1998—slightly better than some of his fellow Albanians thought. Even Rugova loyalists like his adviser Muhammet Hamiti had told me in Prishtina in June 1998 that Rugova resented the blustering, coercive nature of Western diplomacy in those months, and felt pushed into the negotiations with Belgrade—as a result of which he was withdrawing into himself. Some of his advisers like Alush Gashi were principled and intelligent nationalists who, at least in private, were prepared to admit some of the appalling mistakes the LDK had made in the past, and had absolutely no wish to repeat them. Joe Dioguardi of the Albanian-American Civic League was moving the US diaspora into active support for the war, had broken with the LDK, and now supported more radical forces. In any event there was growing support for the war in the US diaspora, irrespective of political factionalism, and an important factor in LDK internal deliberations was always its American wing. Whatever was actually happening with FARK, which was impossible to discover from where I was, its leader Bujar Bukoshi had distanced himself from Rugova and was clearly planning to fight, not talk. In these complex situations among the Albanian leaders, with an endless interplay of international and local actors, the view on the street is all-important. Here there was no ambiguity; in its serious cultured way Tetovo was now ready for total commitment to Kosova. One of my contacts there, a shopkeeper, said that Tetovo would play its full part in the struggle to help Kosova. The simple interpretation of this was in terms of humanitarian relief, but there was another meaning, namely that Tetovo and the Albanians in the key strategic zone of north-west Macedonia at street level were moving towards very active support for the war. This was obvious from the build-up of small arms in the town.

In the Tetovo chaos, with hapless groups of refugees starting to wander the streets, I met the mayor Aladjin Demiri in Arbi restaurant who confirmed that, yes, he was being sent to prison by the Macedonian government and expected to be arrested the following day. He had been accused of various anti-state crimes. There was no story in this now; Aladijn himself seemed barely bothered about it as we sat at a café table outside in the warm evening and listened to reports on the Drenice fighting from a slightly wounded young KLA man who had come down to Tetovo for hospital treatment. If you undertake Albanian political leadership in Macedonia or Yugoslavia, you know from the start that your odyssey may well include violence, death of comrades and gaol. Aladjin had been in prison before, and was not surprised that his President, Kiro Gligorov, wanted to send him there again. The great military and political storm from over the Sar mountains to the north was moving inexorably towards us, and diminishing the importance of an individual in the way that imminent military action always does. Something on the human rights and ethnic conflict issue in western Macedonia that had provided a top foreign story from the region in July 1997 in Gostivar was now, in June 1998, not even worth bothering to file to Wapping. This was becoming a serious conflict, people started to say goodbye to their friends with that warmth and grip on the shoulder you make when you are not sure if you will ever see them again. As these goodbyes were said, the great wooded mountain of Popova Shapka towered above Tetovo, majestic and indifferent.

The summer offensive: Drenice, July 1998

The tide of war was ebbing and flowing, with men and women meeting their fate in the Kosova woods as D-Day soldiers died on the Normandy sand. On the Great Plain the Obiliq chimneys reached up like the arms of a giant under the ground. In Normandy the dead soon had the sea lapping around them, in the Kosova forests they were soon covered with last year's dead leaves. Some met death in silence and isolation, others in front of their families and loved ones. Some died quickly, others slowly. Some had to live with their wounds. Young men fighting for the KLA tried to dig bullets out of their bodies with any implement to hand, in the absence of medical equipment. It rained often that summer, and plastic sheeting became a valuable commodity. The mood of euphoria and liberation in Prishtina in early June had turned by the end of that month to a sense of the immensity of the task ahead and then to a grim realisation by the third week of July that much of the ground that the KLA had originally held was being lost.

I returned to Kosova on 24 July via Macedonia and sat in a Tetovo café in the early evening with a young KLA fighter, Sali, who had come over from Prizren to see Arben Xhaferi and Menduh Thaci. He was thin and weatherbeaten and had clearly been sleeping in the forest for weeks. He complained that there were no journalists in Kosova to cover the horrors of the Serbs' July offensive; Junik had been burnt and the thousands of refugees there from other villages had had to leave to go to Albania. The Federal army was moving tanks and heavy armour into central Kosova and shelling villages from the main roads using truck-mounted artillery. Based on what he and other people I met there said, and a visit to Tetovo hospital, I filed to Wapping that the KLA guerrillas were withdrawing south from the Serb assault into safe havens, some to Macedonia, and that the little summer paths across the mountains were a safe route for the exhausted fighters. It was only a four-hour walk, and many people had family connections on the way.

The view from Kodra e Diellit mountain down to the Skopje plain was lost in the July heat haze. In the mountains communities of pastoralists lived in lonely villages on the steep slopes, half hidden by trees, with neat wooden farm buildings full of newly-cut hay, and little squat mosques with tubby minarets. Social life was a single café built of whitewashed breeze blocks with a beaten earth floor. Their mules stood still in the heat. Above Sipkovica village the Bektashi *tekke* stood but with its roof fallen in; it has never been repaired because a *baba*, a Bektashi priest, is believed to have ascended directly through the opening in the roof to a Sh'ite heaven in the deep blue Sar mountain sky. His spirit helps the shepherds look after their sheep, although anyone who has seen a Sar dog might doubt if he was needed.

As well as being beautiful the Sar has a great sense of freedom. These mountains were to play a vital role in the coming months as allies of the KLA. Fighters walked at night and slept in the forest in the day to avoid Macedonian security patrols. I visited one route across these mountains near a village called Brodec, and with no Serb or Macedonian security forces to be seen, I wondered whether it was a really a necessary precaution. In practice the day was as safe as the night. Occasionally United Nations soldiers appeared who were part of the UNPREDEP border monitoring force, but they were bored Ukrainians whose main interest was heavy drinking and the prostitutes in the Hotel Macedonia in Tetovo. Even if they had been keen and professional, the deciduous forests on the western Sar range were huge and anybody travelling through could hide in them. UNPREDEP apparently tried to make up for its lack of manpower with helicopter patrols to look for the KLA. Again, the Serbs had miscalculated: in winter this retreat and reorganisation of the KLA would have been impossible.

The diplomatic and political tide was turning firmly against the Albanians in these weeks, nowhere more than in London. Veton Surroi told me in Prishtina that Bill Clinton's US Balkan negotiator Richard Holbrooke had recently visited London again in secret, and asked me if I knew what had been discussed. I had discovered from my top contacts that Milošević had been given a virtual *carte blanche* for a violent crackdown on the KLA, as apparently the British were worried by the advance of the extreme right in Serbia, exemplified by the success of the neo-fascist leader Voislav Seselj and his party in the recent Republika Serbska elections in Bosnia. In the blinkered Bosniacentric British official view this seemed to pose a threat to Milošević as a 'peacemaking partner', and to Dayton, Holbrooke's cardinal achievement. It seemed that US policy was once again being unduly influenced by the worst pro-Serb appeasement elements in London, although there was no reason to think Holbrooke wanted this policy himself. I deliberately sent confirmation of this information in an e-mail to Veton, knowing it would be read by GCHQ and the intercept passed to US and British officials, so that it would indicate to them that a sell-out of Kosova could not be undertaken in secret and that complicity by those officials in Milošević's genocidal crimes would be exposed. It was at this time that Veton and I decided to use my access to a key senior pro-Albanian official in London to cause division in pro-Serb London official circles, and it seemed to work well, setting a good precedent for future disruption of their activities. Veton was unique among the Kosovar Albanian leaders in knowing the London diplomatic, intelligence and political scene well, and we agreed on the importance of using fairly ruthless methods to confront these people with the true consequences of their actions. London still had major influence on State Department policy in the region. It is likely to remain an open issue

until decisions are made on whether leading British official figures
in the Bosnian war should be held accountable in court for their
Bosnian policies.

The question naturally arises whether this kind of partisan activity
is compatible with journalistic work, and whether it leads to a lack
of objectivity towards the story. Traditionalists would argue that it
does, since it constitutes a political intervention on one side. In
response I would argue that while this may be true in the abstract,
foreign correspondents' understanding of the government interception apparatus only complements on a small scale a process used
consistently for many years on a large scale in favour of Belgrade and
Milošević, both by journalists with links to the intelligence services,
and the government spin machines themselves. As Janine di Giovanni has written about her work in Bosnia, 'We were guilty, we
knew, of perhaps only covering one side of the war, but for us there
only was one side: the side that was getting pounded.'[10] There was
no reason for the tragedy of the Bosnian Muslims to be repeated in
Kosova. We stated that a certain kind of secret politics was unaccept-
able as a way to dispose of the 'Kosova problem', and that governments cannot use technology to control dissident voices in the
media or suppress stories they dislike. It can also be argued that the
British officials concerned were breaking their contracts as civil ser-
vants by talking to me. But if genocide and widespread ethnic cleansing are being tolerated, is the civil servant faced by the scenario
described by an American historian as that of being 'Hitler's willing
executioners' bound by normal contractural responsibilities? This
was the case in Bosnia, where some members of the British administration, intelligence services and military were undoubtedly passive
accessories to war crimes. There was no reason for this to happen
again in Kosova.

In narrow media terms, also, Milošević's strategy seemed to be
working. Although the white armoured TV trucks still filled the
Grand car park, many agencies had pulled out their crews and very
few journalists were around. The Desk staff on both the *Times* and
the *Sunday Times* at Wapping were very supportive, but in technical
news terms there was not much new to say. In the rest of Fleet Street,
Balkan fatigue had set in. In the more tabloid area of the media the

[10] Janine di Giovanni, *Madness Visible: a Memoir of War*, New York: Knopf, 2004.

fact that there was not a full-scale infantry war being fought in trenches meant that there was no story. In the fields and woods of central Kosova blood was being spilt every day but in small enough quantities and in obscure enough situations to fulfil Milošević's objectives without attracting undue media attention or NATO air strikes. I met David Loyn of the BBC in the Grand Hotel reception one morning and we seemed to be the only foreign journalists around in Kosova at all.

August, with the summer holiday time, was near and diplomacy would be at a halt until mid-September. By then Milošević could have completed his scorched earth policy, with Western minds on the beach. I filed a fairly standard piece for the *Sunday Times* about a refugee family in the forest which made the paper. Waiting for NATO had become bad joke among the Albanians, and the more determined, especially from the diaspora, were joining the KLA, but to interview someone and file a piece would just be seen by some on the Desk as pro-Albanian irresponsibility, and it would be spiked immediately so I didn't bother.

In central Kosova the damage to villages was horrific, with empty farms and bloated stinking corpses of livestock lying around. Whole villages were deserted. I felt an onerous sense of responsibility to try and convey to the outside world the depths to which Kosova was sinking, and it seemed, in Wapping terms, worth going straight to the top. *The Times*'s editor Peter Stothard was not available, but Michael Gove who then edited the Op Ed page was in the office, and I said I would try and do an Op Ed piece on the need for NATO action. I had never written one before and felt uncomfortable about it, but I wanted to put a personal view of the crisis, knowing that the pro-Serb people elsewhere would sit on the copy; they would have been entitled to say too that it was not the job of the news pages to provide platforms for correspondents' personal views. Some people had objected strongly to the Albanian uprising copy I had filed the previous year, and had no wish to expose the paper to the same criticisms over Kosova. A common Wapping jibe against Robert Fisk's brilliant work on the Middle East for the *Independent* was that he wrote literary essays, not news. One or two of the older Desk staff had worked with Fisk and had not forgiven him for leaving *The Times* to go to the *Independent*. Foreign desks have long collective memories. It is, of course, an open question how far Fisk would have been free to take strong anti-Israeli positions at *The Times*, although most of the time people sought a balanced position. Most of the Murdoch empire's central funding came from New York or US-based banks, and some of his closest advisers like the brilliant economist Irwin Stelzer were from that orbit where Israeli security and prosperity were, understandably, important factors. *The Times*'s foreign editor Graham Patterson, a very agreeable man but without the background as a correspondent that most foreign editors have, believed that Milošević was a master politician who would win, as always. It was a not uncommon view at the time, and one which his official contacts repeatedly emphasised to him. The late Sir Edward Pickering, Murdoch's main editorial guru, was a feared figure among top editorial staff. His disapproval could break a career, and I was told he was very pro-Yugoslav. Sean Ryan, the *Sunday Times* foreign editor, was more positive and I had the impression he believed that the Americans would not allow a massacre of the Albanians.

These differences of opinion are interesting because in essence they related to a split within Wapping broadsheets between those who saw *The Times* as a traditional Olympian voice, where news and opinion were rigorously separated, and those who were less concerned about this, and allowed people latitude over the viewpoint they embodied in their news copy. This debate has been central to the history of foreign news reporting and there is nothing new about it. In the nineteenth century *The Times* had famously spiked news of the Batak massacre in Bulgaria in the Ottoman Empire because the Desk of the day found the correspondent, Michael MacGahan, rather biased. On the other hand, if Turkish soldiers are slitting babies' throats with their scimitars, human values dictate that you write the story from the point of view of the baby. I felt the same about the prospect of a Slavocommunist shell coming through your house and cowshed wall and blowing your only cow to pieces. People who have not lived in a Balkan village have no idea what the death of a cow can mean to a family. Sheep are relatively cheap and their loss is not a disaster, but the loss of a cow is a catastrophe, particularly if your family has many small children to nourish.

My Op Ed 'Killing Fields of Kosovo' piece ran on 8 August and had considerable impact, particularly in the United States, where it was posted on hundreds of Internet sites, and helped bring many US Albanian communities into active support for the KLA and the war. I had been in Belgrade two weeks before and it seemed there was genuine fear there among some of the more intelligent people in the Serbian élite that Holbrooke was getting marginalised by Madeline Albright, and that NATO might get more actively involved to try to prevent the whole of Kosova from being ethnically cleansed. This was encouraging. It was time to attack the process of appeasement in a direct way. Others at Wapping felt the same. The *Sunday Times* had asked me for copy for a big foreign story which duly ran on 2 August, saying that NATO was making intervention plans and British troops would be substantially involved. I filed a piece to them on the Belgrade end of the crisis. In Kosova it seemed time to try to state in the daily paper one or two home truths about the issues involved on the ground. The top of the story ran:

KILLING FIELDS OF KOSOVO

James Pettifer says NATO must talk to Albanian separatists

Kosovo, at harvest-time, is roasting. Yet according to *Politika*, the Belgrade government newspaper, it had been a successful harvest this year. But it is a harvest of pain. Mass graves are being found. Cows riddled with machine-gun bullets bellow in their death throes. Wooden houses lost in cornflowers are in ashes. Tens of thousands of people are refugees in the woods and will soon run out of food and water. The sweet smell of hay is lost in acrid smoke.

NATO must act. There has been enough delay and the Belgrade military planners think that public opinion has got used to war. Although the cleansing of Kosovo does not resemble the open savagery of Bosnia, it is no different. A dignified society of conservative, proud Albanian peasants, who asked no more than to farm their land, is being cleansed just as efficiently as the victims of the Bosnian killing fields five years ago.

But the same siren voices from the same official quarters are being heard again, saying that President Milošević is the only man we can deal with, that he is such a good politician he will run Serbia for 500 years (if he lives that long). They say that he does not really intend to drive all the Albanians away in as great an act of ethnic cleansing as in Bosnia and he regards the Kosovo Liberation Army merely as 'terrorists'. And that makes everything different, it seems, in the West. Underlying this fallacy is the view that the Serbs have always been the *Herrenvolk* of the Balkans, and that we try to control them, while they control the region.

This is meretricious rubbish. It is a moral issue. At the heart of the Western 'dilemma' about intervention is the alleged moral equivalence of the
two sides. But they are not equivalent. The Serbs are fighting a colonial war
in Kosova. Few of them live there any more.

As a foreign correspondent in the region I have known the KLA for
three years: it is not now some Marxist/Muslim conspiracy funded by drug
barons in Switzerland. This is the stuff of John Buchan. The KLA is the
Albanian population of Kosova, no more, no less. It is made up of idealists,
cynics, men, women, the old, the young, the desperate and the hopeful. So
are all resistance movements.

The Times still carries considerable weight in the Balkans, and in the
region I have since discovered that my piece had some influence on
later events, particularly the decision of Northern Albanian opponents of the Greek-controlled Socialist government in Tirana to go
ahead with their coup attempt in Tirana in September, which led to
the decision of the United States to push for the removal of Fatos
Nano as Prime Minister in favour of their young protégé Pandeli
Majko. The coup temporarily brought chaos to Tirana, with militants from Tropoja in north-eastern Albania—some of them supporters of the northern-based FARK movement controlled by
Rugova's 'Prime Minister' Bujar Bukoshi—attacking the Prime
Minister's office and trying to overthrow the government. There is
no evidence that Bukoshi ordered this attack, but his followers were
part of the same Tropoja paramilitary scene as those of ex-President
Sali Berisha and shared a common political culture. Although they
did not succeed in restoring Sali Berisha to power, they did force
Nano to give way and resign. It was reported at the time as a further
episode of 'Albanian madness', but in fact all it represented was the
spread of the Kosova war into Albania, and as such was a natural and
logical development. Greece was the dominating power in Albania
after May 1997, and behind Greece lay Serbia and the machinations
of Belgrade. Within Albania there is now little doubt that elements
in the secret police were on foreign payrolls and were involved in the
assassinations of important KLA leaders such as Ilir Konesevsci that
had occurred on Albanian soil. He was travelling to Tirana to buy
weapons to help families defend themselves against the Yugoslav
assaults on their villages. The most important assassination of all in

that bloody summer, was that of Democratic Party leader Azim Haydari on September 12, and I believe it to have been also partly a product of this foreign interference. It is a classic tenet of counterinsurgency theory that in order to destroy a revolutionary movement you·set the leaders against each other by killing prominent figures. Another technique is to criminalise leading figures, so that someone like Haydari, who for all his faults was a patriot and trying to help the Kosova struggle, is regarded as merely an arms dealer and criminal.[11]

I felt the loss of Azim Haydari keenly. We had known each other for nine years. A rough diamond from a strongly patriotic family in Tropoja he had been a wild, cheerful tub-thumping mob-orator in the distant days of the student opposition to the one-party state in 1990. He was a bad-tempered man with a big stomach and a shock of untidy jet-black hair who loved to drink and was not above throwing a punch at somebody he disagreed with. He was a man of the wild north-east. All the year round he wore a long gaberdine white mac, tightly belted. He made friends and enemies at great speed in Tirana and, as the Berisha government lost touch with the people, more of the latter. Although in theory he was a possible leader of the Democratic Party when it was formed in 1991, the foreigners preferred the smoother and more presentable Berisha. Language was an important factor in this decision since Berisha could speak French and some English, whereas Haydari then only spoke Albanian. Unlike many other DP leaders when they came into government, Azim did not demonise foreign journalists, and was cheerfully accessible to interviews or soundings about political developments.

When the Kosova war started, he was soon in the thick of things as a real Tropojan with no inhibitions about the military struggle. There was a price on his head and with his confrontational personality he was not afraid to name prominent Socialist Party names who he believed were in touch with foreign agents—which in practical terms meant the Greek embassy. Greek dominance of the diplomatic scene in Tirana after June 1997 and the advent of the Nano government was deeply resented. The Greek ambassador Alexandros Mallias was an affable and very able man who had opened up Greek diplomatic relations with Skopje in his previous posting. He held

---

[11] See Vickers/Pettifer, op. cit. Also, for background, Vickers/Pettifer, *Albania: from Anarchy to a Balkan Identity*, London: Hurst, 1997.

court in the magnificent ex-residence of King Leka, an Italianate fantasy house with a wonderful garden, far superior to that of the President of Albania himself. To his admirers he expressed everything good about Greek dominance in the region after the overthrow of Berisha, but to his detractors in DP circles who had lost power he was an imperial proconsul.

On 15 September I wrote in *The Times* that Haydari had said what Berisha did not wish to say, and knew he was living on borrowed time after an earlier assassination attempt in parliament a year before. In the same paper Antony Loyd wrote that the Tirana crowd 'chanted anti-Nano slogans and also sang "UCK, UCK" in praise of the Albanian rebels in neighbouring Kosovo, with whom Dr Berisha appears to have uncomfortable connections'. He certainly had. Although the Berisha government had initially allowed the KLA soldiers refuge where I had visited them in December 1992 near Elbasan, nearly all the Kosovars who had trained there had played little part in the later stages of the war. Denis Taylor, on the *The Times* Desk that day, was cautious about the coverage of the Haydari issue, and asked me only for a very short file as a profile of Haydari. I wrote much more about it for *The Scotsman*, picking up a link that had been dormant since the tragic death of my old friend Bob Campbell, the assistant editor. His replacement Andrew Mcleod was a good man, and although I rarely went to Scotland and it paid much less than *The Times*, it was a fact that the Blair government was a very Scottish affair and *The Scotsman* was widely read in Parliament and in government circles. The Defence Minister and later NATO Secretary-General George Robertson was rumoured to read it with his breakfast.

The upheaval in Tirana gave further succour to Milošević in his Kosova clampdown. As in the spring of 1997, Tirana's difficulty was Belgrade's opportunity, and Milošević moved towards a final military 'solution', with a scorched-earth policy in central Drenice. However, the war was not doing Serbia much good. *The Scotsman* asked for a piece on the economy and I filed that the nationalist leader Vojislav Seselj had said on Serbian TV the week before that the campaign in Kosova was costing about a million German marks a day and that some estimates put the cost of the five-month conflict as high as

1.2 billion marks. About 100 communities had been affected and as many villages had been destroyed. About 100,000 people had fled their homes.

In Belgrade the strategy was to have a quick military victory and then do a Kosova deal with Holbrooke and Rugova, with Serbian admission to the World Bank and International Monetary Fund traded against a settlement in Kosova. All economic sanctions against Yugoslavia were to be lifted. In Belgrade Tahir Hasanović, a New Democracy Party leader, told me that Milošević wanted a seven-year term as President, as in France. The dictator was clearly optimistic that what he saw as his special relationship with Holbrooke would deliver it for him. Was what Tahir said reliable? As he had once been the boyfriend and almost the fiancé of Milošević's daughter, he should know, I thought. Slobo was said to have vetoed the marriage because of Tahir's mixed Serb, Turkish and Jewish background. The fact that he had been a star leader of the League of Young Communists in Sarajevo along with Montenegro's Milo Djukanović didn't seem to matter; in the end Serb blood hygiene mattered more than ideology. Belgrade liberals were sitting on the Kosova fence, saying that no country could allow 1,000 armed terrorists to occupy its territory, but also rejecting Milošević's purely military 'solution'.

Few people in the Belgrade political élite had any real idea about the nature of the situation on the ground. It was universally believed that the KLA was an import from Albania. Most of them had never been to Kosova in their lives, any more than most British people from the mainland have ever been to South Armagh or other 'bandit country' areas in Northern Ireland. I often wondered what Milošević really knew about Kosova, apart from how much money was made in the Trepce mines and the number of votes Kosova delivered for the Socialist Party of Serbia at election time. Apart from the standard problem for the Serbs that their understanding was obstructed by the forcefeeding of myths about events there in 1389 six hundred years before, there was very little real information about the war in most Serbian newspapers. Many Serb television and press reporters did their best, but they had significant security problems in the KLA areas, and the government in Belgrade took a close interest in what finally appeared in the newspapers. For many reporting consisted of being driven around in an army vehicle and told how safe and normal everything was, hardly a sound journalistic technique.

In connection with the Belgrade strategy, I wrote in *The Scotsman*: 'Whether this is a viable scenario depends almost entirely on whether the KLA can be wiped out as a fighting force within the next two or three months.' Progress was significant in this direction, from a strictly orthodox military point of view. The KLA stronghold Malisheve, where press conferences had been held in June, was overrun by Serb heavy armour after being surrounded. But this was not an orthodox war. Even if it was a disaster, it was not a catastrophe for the Albanians; the KLA lost much territory but few fighters.

The refugee nightmare in the forests continued. The people were living like medieval outlaws. September was as wet a month as August, and conditions were appalling. Every small action of daily life was a struggle against the mud, and winter was coming. The cheerful chaos of the first camps three months earlier had turned to grim and sullen expectation of a hard winter and a fight for survival. The campfires with their acrid smoke that made eyes water were enough for cooking and keeping warm in summer, but of no use in the full Balkan winter. Superbly dedicated and efficient Swiss Red Cross officials had begun to bring in substantial quantities of food, but they could do nothing at all about the problem of shelter. The Red Cross had all kinds of operational difficulties, as did reporters, refugees and everyone else. The density of the woods with the trees in full summer leaf meant that you could miss someone standing a few yards away, the afternoons and evenings were increasingly cloudy and dark, and there were virtually no maps of Kosova, these being a monopoly of the Yugoslav army cartographic department. Vehicles sank deep into the mud, and those trying to drive along the beds of shallow streams soon found them swamped by raging torrents after a big storm. Some internationals had Albanian-language interpreters from Tirana, who said they had real difficulty understanding the dialect of the Drenice villagers. Dirty water was everywhere and clean drinking water hard to find, as the Serbs had poisioned the wells in the villages with animal carcasses and pesticides. Even with the best efforts made to store food, the damp caused flour and rice to become mouldy in a week or two in people's improvised plastic bivouacs.

The scale of the misery in central Drenice was often hidden even from the journalists who were there by the forest itself, which stretched over hundreds of square miles. In its deep leafy dells and shadowy glades it held the future of Kosova, the children trying to learn to read and write in improvised schools under the dripping oaks and beeches. As a result of the deteriorating conditions—the United Nations Children's Fund announced that there was a major problem of respiratory infections among the forest-dwellers—and the looming autumn and winter, migration and population movement intensified. The narrow Kosova timber carts started to make their way through the forest to the west towards Albania. The KLA had split into smaller groups and, instead of trying to fight a set-piece war, started to harry the Serbs in hit-and-run raids, and had some success around Mitrovica under the talented Commander Remi, and in central Drenice where it had recaptured territory previously lost. One could say that the Albanian military show was on the road again after the dark and dire days of July and August. The television in the Grand Hotel Media Centre was still carrying stories of military success, but Kosova Serbs did not believe them. My driver Mr Bajramović said that Rugova was being subjected to a torrent of criticism on the Albanian side for his refusal to visit the combat zones and see the war damage for himself. I checked and, as always, Mr Bajramović was right. It all seemed rather sad and pathetic. Eventually the US Balkan envoy Chris Hill more or less dragooned Rugova into an armoured personnel vehicle and they drove together to Drenice. The hail and freezing rain that the country boy soldiers of the KLA endured were not for their 'leader'.

From Prishtina, it was very hard to find out what was happening but the Red Cross workers believed that thousands of people had started to move to Albania and Montenegro. Afterwards I discovered that about 15,000 people had left Kosova. On the ground it seemed a hopeless situation as the Serbs created chaos and the international community were not taking any effective action to prevent it. However, we now know that more was being done than any of us in the depths of the Kosova forests realised. The inspiring political leadership of Hashim Thaci and his colleagues, with the redoubtable Ramush Haradinaj in command in Dukagjin in the west, was beginning to have results. Thanks to the resolve of Americans like Madeleine Albright, NATO was not willing to preside over another Bosnia, where British appeasement of Serbia and European ineffectiveness led to genocide. The possibility of large-scale refugee and internally displaced person movement to neighbouring countries, particularly Albania, set alarm bells ringing in Western foreign ministries. This would spread the crisis and affect Albania's precarious stability, and the coup attempt in Tirana two weeks earlier was fresh in official minds.

It is not widely realised how far EU policy towards Albania was, and is, affected by fear of population movement and asylum-seekers. The diplomats' fear was that Kosovar refugees in Albania would lead to a second, successful uprising against the Socialists and a new, pro-KLA government in Tirana. Mass migration from Albania would follow. Seen in retrospect this was probably an alarmist perspective, but it had an unusual effect among Western diplomats for myths in the Balkans in encouraging action rather than preventing it. The fitful attempts by Chris Hill to open negotiations between the Serbs and Albanians had come to nothing, and NATO was moving on to a much more advanced planning stage. In New York Holbrooke was becoming marginalised. The local media in Prishtina were becoming much more radical, with Veton Surroi's *Koha Ditore* newspaper openly supporting the KLA and leaking details of Hill's pro-Serb 'peace plans', which envisaged Kosova as part of a future Yugoslavia. Hill was enraged with the editor, Baton Haxhiu. In turn this had a major effect on rank-and-file opinion in Rugova's party, and recruitment of LDK people into the KLA increased. Rugova himself, like Holbrooke, was becoming more marginalised, and rarely left his house.

US military advisers and private sector military contractors were working with the KLA to reorganise the force, and make an effective functioning central command structure, although this was not widely known at the time. Agim Ceku, an outstanding Kosovar Albanian officer who had worked with the Americans in the war in Croatia, became the head of the 'new' KLA. This had a noticeable effect in the atmosphere of newspaper offices. The *Sunday Times*, with its orientation towards the United States, began to bring the possibility of NATO intervention into many stories, so that, for instance, my copy about the boy in the forest that went into the paper with the headline 'Winter bites early in Kosovo' also carried news that NATO was renewing the threat of air strikes and cruise missile attacks on Milošević's forces. It did not include material I had filed on the renewed fighting around Junik and the appearance yet again of a 'new' Albanian military force—the FARK army of Rugova associate Bujar Bukoshi—in the fray.[12] I think this was because the Americans now saw the KLA as the only show in town. The military situation in the northwest was certainly critical. A friend in Prishtina told me that there was nothing left of Junik now. This was difficult to believe; it was the largest village in Kosova, and had some remarkable stone tower-houses dating from the early Ottoman period. The *Realpolitik* on the ground was that while they had achieved their objectives there, Milošević and his generals had wasted precious time in July in central Drenice when they had a *de facto* free hand to smash the KLA.

In the *Times* office the atmosphere was different, and on some occasions there seemed little interest in the story. For all its virtues, the paper was dominated at that time by a much more 'British' ethos, and it was clear that the traditional British-Serb link dominated much thinking. The 'Americans' at Wapping were often those closest to the Murdoch management structure, or Australians like Des Houghton who was in Wapping on secondment from a Murdoch post in Australia. The *Sunday Times* was often closer to US policy positions on international issues than the daily paper. Des had quite a cordial relationship with the intelligence people who rang up on occasion to comment on the GCHQ electronic intercepts they had received of correspondents' copy, usually attempting to influence what went into the paper, but he thought the Foreign Office equivalents were idiots. At a social event I met the former Belgrade correspondent Dessa Trevisan, who was not very complimentary about my displaced persons story and said that the Albanians would have to show whether they could live in the forests as long as the Serbs had done when fighting the Germans. The conflict dragged on in and around Wapping as much as in the Drenice forests.

---

[12] The FARK paramilitary organisation was set up in 1998 by the Kosova Albanian leader Bujar Bukoshi, a doctor, who had been Prime Minister of Kosova for a period in the mid-1990s and was a leader of the Kosova Democratic League. FARK was in essence the response of the LDK to their failure to control the Kosova Liberation Army, and it was funded by LDK money. It clashed in the summer of 1998 with the KLA over munitions supplies, recruits and spheres of influence, particularly in northwestern Kosova. Many FARK soldiers left at that time and joined the KLA during the American-advised reorganisation of the KLA.

In Prishtina many people had predicted that the conflict would spread to Macedonia, and in the last week of September an important local Albanian leader there, Beqir Limani, was killed in a shoot-out with police in Kichevo, a town about 50 miles south of Tetovo. With parliamentary elections due on 14 October, the Macedonian security apparatus was sending a message to the Albanians. I had seen a senior Serb intelligence official I recognised in a Skopje restaurant talking to a Macedonian friend of mine, a prominent journalist, who told me afterwards that there was increasing coordination between Belgrade and Skopje over the Kosova war. It went without saying that there was similar activity on the Albanian side. Beqir Limani's uncle was Fazli Veliu, leader of the Macedonian Albanians of the diaspora organisation, whom I had not met at that time. A Swiss-based businessman and LPK leader, he later became, along with Ali Ahmeti, one of the two or three most important Albanian leaders in the 2001 conflict in Macedonia, and was the founding father of the Macedonian Albanian National Liberation Army. He came from an exceptionally militant village called Zajas, a picturesque but dirt-poor little place near Kichevo. It bred nationalist activists like a lawn grows clover.

I filed for *The Times* and was told by the Desk that the copy was OK and had made the paper, but when I returned home I could find no sign of it. The whole subject of Macedonia was ring-fenced then, in a way I found irritating, and I began to direct more material to the Sunday paper, *The Scotsman* and American papers which did seem to be interested. I managed to get something in *The Times* a little later about the visit of Robin Cook, the Foreign Secretary, to the Kosova-Macedonian border, but began to feel that the underlying atmosphere was discouraging. On returning to London I was told by a friend who was high up in Wapping that the hardline pro-Serb people and also the Foreign Office were putting pressure on the managing editor, George Brock, to stop the paper taking my copy at all, but this, especially in retrospect, appears absurd. Brock seemed a model of probity and common sense, but Wapping had a complex political underworld, like the offices of most influential media organisations. From a very different point of view to mine, this is well described by Andrew Neil in his book *Full Disclosure* (London, 1997) on his time as editor of the *Sunday Times* in the mid-1990s, which is illuminating about the atmosphere in News International and especially the often bizarre atmosphere within the plant at Wapping, but marred by his neglect of the intelligence manipulation and 'spin' factor in the modern media, and an exclusive concentration of the difficulties of working with Rupert Murdoch.

Since 1997 I had come to loathe most diplomats in Albania, and believe that many are enemies of a free press. Since my problems at the *Independent* I simply got on with work and tried not to get involved with them. I was quite often interviewed on CNN when in England and this did not help either, since the Murdoch news channels were serious rivals of CNN and I was often billed as a *Times* person. There was a palpable feeling of tension around and I tried to avoid going into Wapping at all, finding it more stressful than working in the war zones. There is something about a long stare across the office from a senior manager at Wapping that beats a long stare from a heavily armed Balkan border guard.

It is of course quite reasonable to ask: does all this matter to anyone other than journalists? Does foreign news matter any more? I believe it does, not because there were strong and contrary views and politics in the *Times* office—there always have been and always will be on important issues—but the strength of the outside pressures sometimes seemed overwhelming. The Desk and senior people at Wapping were only trying to keep their sanity amid it all, and the long stares weren't personal. In this context the traditional objections of the liberal left to the Murdoch ownership seem irrelevant. Rupert Murdoch did not tell anyone at *The Times* what to think about Kosova, but hundreds of spin-doctors, spooks, lobbyists and spin-oriented diplomats (most of them paid by the British taxpayer) certainly did, and their blatant partisanship, conscious suppression of facts, attempts to smear individuals and totalitarian attitudes were and are the real threat to press freedom. Rupert Murdoch provided money, an energetic and usually positive atmosphere, and some superb Desk and technical staff of all kinds to back up correspondents in the field. *The Times*, then under Peter Stothard, worked on the basis of a wastage of ideas (Beaverbrook's definition of a good newspaper), and even the best stories had to fight their way on to the page. I dare say Murdoch has his faults, but having seen my father come home after a session doing business with the late Robert

Maxwell, I doubt whether Murdoch is quite the unique monster some of his critics claim. The mishaps of the *Telegraph* group proprietor Conrad Black which became public in 2003 are likely to improve historians' views of the Murdoch period of *Times* ownership. (Maxwell's speciality was bullying and bellowing abuse down the phoneline, usually when Mrs Maxwell's Jaguar had broken down.) During these years an exceptionally civilised and able *Times* editor, Peter Stothard, presided in the magic chair and backed up his writers. Over Bosnia the enemy won for a long time before people like Martin Bell, Antony Loyd, Maggie O'Kane and many others told the truth. Over Kosova the government media machine failed, and this caused it pain.

Gambling with Mr Arkan: November 1998

According to an English radio report I was listening to, Kosova was improving. The Foreign Office spin-doctors, through their influence on the BBC World Service, were pushing heavily the line that the Kosovo Verification Mission was the answer to every problem in Kosova, if not the world. The KVM party of international observers of the 'ceasefire' had come to Kosova as a result of the Holbrooke-Milošević agreement in October, a few weeks before. Was there a ceasefire? It did not feel like it. In Belgrade I learned that a brave Serbian journalist, Djuro Slavuj, and his driver Rank Perenić had disappeared while covering the war near Rahovec; a memorial meeting had been held in the Grand Hotel for them. I planned to travel down to the front on the train from Belgrade. An effect of the conflict was to wreck normal public transport over the whole of southern Serbia. The fierce elderly lady in the station ticket office said that the train via Sandjak to Prishtina was 'dangerous' and would probably not run. She added that the road between Sandjak and Mitrovica was shut because of fighting between the KLA and the army, and buses were not using it. A phrase from very old days at the *Independent* and its East European editor Steve Crawshaw ran through my head: 'Take the temperature of the street, James, always take the temperature of the street.' Clearly the place to do it in Belgrade was the bus station. I made the two-minute walk to the long-distance coach office. Here was the usual mass of people, and I felt the usual *frisson* of excitement at the sight of the rows of patient loyal Jugotrans buses, the hewers of wood and drawers of water of the decent side of old Yugoslavia, made for the people and used by them without a bourgeois foreigner in a pretentious four-wheel-drive in sight. My classicist friend Professor Richard Seaford once coined a new word for the state of post-1999 Kosova, saying that since everyone believed the ancient Greeks had invented all the normal political terms like democracy and oligarchy, he would add another: *leukatessara kuklakratia*, meaning rule by people who drive white four-wheel-drive vehicles.

When I asked for a Prishtina ticket, a man behind me in the queue said that the KLA was moving into Sandjak. The ticket office dragon, a very large lady with a picture of the Chetnik leader Draža Mihailović on her desk, breathed a little fire and revealed that if you really wanted to go to Kosova there was a bus on the alternative route via Prokuple, a dull town in southern Serbia, where you ran down the main road into Kosova near Podujeve. This was not safe, but it was possible. Reports of the KLA's death, as of Mark Twain's, had been much exaggerated.

The journey down was grey and wet, passing through damp green tunnels of arching trees over the road, and occasional stops for the driver to stretch his legs. On arriving in south Serbia he started to play nationalist songs with a strong beat, but nobody took much notice; we had come a long way since the heady, confident days of 1992. Then the music would have led to a lot of quiet drinking of slivowitz on the bus, and toasts of 'Onward Serbia', the cry of the Croatian and early Bosnian wars. Now that war had become everybody's way of life, it seemed no cause for celebration. However, war was always a way of making money, as we were soon to discover.

The bus slewed to a halt near Kurshumi where, at the back of a little gravel car park, an improvised café had been set up, with a tin roof and a couple of white plastic tables and chairs. It was in the middle of nowhere with thick forest stretching a hundred miles south before there was any kind of civilisation. I certainly could not expect civilised behaviour here; killing somebody did not amount to much, and there was that ache in the back of your head that told you this was frontier country, 'without the law'—where in fact most people do not know what the law is. A few empty beer kegs lay in the long grass. It was not apparent why we were stopping, but soon some out-laws appeared.

Two tall Serbs came out, and we were shepherded off the bus. They looked like Arkan's sort of men, as indeed they were, and the café had a picture of the leader with some of his 'Tiger' soldiers at a parade. Arkan looked quite docile in his paramilitary fatigues; often he looked more menacing in a suit, his body language sending a message of someone harbouring much suppressed violence and re-sentment. Then a strange thing happened. About a quarter of the bus passengers were Albanians or Roma, and they understandably looked very frightened, and were herded into a corner of the garden by a group of rose bushes. The men squatted and lit up cigarettes with fumbling fingers. The women stood a little way behind. Every-body knew what to do. The women could expect no protection from their men, but they must look as if they could. The Serbian passengers and another couple of foreigners were herded to the café chairs, and a pretty girl appeared and took orders for drinks. They turned out to be free, this was clearly not a café, but a philanthropic institution, owned by Arkan the benefactor of (some of) mankind. We waited. An unpleasant large mastiff appeared and ran at the Alba-nians, but fortunately for them it was chained up, and had to make do with barking aggressively at them, as high as a man on its hind legs. The dog wanted meat, blood, vibrant flesh—he was a warlike spirit with his spiked collar, but all he could have was a barking session.

I felt the hair on the back of my neck crawling, and went into the woods for a pee. That took thirty seconds, but I wished I could pee for half an hour until the bus engine started. The woods were at their warmest autumn mixture of faded greens and yellows and browns—it was like walking into an Impressionist painting, I wanted to walk through the beautiful canvas and hide the other side, but I could not. Coming back, I headed for the bus but there was no escape.

'*Novena?*'

One of the men said the Serbian word for journalist. I nodded, as denying it was pointless. He waved me towards the café, and we sat in state while another of the gangsters carefully carried a round plas-tic table towards the huddle of Albanians. I was going to be made an honoured spectator, shown who was in charge in south Serbia, made complicit in their ritual. Serbs are brilliant at drawing you into their social world so that you seem to share their assumptions, as so many British diplomats have found, Mephistopheles with so many docile Fausts in Austin Reed suits. The man went back into the café and fetched a round wooden tabletop of about the same size and fitted it on top of the plastic table. In the middle of it was an arrow, and round the edge numbers and astrological signs were painted, it was an improvised roulette wheel.

'*Shiptare*!', he bellowed at the nearest Albanian, a feeble middle-aged man with a bad foot and disintegrating shoes who froze and let his cigarette slip through his fingers into the grass. '*Shqiptare*' is the abusive Serb word for Albanian with roughly the same sense as 'Nigger'.

'*Haide, shqiptare, haide*'—meaning 'come', actually an old Ottoman Turkish word in universal Balkan use.

Nobody moved. The Albanian women looked terrified, one clutched a baby so tight that I wondered if she would throttle it. Then a henchman in a black leather jacket marched over the grass, grabbed the man by his collar, and dumped him quivering by the table. The Serb in charge put a wad of notes on the table, removed his gun from his belt, and banged it on the table. The Albanian knew what he had to do, or he would be taken into the woods and shot. He reached into the inside pocket of his grubby old jacket, and took out his wallet. The Arkanite grabbed it, removed the money, threw it on the table and spun the wooden arrow. It landed on some number or other, the *maître de casino* roared with laughter and pocketed the notes. Nobody came forward when he waved, so he spun the wheel madly again and banged the sidearm on it. The Albanian men, only three or four of them glanced at each other like sheep before the slaughterhouse door, and moved forward together. Balkan sheep are very good at grazing together, whereas English sheep are scattered in neat fields, rural individualists. Balkan men live on the same hillsides as sheep and learn from them. In Albanian society you do not leave the group unless you have very good reasons. The individual may be killed, the family or group must carry on.

The Albanians carefully put a pile of wallets on the table, the gun was banged down again, the arrow spun, and almost casually the money was taken and they shambled back to their women and children, who were frozen in cheap short skirts and thin jumpers.

One of the women had very nice legs. A man I had talked with at a previous stop was a miner who had moved with his wife to the big copper mine at Bor, in north-eastern Serbia by the Danube, after the closure of Trepce. It was very ironic, losing their own great mine, and having to slave in the depths of the earth for Milošević in a foreign country. I wanted to talk more with him but he was unhappy about talking to a foreigner in Albanian. I had heard that most of the Bor production was being exported illegally, in defiance of UN sanctions, through Romania. I loathe Romanians, they are the shysters and liars of the region. It would have been nice to nail them with a sanctions-busting story.

The grim ritual was ending. Arkan's men had performed their domination ritual, all for a couple of hundred Deutschmarks at most. The tallest Serb picked up the roulette wheel table-top, and ran towards the Albanians menacingly, but also laughing. They scattered in the direction of the bus. I got up and followed them, realising as I did so that I had peed more into my pants. Some one tossed the empty wallets to the dog, who attacked them and started to chew them in the absence of anything better. It was a normal kind of day in Milošević's Serbia. Everyone had a disappointing, irritating little problem. The dog hadn't bitten or eaten anybody, the Serbs hadn't got much money, the Albanians had lost some and been humiliated in front of their wives. The women had been scared stiff but none of them had been taken to the wood and raped. At least everyone was still alive. I thought of Miki Vasić's cheerful greeting in the Grand bar a little while ago when I had run into him after a gap.

'James! You still alive?'

It seemed like it, although what kind of 'life' there was in Kosova then is a matter of debate. Miki said that to everybody. It was designed to tell foreigners that Kosova is a tough, violent society, the hardest place of all in the Balkans if not the world; death is near, killing somebody was nothing special, and he, Miki, had the heroic spirit of the Kosovo Serbs, and could cope with it all. It also meant that he had read my *Times* Op Ed piece and heard what people thought should happen to the writer, along the lines that I should be dead and floating face down in Lake Batllaves. It is the same on the Albanian side, there is a common saying that a boy cannot become a man unless he has killed somebody. But if nobody was actually dead today, the actors in this strange roadside drama were rehearsing and their murderous play would soon open. As Antony Loyd has written, life was getting that mad feeling it has before a war intensifies, a sense of collapsing restraints, when anything can happen.[13]

The rest of the journey was a relief, although in theory it was through dangerous bandit country where neither the KLA nor the VJ was in control, and a firefight for control of the road might happen at any minute. We were soon in Kosova, the driver made a run for it through the very dangerous Merdar crossing, driving ridiculously and dangerously fast—we were more in danger of crashing into a roadside tree than from snipers. The soldiers on both sides knew the bus carried both Serbs and Albanians, unlike the solidly Serb trains. The KLA often laid down small arms fire on the railway line, but never attacked buses. Even the most muddled and informal wars such as this develop internal rules and *modi operandi*, and both sides knew that shooting at a bus full of ethnically mixed civilians was off-limits. Then the driver had to slow down; just before Podujeve town, a huge tank transporter had gone off the road into a ditch and the tank was balanced precariously above the fields. We stopped in a line of traffic for a few minutes. I pinched myself. The tank was going *into* Kosova, and the radio had said that the Kosovo Verification Mission was making sure that all the heavy armour was leaving, as the Holbrooke-Milošević October deal had stipulated. I felt relaxed again; on the bus, as always, you found the truth. A Jugotrans bus was taking me into the parallel worlds of this stage of the war: Kosova as it actually was and Kosova as the diplomats said it was. After nine years here I found it deeply familiar, even somewhat comforting.

After this nerve-racking reintroduction to Kosova, reporting on the Verification Mission was easy, a mixture of comedy and tragedy in about equal proportions. The first thing anyone knew about it was its bright orange vehicles and outfits, looking like well-turned-out Dutch sanitary workers, moving along the main roads and observing the ceasefire, or at least that was the theory. It was also the theory that Milošević had withdrawn much of his military *apparat* from Kosova, but the practice was rather different. The heavy stuff was being hidden in empty factories, barracks and forests. The KVM

[13] See Antony Loyd, *My War Gone By*, London, 2000.

was digging in too, ready for the fierce winter. The headquarters of the Mission was out on the plain in, of all places, the hotel that had been taken over by Bosnian gangsters two years before. Heaven knows what had happened to them. Now, as if by magic, it was a very professional and very American operation, the boss was a cheerful US official called Richard Huckerby. He worked with another American, a diplomat called Shaun Byrnes. The yard was full of weird but magnificent bright orange Hum Vees, squat armoured monsters with deep roaring diesel engines—they consumed about a gallon of diesel every minute. I stood speechless as the rest of the press pack milled around the yard, and younger US officials tried to shepherd people into some sort of order before Mr Huckerby said his few words. In a phrase this was it, something the Albanians had dreamed of for many years: the military and intelligence machine of the world's only superpower had openly arrived. The willingness of the Kosova Liberation Army soldiers and the people who worked with them to die had achieved more in two years than the Democratic League had in ten. A black technician in overalls was fiddling with one of the numerous aerials bristling out of the hotel roof. Uncle Sam seemed to be putting down roots and to have come to stay. I wondered if Milošević, hundreds of miles north in Belgrade, realised this.

Compared to this impressive headquarters, the actual monitoring in the field was a shambolic affair, with many of the orange jackets in their Land Rovers young and inexperienced diplomats, and I spent half a day in the rain watching a supposed VJ withdrawal operation at Prishtina railway station when absolutely nothing happened at all. The British officials on the whole were the most competent, because they were nearly all former army officers, many of them actively engaged in military intelligence under KVM cover. The press watched the monitors, who disliked the media and drove away. Individuals monitors were often intelligent people who knew perfectly well that what was happening on the ground had little connection with the spin in the media, particularly the BBC which was reporting extensive withdrawals and full compliance by the Serbs. This was absurd. The Serbs didn't take the monitors seriously, and got on with hiding their heavy armour in woods and inside factories and other places where the KVM were not supposed to go. I took a bus along the Prishtina-Peje road to check things out, and did not even need binoculars to see the heavy armour being taken into forest hideouts on a hill opposite the chicken farm half-way along the road. Milošević was making a fool of NATO. This was duly reported, and within a day or two the KVM monitors were forbidden to talk to journalists, even to borrow a cigarette-lighter.

Some monitors realised after a time how they were being used by the pro-Milošević spin machine: they began to resent it, and were privately quite helpful to journalists. The Prizren office of the KVM was in an echoing empty factory where monitors had commandeered the old manager's office. Several weeks after it was supposed to be in full operation, furniture was still being moved into the office. The British chief monitor was a very intelligent young serving officer who had just come from undercover work in Northern Ireland and was only interested in monitoring the KLA, whom he clearly saw as little different from the IRA. I had been told by a local Albanian contact that large amounts of Serb military equipment had been taken from a local camp and hidden inside a large factory on the Prishtina road. I asked him if he knew about this.

'Yes and no.'

'Are you maybe intending to go to have a look?'

'I would need the bosses' permission to do that.'

The 'boss' turned out to be a Norwegian ex-officer who seemed to have no interest whatsoever in what the Serbs were doing and doubted the legality of inspections inside state-owned buildings. Once again the deeply familiar paradigm appeared—of well-meaning international agreements to try to control Milošević that collapsed in practice. This was because of the skill of the Serbs at evading them on the ground, the fact that legally the Serbs were the sovereign authority, and the general pro-Serb inclination of the military culture in most EU armies.

On the other hand, it was clear that in those October and November and early December weeks the harrying of the KLA had slowed, if not stopped. It was not difficult to move around the countryside unobserved, and it was possible for the refugees to return home. This certainly was a real gain for the Albanians. The domestic returns were heavily pushed by the internationals as a great success, even if many or all of the people's animals were dead or had escaped, and serious damage had been done to their goods and property.

It looked as though the Kosova problem was once again going to be swept under the carpet, but this was unduly pessimistic. The Americans who were working with the KLA knew exactly what was happening, and were continuing to give aid and training advice in the wilds of northern Albania, with the result that a much more organised and effective force was emerging. The British monitors were generally strongly anti-KLA, but in the chaos of the war you only knew what was in front of you, and this was not apparent then in Prizren. However, it was becoming clearer than ever that there were differences between British and US perceptions of Kosova reality, something that was to emerge with great clarity in the disagreement between General Wesley Clark and the British General Mike Jackson over how to handle the Russian grab for Prishtina airport in June 1999.

In Prishtina the agreement had proved to be something of a boost to Rugova and the Democratic League. I went to see Rugova in his office and met the key LDK leader Fehmi Agani and the archaeologist Edi Shukriu at the door. Agani was neat and spruce with well brushed white hair and shiny brown shoes. Although a sociology professor, he always looked like the secretary of a provincial English golf club, and the internationals loved him for it. However, he was not quite what he seemed and had developed his own contacts with the KLA, particularly the remains of the Jashari family and the Prekaz militants, a major factor in the decision by the Serbs to murder him as soon as the NATO bombing campaign started. He was bubbling, warm.

'We will have an independent Kosova, James, we will. And we will give honorary citizenship to the foreigners, the journalists, all the people who helped us.'

He effused at some length about my *Times* Op Ed piece. It was very nice of him, but it was also tragic. He was very intelligent and I think he knew in his heart that the Serbs would never give way unless they were forced to, and the war was not at that point yet. This was the last time I saw him alive.[14]

Edi was chain-smoking as usual as we had a cup of tea in a side room. She grumbled that with the war she never had time to open

[14] For perceptive observations about Fehmi Agani and the LDK see Ismail Kadare, *Il falla ce deuil pour se retrouver,* Paris: Fayard, 2000.

an archaeology book. It was like the very old days in that there seemed to be a modest amount of life in the LDK leadership again. Her hope was that some sort of internationally supervised negotiations with Belgrade might produce a Serb withdrawal and they might become the Kosova government under international protection. This was very much a Prishtina perspective: from talking to the villagers north of Prizren it was obvious that the last thing they wanted was the old days back again, and the people they called the Gjakova mafia having a monopoly on power, even if they were Albanians. Fehmi was a very good man, and unlike many of the LDK big cheeses quite disinterested and careless of his own safety and comfort, but he found it hard seeing a new leadership generation coming forward. As the bitter military fight for survival went on, the new people wanted much more than a return to 'autonomy' in some sort of Yugoslavia under the old 1974 arrangements. In many ways, Fehmi was the good heart of the LDK but he was someone who never completely escaped the dependence on Rugova that in those days so discouraged initiative and new thinking among many of his followers.

I went down to Tetovo to see what was happening there. Within five minutes of getting off the bus I met Aladjin Demiri who was out of gaol for the weekend on parole. He looked serious but was suntanned and had a nice gold cigarette holder—even in gaol the mayor kept his French and Sarajevo culture. Menduh Thaci was in a combat jacket and looked very busy with the war. For the first time since the turmoil in July 1997 the red Albanian flag with its proud and threatening double-headed black eagle was flying again in Tetovo. The Slav minority sat endlessly drinking beer and playing bingo, quite marginalised by events. The VMRO party of the Macedonian-Slav majority had just won the elections, and Arben Xhaferi's ethnic Albanian party would be asked to join a coalition, thus there was the sense of a new era starting.

The moneychangers stood in the north wind with no business. The town was cool and late-autumal and there was a dusting of first snow on top of Kodra e Diellit mountain. The next day dawned with Tetovo at its most seductive, a bright morning, with grey mist swirling up into the Sar forests. My hotel room was warm, calm and austere, an island. In the market the jars of honey with the comb inside and the deep red paprika looked warm, but the outlook felt icy cold. Winter was coming again, and the Albanians would have to make great efforts to keep the KLA campaign moving. It all had to be done under cover and by remote control. Macedonia was like a hotel annexe, when all the visitors are staying in the main hotel, the Hotel Kosova. Nobody could have dreamed that in a few months the Tetova streets would be jammed with thousands of refugees, Kosova would be half-empty and Prishtina café society would be reinstalled in the Arbi restaurant here after its ejection by the Serbs from Spaghetti Toni's in Prishtina. Journalists would sit and drink coffee in Tetovo with the supersonic boom of NATO planes going through the sound barrier as they accelerated home to their bases in Europe and America. The development of a Balkan war is often beyond the grasp of even the most fevered imagination, and that was true of Kosova and Macedonia between the autumn of 1998 and summer of 1999.

Nevertheless there was a good deal happening in Tetovo although, perhaps appropriately for a conspiratorial town, much of it was taking place in the underground, parallel to the Koranic world of the Unseen, the mystical world so beloved of the Sh'ite dervishes and their dissident followers who built the great *tekkes* and mosques there in the town's eighteenth-century heyday. I had an interview with the PDSH leader Arben Xhaferi in his office, where heavily-armed shaven-headed bodyguards stood on the stairs, and the fighting but dead Jashari family looked down at us from a photo on the wall. As always he asked for up-to-date news from Kosova in exchange for giving the interview. His wise gentle face, with crinkly hair and a black head, was taut and his speech had become slower, as it did every time you saw him, with the grip of his aneurism and Parkinson's disease increasing its hold. He was a rock of personal intergrity with an acute political brain, and as a result of his personal charm and gentle manner was seen by Skopje diplomats as the Macedonian Albanians' equivalent of Rugova. This was a serious misjudgement; he hated Rugova personally and his central political ambition was to avoid a split between 'moderates and 'militants' in Macedonia such as had so bedevilled Kosova over the last ten years and made the whole struggle such an epic of stress and violence and

political difficulty for all concerned. Xhaferi was almost wholly successful in this, and laid the political foundation for the opening of
the Preshevo campaign in 2000 and the successful struggle of the
National Liberation Army in the small war in Macedonia in 2001.

Xhaferi may well be seen as one of the master politicians of recent
Balkan history, but that autumn he lived in a nightmare of daily frustration and stress, having to take vital decisions in Tetovo that would
affect the future of the war without ever having secure communications of any kind with the political leaders of the Albanians inside
Kosova. He knew that his mobile phone was probably one of the
most listened-to phones in the world, and used couriers as a result,
but it led to an ever greater isolation. He was a most sensible, sane
man in spite of it all, but he asked for news like a junkie asking for
dope, eyes nervous, intense, searching as he made pictures in his head
of a war only thirty miles away up the road in a country that was his
but which he could never visit. He was also besieged by foreign diplomatic and international community visitors, and had to keep up a
façade of studied moderation and non-involvement in the effort to
keep foreign observers out of Tetovo. The German soldiers there
were part of the Tetovo furniture and did not involve themselves in
local politics. His subtle political achievement for the Albanian cause
in this period was extraordinary, in such marked contrast to the failures and inertia of Rugova.

The central issue in Tetovo was weapons supply, which was at last
being faced by the Albanians, and the public transport routes were
moving substantial quantities of small arms and ammunition into
Kosova. Once again the humble bus was central to the Albanian
political and military fate. The business skills of Tetovo number-two,
Menduh Thaci, were being used to crack open the Serb security system at the border. I took the bus up to Prizren to see how it worked.
We chugged out of Tetovo bus station and wound through the town,
past the little shops, like one with the evocative name 'Vukovar 2',
owned by someone who had lost everything to Serb shells there and
opened up again in Tetovo. Albanians have as many faults as anyone
else—their detractors and critics would say they have more—but
they have a peculiar indestructibility born of their hard mountain
origins. If your family loses more or less everything in a war, you
move somewhere peaceful and start again with what little you have

left. There can be heroism in shopkeeping in wartime as there is
with a gun in a trench.

The bus managed to go about a mile up the road towards the border with the towering peaks of the Sar above us on the left, then
stopped at a garage, apparently for diesel. But that was not all. A
compartment under the luggage space was opened and several
extremely heavy cardboard boxes were loaded up. The bus was carefully washed—if you are smuggling weapons it is nice to have a clean
bright bus in which to hide them. On the left as we went towards
the border were militant villages like Poroi, where it was rumoured
there was a fully-fledged local KLA fighting unit, not merely a logistics and supply system. On the right was the Jugochrom factory, a
business with its roots in the rich minerals of the Sar mountains
above us. As always in Kosova it was hard to tell where the war began
and ended, or what was the difference between peace and war.

At the border the bus stopped for a long time, and everyone was
very tense. One or two hungry stray dogs hung about the bus door,
but it was not their day as nobody was allowed off the bus to feed
them. In a small hut run by the Macedonian customs prolonged
negotiations were taking place, presumably about the exact price
that would be required for the bus and its contraband to be allowed
through the border post. Then we were waved off for passport
examination, and all seemed to be going smoothly.

This was over-optimistic. As the only foreigner on the bus I was
frogmarched by the Serbian officials over to their little hut, where a
relaxed and friendly and obviously quite senior Interior Ministry or
secret police official sat in a cloud of Beaujour smoke. He spoke
quite reasonable English and after looking at my passport and asking
whether James Pettifer was related to James Bond, stole my little
packet of cigars and began smoking them. He then proceeded to go
through everything in my bag in minute detail, looked at my camera
and made a note of its serial number, and then unfortunately found a
Waitrose plastic bag stuffed with all the background material of
newspapers, press releases and handouts that were the raw material
of wartime history which I was taking to my archive in Bath. He
obviously regarded them as very significant.

'James Bond? Yes, I think so.'

He smiled sweetly and began to gather all my precious documents
away into his drawer. It was a waste of time saying that all this was

· material acquired in the course of ordinary work and that none of it was secret or the property of the Macedonian or Serbian government and that the newspapers were on sale in every kiosk in Tetovo or Skopje. I felt like getting angry but it would have been a bad idea; I needed to get to Kosova and with a double entry visa this bus was the only way. Outside the bus driver and passengers were getting agitated. The driver was beckoned in and I was thrown out of the police office, more money changed hands, and the journey into Kosova began, past the group of little white houses at the edge of Gllobocice village, with neat rows of plum trees and scrubby vines on beechwood posts in the gardens.

The whole search had actually been a charade, so that it would seem as if there was a border in operation. In fact the border had been bought by the power of Albanian financial resources, the money that poured into KLA funds from rock concerts in Switzerland, Hamburg and the Bronx, and as a result the guns were about to reach their destination. The Serb Interior Ministry official needed money as much as anyone else, and took it. At Balkan borders there is a price for letting a truck full of weapons through as much as a truckload of timber or candyfloss. Smuggling is in everybody's blood as much as sea-fishing in a Breton coastal village. On the Macedonian borders that autumn the police and customs were making a fortune out of weapons smuggling. A price for a cargo is negotiated beforehand, a down-payment made, and the balance paid when the vehicle crosses the border.

We wound downhill through the forest on the lower slopes of Black Nicola mountain, and after a few minutes drew to a halt. Above us on a grassy slope was a young man with a woolly hat and military uniform. He had a mobile phone and began using it. Then in a trice the boxes were hauled out of the bus's luggage compartment and thrown on to the grass verge, the driver scrambled back to his seat, and the bus surged forward, now several hundredweight lighter. Behind us, no doubt, the young man and his KLA comrades were collecting their ammunition. Ammunition is hugely heavy and is lethal to move around the steep Sar slopes. I had been told in Tetovo that the price for it had been rising. This is nearly always a sign that a conflict is intensifying; if the price falls, holders of ammunition are in the market selling as they do not expect a conflict in the foreseeable future. The Balkan mountains have their market conventions as much as Wall Street. Stored guns are stored value for almost indefinite periods, but ammunition, being so heavy and therefore costly and exhausting to move around, is traded more quickly over a short time-span, often in smaller quantities, and the price fluctuates much more than that of weapons.

Out in the Drenice villages, people were living in conditions that looked like a movie set for a film about displaced persons after the Second World War. I drove out of Prishtina for a day with a friend, and we wandered among houses without walls, some with gaping shell holes in the roof, and others that were about to collapse completely. There were almost no farm animals to be seen except chickens, and most houses had the Serbian Orthodox cross daubed all over them with black paint. There were new graves in the cemetery. The sewage ditches had been broken by heavy VJ vehicles and stinking sewage ran in little rivers along the streets in the mud. Traumatised people wandered around their big farmyards, once the tidy domestic fortresses where eggs were laid, fruit picked and sheep kept safe. Now charred wood and broken wattle fences were all that remained. Last year's hay was grey and rotted in conical haystacks, the beasts that should have eaten it were long since dead. As if in a daze people wandered around, picking up bits and pieces of things from their old pre-war lives and then dropping them, like primates wandering into some human settlement and not knowing what human tools and possessions were or where to put them. The older women looked particularly zombie-like: all their normal lives and security were focussed on the house and the yard. Life would have been better for them in the Middle Ages or under the Ottomans. The saccharine voices of the State Department people about what a wonderful agreement it was was that enabled people to return to their homes came to mind. They made returning sound like coming home to a suburb after a minor burgulary. How unlike that it was.

We found a very young KLA soldier at a street corner and asked to be taken to meet a local commander. There seemed to be no one around, but he was prompt and efficient and it was clear that a new pattern of organisation was emerging. He asked for some cigarettes and I gave him Marlboro Lights. There was certainly no sign of the

MUP or any ordinary Serbian police force or VJ in the area; in a military sense the situation in central Kosova in November 1998 had in many ways returned, territorially, to how it had been a year before when the Serbs controlled the main roads and the towns, but the Albanians dominated swathes of countryside and forest. There were rumours of a new Holbrooke initiative, even in the villages, but down here there was no way of knowing what was happening in Belgrade. I had come to distrust the BBC more and more, and usually listened to the Voice of America on my tiny Sony short-wave, but in spite of being much more objective and less 'Yugoslavist', the VOA did not have the same depth of correspondents. News of any kind, good or bad, was in short supply in the field. Anyway, it was difficult now to imagine what Holbrooke and Milošević would talk about. Repair grants for shellholes in walls? It all seemed rather silly.

My mind went back to visiting a village nearby with the same friend about a year before. The local schoolteacher was a friend of his who was involved in a project to collect Drenice folk songs. We had been to her family house, and sat on the long sofas on beautiful embroidered rugs and talked about preserving something from the world of culture and the spirit. The house was neat and bright and incredibly clean and tidy with whitewashed walls. She was neat and modern and wore jeans and could have been living in a fashionable part of London or New York. Now we were back, but wondering about how the fabric of Drenice life would survive at all. Although the KLA was much better led and organised now than a year before, and small-arms stocks in the villages were much higher, there was still nothing to stop Milošević once again using his heavy armour and rocket-propelled grenades to wreck the villages. The villagers told us that not everybody had come home, and some people were staying in the forest as long as the weather allowed. They did not trust Milošević in the way the European diplomats did, and events proved the Drenice people right.

In Prishtina the media were back to cover the Serb withdrawal, there was a long waiting list at the Grand and I shared a room, packed like a sardine, with Chris Bird from *The Guardian*. I had not met him before, his partner was the Reuters person in Belgrade, and he was deep in Rebecca West. Like Antony Loyd, he was a fan of the Lada, preferring the lightweight Russian four-wheel drive to the heavier European 4WD counterparts. After the terrible summer of isolation for the Kosovar Albanians, the war had become internationalised again. Milošević did not like it—it was not what he expected. The machinery of direct repression was moving in, with the *Koha Ditore* offices guarded by heavily-armed MUP with Hecklers and flak jackets. The *Daily Telegraph* and BBC correspondents had been raided and their equipment seized, and apparently in Brussels at NATO an American general was briefing NATO ministers after a meeting with Milošević. At Valljake, south of Kline, I watched the army reoccupying a barracks it had been forced to evacuate in May. The parameters for intensification of the conflict were being set.

The day for the final withdrawal of Serb army vehicles arrived and the November weather was filthy. I stood by the Obiliq crossroads just north of Prishtina and peered into the thick cloying fog that left your clothes soaked through after an hour or two outside. The day's story ran: 'Hundreds of Serb army vehicles are on the move in Kosova today, as Serb commanders have set up a large window dressing exercise to confirm to NATO that promised troop withdrawals are actually taking place. Appalling weather conditions make life difficult for the OSCE observers in post.' I added, among other material, that they were reoccupying the Valljake barracks, and the KLA ceasefire was holding. Adem Demaci, the KLA's political spokesman, said that the KLA had recovered control of about a third of the territory lost to the Serbs in the last two months, as the weather created problems for the Serb forces. I ended the piece by saying that a lot of it looked like UNPROFOR in Bosnia all over again, with the Serbs pulling the wool over the eyes of the international community. Back at the Press Centre in the Grand the bar was doing a roaring trade as people tried to thaw out from the wet and cold. The British Foreign Secretary Robin Cook was on television and said nothing. The Albanian scene was dominated by much talk of a major crisis between Veton Surroi and the Americans, after Surroi had published the stolen Holbrooke-Hill 'peace plan' in the newspaper. The LDK had seen it, but chose not to publicise it, although it envisaged a solution for Kosova within Serbia. Surroi was now openly opposing the Rugova people. I wrote in my notebook that night: 'There is no information in this town on what Rugova feels, says or thinks. But I know why Robin Cook was talking to Agani and Co. in Macedonia—he wants to heal their breach with Rugova and end Rugova's isolation.' In the Media Centre some of the French journalists were getting drunk with the Serbs. Not much was changing in Kosova.

The following morning a photographer friend on *Koha Ditore* who had just come back from Albania ran into me in the street and we had coffee. A cameraman then arrived, who was travelling with him. They said that Bukoshi was now mobilising his little FARK army in Tropoja as the official wing of the 'Kosova government', but that FARK only amounted to 2–300 fighters. This was very puzzling. I had not been over the mountains into Albania for a while but I thought that FARK had more or less dissolved itself the previous autumn, and many of its soldiers had joined the KLA. The two reported that it was a media-sensitive operation, and that FARK had British SAS-type soldiers as their military 'advisers'. It sounded as if someone in Whitehall had realised that the ice was about to break and NATO would at last become seriously involved. A stooge army would be needed to try to take credibility from the KLA and give the pro-Serb British an opportunity to cause trouble in the Albanian movement, with a right-wing group, secretly controlled along classic counter-insurgency lines. Later I learned that Paddy Ashdown (former Member of Parliament and leader of the Liberal Democrats) had become Tony Blair's special adviser on Kosova, and he thought that it was time for us 'to do' something with the KLA. This was not necessarily a discouraging sign, since Ashdown was an ex-MI6 officer and tended in his newspaper articles to reflect the views of the more intelligent people in that organisation. It was another signal that the current very unstable political and military equilibrium could not last much longer.

6. Peace and War in Kosova

In January 1999 the sense of an endgame was never far away. The time that should have been a much-needed rest was interrupted by a flare-up of the old 1997 controversy with the Oxford Helsinki people, and the issue of Whitehall's efforts to control foreign reporting. It was becoming clearer, in the view of *The Times*, the *Sunday Times* and many other people, that some editors had been willing to provide journalists' cover for MI6 agents in Bosnia who had then filed material of a highly pro-Serb nature to fit in with the policy of the Major government. It was equally clear to those of us who worked in Kosova over the years that exactly the same processes were still at work as in Bosnia.

On 18 December *The Times* had run a story about the legal victory I had with Miranda Vickers in 1997 over the Oxford Helsinki Group, and attacking the then editor of *The Spectator*, Dominic Lawson, in this context. I had recently, in that summer, done some work on a *Sunday Times* story investigating the activities of one 'Keith Craig', the pseudonym of a MI6 officer who had been involved in recruiting local journalists in Bosnia to work for MI6, in alliance with a Russian defector based in London, also working for MI6, who had run a fake news agency, paid for by MI6, to try to spin international coverage of the Bosnian war in a pro-Serb direction. The story had not made the paper for legal reasons, but in the course of it we had discovered material that interested me a great deal about the 1993 arms plot that confirmed my suspicions of British involvement. I always enjoyed working for David Leppard anyway, one of the most gifted journalists in Wapping who was determined to carry on the best Insight traditions of the *Sunday Times*. It seemed that the an MI6 officer had been posted to Skopje immediately before the arms plot, and been involved in setting up the framework for a counter-insurgency operation against the Albanians in Macedonia. This seemed perfectly consistent with what I already knew, although I was

214

surprised, perhaps naively, how far the then Tory government was prepared to go to support the ex-communists in Skopje. It seems that its original plan had been dropped, and the arms plot substituted.

I had a pre-Christmas drink in London with Miranda Vickers and we sat in O'Riordans at Brentford by the river and wondered where the war really was, in Kosova or in Whitehall. In some ways there was more adrenalin with the London allegations, since they were part of a series of great stories, but many of them were difficult to get into the papers at Wapping because of legal problems or shortage of corroborative documentation. The Insight team was determined to do a story showing how the Major government had connived with arms sales and military training for Milošević, but although several good people worked on it for two years, on and off, it never made the paper. John Witheroe, the *Sunday Times* editor, and Peter Stothard of *The Times* both had courage and were used to standing up to government and legal pressure, but the enormity of the implications of the allegations brought all concerned to breathe deeply, in that they confirmed that the Conservative government had been in active collaboration with vicious neo-communist regimes in both Belgrade and Skopje. British operatives had been used in Macedonia to frame up innocent post-communist Albanian political leaders as little more than appendages of Milošević's terror apparatus. It meant that the agony of Bosnia had been quite unnecessarily prolonged, and Britian was an accomplice to genocide. Now, a period of years after the end of the Bosnian war, these matters are much better understood, but at the time it was difficult.

In London Sir Reginald Hibbert had organised a meeting with the London KLA representative Pleurat Seidiu, attended by all representatives of British friends of Albania. He took the view that the central task in London was to establish the legitimacy of the KLA. Aged nearly eighty he was making a unique contribution to the war effort, although he had not been in Kosova since being there in the Second World War as a young British Special Operations officer. The meeting went well, although some of the older people of the Second World War generation found difficulty sitting in the same room, let along around the same table. Returning to the Balkans, in Belgrade the *kocheva* was blowing, a particularly cold and bitter winter wind that comes down the Danube valley from the Carpathians. While waiting to fly out of Gatwick I had read in *VIP News* that

armed Serbs were blocking the road down to Prishtina. Eight VJ
soldiers had been taken hostage and were being held in a village near
Podujeve. This would be the first serious test for the Kosovo Verification Mission. In my bag were proofs of my Macedonian book and
I did not know if I would have time to read them. I flew to Sofia
first since I needed to see my publisher there; the city was cavernous
and poor but as always friendly and non-threatening for those not
caught in the crossfire of the Mafia's quarrels.

Yonko Yonchev, the publisher, was calm and measured and progress with the book was extremely slow. That was Bulgaria—it somehow got there in the end but you often wondered how. In Sofia it
feels as if you are on the edge of civilisation, and might fall off at any
time. There is the central plain and Hemus mountains and the Black
Sea coast, then nothing but the vast Asian steppes. My sculptor friend
Blaj was engaged in an ancient ritual brought from wild origins in
Central Asia when I arrived at his apartment: he was hiding the
umbilical cord of his new-born son in a sculpture so that he would
follow his father's vocation—an old Bulgarian custom. The Bulgarians have a marvellous rich national folk culture to sustain them in
their poverty and difficulties.

Sofia station was an an ugly Stalinist concrete construction, and in
it the dope dealers were peddling fine Lebanese Black cannabis, and
the muggers watched the deals to check who had enough money to
make a mugging worthwhile. The train, freezing cold and dark, ran
to the Bulgarian-Serbian border over the Dragoman pass, with its
vast, snowbound, trackless forests. The pass had been a great thor-
oughfare and artery between Bulgaria and Europe in Ottoman
times, and the setting for Eric Williams's excellent Cold War thriller,
but the region but had more or less died as a result of Warsaw Pact
borders and was only now beginning to revive after the end of communism in Bulgaria in 1990. Milošević had quite good relations
with the Bulgarians, many of whom united with him in Orthodox
chauvinism, racism and a common distrust of Islamic people like the
Turks and most of the Albanians. As always in the region, the fault
lines of religion that lie below the surface often determine what
happens. The Bulgarians had treated their Muslim and Turkish
minority very badly in the 1980s under the communist dictator
Todor Zhivkov, and had learned little from the experience.

Suddenly there was a commotion on the train at Pirot, the first
stop in Serbia after the border. The border had been routine, the

heavy Bulgarian border guards were swaddled in huge parkas and looked as if they were in the Yukon. The train sped forward in a cloud of blown snow. The blizzard had let up but there was so much snow around that it was difficult to tell the difference. Pirot was in the deep forgotten Balkans, a valley in Serbia next to a Bulgaria lost in economic crisis. The town was inhabited mainly by ethnic Bulgarians, square gorilla-like black haired men with brawny arms and pudgy hands, and immensely strong blowsy blonde girls lifting huge bags and suitcases of contraband. The Bulgarians could be the champion rugby players in the world if every player was a front row forward. They liked lots of drinking, wrestling, weight-lifting and sex, in no particular priority. The Serbs despised the Bulgarians philosophically for their crude 'Asiatic' behaviour, but needed them here. The smugglers were getting off the train with cheap Turkish clothes bought in Sofia. The cause of the commotion was not this local mafia in cheap shell suits and odd coloured skirts. Smuggling was accepted, but an old lady had died of hypothermia on the train. She had fallen asleep by a broken window and the draught and wind chill effect had frozen and then killed her. Broken windows on trains can be dangerous in any Balkan winter, it is always a good idea to carry tape to seal them up. She was a stiff, literally, as she was hauled out of the carriage, and carried into Pirot station in her miserably poor dark clothes. Icicles a meter long hung from the guttering. The Morava valley seemed to be a giant refrigerator, hundreds of miles wide, and we were deep in some obscure and forgotten compartment.

After a while the police and customs men allowed us to escape, probably leaving the old woman to an obscure pauper's grave in the mountains. It was a very sad, if painless way to die. We wound slowly north through the woods and snow-covered cabbage and maize fields up the river valley, with its limestone gorges and deserted woodland, then crossed open prairie land and halted at Niš, birth-place of the Emperor Constantine and a great military town of the Romans, now home to the Prishtina Corps of the VJ, the garrison town of Slobodan Milošević for all south Serbia. All Kosova international telephone calls are routed through Niš, and tapped, as I discovered some years before when Mike Evans, the defence correspondent, was in charge of the Desk, and I by-lined a story from Tetovo. It was filed from near Niš and the Desk Editor that day picked up the difference, I presume because the Foreign Office had rung in after the phone intercept was passed to it by the Serbs, such was the closeness of the liaison between the Serbian and British secret intelligence services at the time.

I transferred to a coach to Belgrade. The bus station at Niš is huge and modern and communist and efficient, with the tough young uniformed staff with threatening haircuts glaring at any *stranatz* from behind armoured glass windows, and a loudspeaker system out of Orwell's *Nineteen Eighty-Four.* Nobody in Niš bus station stood any chance of being ignorant of the Belgrade government's thoughts. An Ottoman wall runs along the perimeter. Although there was the usual variety of humanity among the Serbian staff, you could be sure they all supported the Socialist Party of Serbia. A new picture of Slobo hung in the front of the coach. I slept fitfully. There was no sense that the regime was threatened by what was happening in Kosova, only sixty miles away as the crow flies; most people in Niš had no information at all about what was being done in their name, unless they had family members in the army or the police. Kosova was thought to be a bad and dangerous place now with so many Albanians there. Not many of them had ever been there, and and it was just better not to think about it but to concentrate on the daily fight for economic survival, an attitude the government encouraged with its news coverage.

Hours later Belgrade suddenly loomed in the dim winter light, and I alighted in the central bus station to the clacking sound of the roosting birds. I checked in at the press office and headed south. Belgrade contacts told me that US policy was in chaos, and Milošević was worried that Richard Holbrooke had been marginalised in the State Department. Madeleine Albright was taking charge of Kosova policy and working closely with the pro-intervention General Wesley Clark, which meant more NATO involvement. The Belgrade chattering classes were now talking about Kosova, and the economic crisis was forgotten. I was not very impressed by these stories, the economic crisis had never touched these fat cats in the first place, in fact some of them had grown considerably richer in the wartime years. A contact in Tahir Hasanović's party told me that the British diplomat David Slinn was in town and working on the 'Kosovo sedition' (Slinn also spent time in Prishtina, and I doubt that he used those words over dinner with Veton Surroi). Milošević was attacking the press, *Nasa Borba* was shut down. The local OSCE office was publishing the Kosova 'alert status' in the Belgrade papers, Mitrovica and Podujeve rated 'two', but everywhere else 'one' or 'zero'. The snow was so deep between Ferizaj and the southern border that it was often difficult to enter or leave Kosova by road. People came into town with oak branches for the customary Serb Christmas rituals. Things seemed pretty normal, a people plodding on regardless in this brutal winter towards the next stage of their war. I took the dawn train down to Prishtina through Serbia in deep freeze.

In Kosova the KVM was congratulating itself on its first real success, the release by KLA commander Remi's men of the VJ soldiers held in the Llap hills Antony Loyd was now working with Remi, a sign of the respect this new military leader enjoyed in Wapping as a brave frontline fighter against dictatorship. The Verifiers now had a new and able American leader, William Walker. It would soon be a name to conjure with, a name for Kosova street plates after July 1999. I filed to *The Scotsman* that this release was a real success for the KVM, but that although the military stand-off might have been relaxed, the October ceasefire brokered by Richard Holbrooke was now in tatters. Milošević was building up his heavy armour again, and without a re-start of the stalled 'peace process' further conflict was inevitable. Adem Demaci was in Albania, building up support for the KLA among the Albanian political parties. I was doubtful about what he would achieve; the Foreign Minister was Pascal Milo, a Socialist academic I knew, cultured and intelligent, and a southerner with a known distaste for Kosovars. In the end it probably did not matter. The central point was that it was Adem Demaci as the KLA spokesman and not Rugova who was presented in Tirana as the Kosova spokesman.

In reality there had been almost no progress on the peace plan since mid-October 1998. The main danger for the KLA was being blamed for what in reality was general inertia. William Walker in the OSCE head office held a press conference in which he expressed his concern at 'the growing radicalisation of both communities in Kosova', and called for an acceleration of the political process. The place was full of thinly disguised British military intelligence officers and Signals NCOs with strong Scottish accents and stronger cups of tea. The head of Rugova's information service and one of his closest associates, the journalist Enver Maloku, was shot dead the same afternoon. He had been a Gorani from the Slav-Muslim minority in Kosova who was accused by some people of having once worked with the Serb secret police. It was widely believed to be a revenge killing by someone in or around the KLA. I had a dim memory of having met him some years before, but could remember little except that like several of Rugova's aides he wore an English-style sports jacket. When I asked a *Koha Ditore* journalist who he thought had done it he shrugged his shoulders and said that possibly Maloku was involved 'in dirty things'. The Serbs still had agents in many parts of Kosova, mostly within the LDK but in many other organisations as well. The angle of his shoulders spoke volumes.

Thousands of people crowded into Maloku's home village of Bradash for the funeral, but Rugova did not attend, his aides being afraid for his security. The twenty-fifth Albanian corpse was discovered in one of the villages near Prizren, after another massacre by the Serbs: aged thirty-six and from Peje, Emin Basha was tortured and executed. According to the verifiers, there were now over 30,000 displaced people in the Llap region alone. It was a grim and bloody week. I got drunk one night with a CNN cameraman in the Grand bar after reading a statement from the Contact Group in London saying that although there had been more 'clashes' in Kosova, 'the threat of force was having some effect in Belgrade'. The statements of the Contact Group and the inanity of the non-American part of the IC were a greater incentive to drink to excess than the dangers of the war. Rugova had agreed immediately to the Contact Group's proposals for talks with Belgrade; Demaci said that the Yugoslav army must withdraw first. Maloku's murder felt like an undercover Psy Ops killing, to dent any confidence Rugova may have had and make him pliable. This may seem far fetched at one level, but as NATO intervention approached, the dark side of Kosova politics was such as to have made instant sense to Al Capone. Russian ex-KGB agents were known to be fighting with the Serbs in southern Drenice, and one of them might have been the person who followed you through the dark streets to your apartment. Rugova seemed to me not to have any contact with the reality of Kosova at all, but nevertheless he received universal support from the diplomats. A Dutchman asked me if it was true that Demaci had a stubborn personality and that this was the problem. We did not answer and moved to the other end of the bar. However hard you worked, it seemed impossible to write the story with any degree of effectiveness, the tide of blood was flowing ever more strongly but the rigidity of most European diplomats was undiminished.

It was also an empty Prishtina, the streets more or less deserted. The atmosphere was intolerable. All the chattering classes wanted to talk about was whether there would be a sell-out to the Serbs to avoid a war during NATO's fiftieth anniversary celebrations in April 1999. I went to Prizren and found the town in a deathly cold hush, as if waiting for the end of the world. Nobody knew how, or if, the KLA on Mount Pashtrik was surviving in ground temperatures of at least twenty degrees below, plus the wind chill factor. I wanted to file from the lowland villages north of Prizren, like Randobrava, that had been in the front line for months and were full of particularly uncompromising Albanian families. I thought it might be practical to get there and back to Prizren in a day. It seemed like a millennium since we sat in the Turkish restaurant by the Prizren river Lumbardhi on a warm summer night and listened to Sabet Jusefi talking about old days in the movement in Switzerland, how Yugoslavia might have had a chance if the West had supported the Marković government more actively, and how the government should clear the piles of rubbish accumulating on the opposite river bank. In fact it was only a couple of years ago. The neo-Ottoman music had been so good, with the female singer making her voice roll and ululate, that I asked the boss for the name of the band, and he insisted on giving us the tape.

Prizren has always prized the struggle for the Way, there was a Dervish *tekke* within 100 metres of the restaurant. The spirit of the Ottoman past wound around us like the green creeper on the mosque roof. The friendly little *tekke*, the people's shrine, and the elegant aristocratic eighteenth-century Sunni mosque of the Turkish élite a little further down the river were a product of a much greater civilisation than that of Tito's Yugoslavia. The Prizren Serbs appeared to be planning a last stand, and there were rumours that Seselj was sending in weapons and paramilitary people from Belgrade to defend them. It seemed credible, from what I could discover, but there was not enough solid evidence to file on. Given the continual Foreign Office pressure on my work, it was just the sort of copy I avoided filing. My opinion about the rumours and allegations would not suit Whitehall, and it was only a short step to being accused of exaggerating or even fabricating events. I tried to get to Randobrava but no driver would go near for any amount of money. A contact said that the Serbs were planning to murder a whole village up there as an example, and it was too dangerous even to consider. It was doubtful, but six weeks later he turned out to be right, the Serbs massacred eighty-nine out of 124 inhabitants of the village of Krushe, a few miles from Randobrava.

A visit to the KVM mission in the old factory on the outskirts of Prizren was not encouraging. I met a good and efficient British army officer, Mike Morwood, working under a Belgian, Michel Maisonneuve. Relations with the Serbs were clearly tense, and Morwood admitted that in practice they could not go anywhere or do anything the Serbs disliked. He seemed to see their main role as monitoring the KLA, and in particular 'infiltration' from Albania. This seemed very partial, and also improbable in practice given the weather conditions on the border that week. He was an honest man and admitted that 'we have freedom of movement problems along the border', only to revert quickly to the OSCE official line and add that the VJ were 'very cooperative'. The Verifiers were clearly falling under *de facto* Serbian control. A new development was the burgeoning of Yugoslav minefields. This provided good copy for *The Times* a week or so later:

LANDMINE BAN IS DEFIED ON THE BORDER
Serb military engineers in Kosova are laying tens of thousands of internationally outlawed anti-personnel landmines along key corridors on the Albanian border in a desperate attempt to stop the flow of weapons and ammunition reaching Kosova Liberation Army units.

The minefields are in the hills near Gorozup, above the River Drin valley, 18 miles west of here and east of the KLA strongholds in the Tropoje region of Albania, near the border with Montenegro.

A team of experts from the International Committee of the Red Cross is compiling a report on the situation to be sent to western governments. A Red Cross spokesman in Geneva said yesterday 'Reports coming from Kosova concern our delegation a great deal.'

Yugoslavia is one of the largest manufacturers among the 25 countries that still make mines. The December 1997 Ottawa accord bans their use, and Yugoslavia is among the 123 signatories to the agreement. But in Kosovo seven types of sophisticated anti-personnel mines have been found by munitions experts attached to the Kosovo Verification Mission run by the Organisation for Security and Cooperation in Europe.

In accordance with an October 1998 agreement on Kosovo, Yugoslavia is allowed to maintain a three mile no-go zone along its border. Privately OSCE members say it is far wider in some places.

In theory Serb army escorts ensure the safety of all border visits by monitors. In practice this allows the Serbs to lay huge minefields. 'We have to work with them on that basis,' one former British officer said.

Serb military sources see the mines as a regrettable necessity, given the inaccessible nature of the boundary between Albania and Montenegro.

For now, the hostilities have been brought to a standstill by the worst winter in ten years and the hope that the Paris peace negotiations prove fruitful. But, whatever the outcome at Rambouillet, the menace of the minefields will remain.

The shootings and violence of the VJ against the north Prizren villages was not mentioned by the verifiers, and although these events were taking place only a few miles away, there was a sense of the KVM slipping into total irrelevance having been a vital step towards peace in October 1998, only two months ago. It was a copybook illustration of the short life-span of an IC mission in wartime, and in the kaleidoscope of the Kosova struggle. Where the mines issue and control of the VJ was concerned the KVM had taken on aspects of the role of the UN in the Bosnian crisis, where the Serbs quickly learned to control the verifiers and incorporate them into both their political discourse and practical activity. In Prishtina researching the story had been a nightmare, and it had only been possible to file anything because the British officer in charge of the OSCE mine observation unit was away somewhere and his Albanian interpreter who disliked him for his openly pro-Serb views unlocked his office and showed me the otherwise secret records of KVM observation of minefield activity. Not surprisingly nothing about this had ever been released to the media, since it showed that the OSCE knew the Serbs were in breach of international law and the international community was doing nothing about it. The OSCE spin on this story was to suppress any criticism of the Serbs, or even the most basic factual reporting of what was happening. In the end the international community had to pay vast sums of money to clear these minefields after July 1999, and the task is still not complete. The OSCE and IC complicity has cost several Kosovan and Albanian children and some adults a limb or even their lives, often from following their animals into undergrowth.

In the bar of the Hotel Theranda in Prizren a couple of Serbs were musing gloomily into their slivowitz, saying how far away they were from the parts of Serbia that mattered. Right down here in south-west Kosova, on the edge of the Muslim domains as they saw it, they were far from safe cities like Niš or Belgrade. Serbs are very bad at being away from their homes, but in their hearts they already knew, I believe, that Kosova might not be theirs for long. In a very dim and inchoate way this postman was already thinking of an escape route, how he and his family could leave when the war spread down into the cobbled streets of his city from the frozen heights of Mount Pashtrik. It would be good for a Serbian family to be near the express bus station for escape to Belgrade. Like the rest of us, they were not yet thinking the unthinkable, of a full-scale NATO military commitment against Milošević, but down here in this gloomy back-of-beyond pub it was easier to see what the dramatic and far-reaching implications of that would be than in Brussels, Paris or London. Once NATO was involved in military action, it would be in its first war, and would have to win it. That could mean liberation for Kosova—or so it seemed that January. As events turned out, the rumours about Seselj's people were true; I should have been less cautious and filed something, because one of the first things that happened in Prizren after NATO started bombing two months later in March was that Radical Party paramilitaries set fire to the little wooden museum building where the League of Prizren had been founded in 1878, and it burnt to the ground. Next they ran barbed-wire entanglements around the main Serb suburb on the hill below the castle, and controlled the town for the next six weeks. But forecasting is dangerous in daily news journalism, and 'oracle' is a term of abuse. The future is only for tomorrow's paper.

I went back to Prishtina feeling that individual news stories from Kosova were likely to become less and less important. There was an overwhelming sense of the war moving, in Homeric terms, from the realm of the humans to that of the gods—away from foot-soldiers who had worn out their boot-leather in the Kosova woods and muddy fields for the last ten years towards the masters of high-technology warfare, whose feet had never touched the Kosova earth and never would. Print journalism tends to lose its way just before a major war only to renew itself once the conflict starts, but a NATO air war would be dominated by the television cameras. It was diffi-cult to imagine any conceivable news story or analytical exercise I could write that would make the slightest difference to anything that was going to happen in the next stage of the conflict. This was not so in the summer of 1998, when in many ways the Anglo-American media saved Kosova.

The burnt-out houses, blackened timbers and shelled mosque along the road fifteen miles from Prizren looked exactly like the Brcko corridor in Bosnia, a scene of devastation where a house had a bed hanging out of a bedroom wall at a crazy angle and a shell hole in both sides. A few people stood ankle-deep in dirty brown water trying to rescue a sheep from the stream. The VJ patrols were a few yards from the road into the woods, presumably laying mines, while an occasional burst of fire came from KLA fighters deep in the forest. In one sense it was new, as scenes of unfolding war always are, and in other ways it was part of a pattern of conflict where in putting it into my blue notebook I was rewriting something that I had already seen so many times. But there was one new and ominous detail; on the top of the hill above Suva Reka a large artillery piece was being cov-ered in tree branch camoflage, but its turret pointed straight into the town. Some time in the near future, Kosova was going to be blown apart. The fact that it was pointing into Suva Reka was particularly ironic as this was a solid LDK and Rugova town, with everyone working in the big rubber and tyre plant, but support for the old leadership was not going to do it much good. The thought brought on feelings of overwhelming tiredness and irrelevance as the bus rolled down from the Cerraleves hills on to the central plain. In the past ten years I had seen so much violence, repression and unhappi-ness here that it was difficult to imagine that worse could still be to come, but it was.

Suva Reka was duly taken apart two months later. As the Hague International War Crimes Tribunal indictment of Slobodan Milošević dryly states,

On the morning of the 25 March 1999, forces of the FRY and Serbia surrounded the town of Suva Reka. During the following days, police officers went from house to house, threatening, assaulting and killing Kosovo Albanian residents and removing many of the people from their homes at gunpoint. Many houses and shops belonging to Kosovo Albanians were set on fire and a mosque was damaged. The women, children and elderly were sent away by the police and then a number of the men were killed by the forces of the FRY and Serbia. The Kosovo Albanians were forced to flee, making their way in trucks, tractors and trailers towards the border with Albania. While crossing the border, all of their documents and money were taken away.

On 31 March 1999, approximately 80,000 Kosovo Albanians displaced from villages in the Suva Reka municipality gathered near Belenica. The following day forces from the FRY and Serbia shelled Belanica, forcing the displaced persons to flee towards the Albanian border. Prior to crossing the border, all of their identification documents were taken away.

The Serbs murdered no less than forty-four members of the Berisha family in Suva Reka on 26 March in one of the worst crimes of the entire war. All the *fis* were murdered in cold blood, from Ismet Berisha, aged two, to Sair Berisha, aged eighty-three. They gave all they had for Kosova, and died with dignity at the hand of the Serbian barbarians. I commend the example to those in London and Paris and Brussels who still claim that those of us reporting in the field in Kosova exaggerated the evil of the Serbs' activity.

That evening was spent in Tricky Dick's, the main Prishtina watering-hole for the media at this stage of the war, a friendly but gloomy bar opposite the Rilindja tower block that used to house the Kosova papers and radio until the Serbs closed them down in 1993. Philip Schmucker, always a bastion of common sense, was grumbling about the *Telegraph* group. Tom Walker said the town was full of stories of KLA plots, and that thirty-six people had been killed near Prizren in a single land-mine incident.

As I had gone in I looked back at the Rilindja tower and wondered if its coordinates were being fed into some targeting computer in Strategic Air Command somewhere like Omaha, Nebraska. It looked worn and ugly against the night sky. Perhaps the battered old

Yugoslav concrete had a soul that knew something was coming. Tricky Dick's had been renamed after the US Balkan negotiator Richard Holbrooke and in a complex, obscure and totally Kosovska operation had been taken over by a cooperative of journalists, some Serb, some Albanian, some foreign. It must have been the only war pub in the world where the hacks could recycle some of the costs of their drinking, and feel they were making a good investment of their proprietors' expense allowance funds. Those involved felt that this was an idealistic return to the positive old Titoist principles of workers' self-management and control, on a strictly multi-ethnic basis. The fact that the pub was named after Richard Holbrooke was perhaps a sign of the real Kosova Albanian attitude to a man they had never trusted much after Dayton in 1995, and to the omission of Kosova from the Dayton negotiations. Holbrooke was nevertheless a fixture in the Kosova scenery for a long time, and in the international soap opera aspect of Kosova life, where almost every major politician in the world comes to Prishtina, it is necessary to be a pretty big name to make waves—or even nowadays to excite much local interest. To have an important watering-hole named after you is an achievement of a kind, if ironic in this case.

'Who is in today?' was a common question among friends during the summer of 1999, when there was a succession of star visitors. Eventually and somewhat reluctantly Holbrooke came to visit Prishtina and the pub, in that year, accompanied by a jocular Bernard Kouchner, the first post-war United Nations Kosova administrator. However, from a Machiavellian viewpoint Holbrooke was perhaps a slightly better friend to the KLA than his Albanian critics have realised. He allowed himself to be photographed with the KLA leader Jakup Krasniqi in early 1998, and gave it respectability at a wobbly time. The October deal with Milošević gave the military reorganisation of the KLA vital breathing space. Holbrooke was at least honest. When he first came to Kosova in the summer of 1998 he said he had 'no idea' how to solve the conflict, and he did not, like some minor US diplomats, involve himself in repeating the ritual blather from the Contact Group.

The next day I thought I could possibly get a story from Gjakova, The copy I filed to *The Times* ran immediately in the paper, though cut about somewhat by the subs. The Serbian form of the name of the town was inserted and the copy about the arrest of the young men cut:

ON THE MURDER MILE IN BANDIT COUNTRY

Terror comes unexpectedly, even in bandit country in western Kosova. It came when I was on the Prizren–Djakovica bus, with about twenty Albanians, in the grey gloom of a January afternoon.

The road seemed clear, then the driver suddenly hit the brakes on the icy slush. '*Mott*', he spat out an Albanian obscenity. In front, a blue Serb armoured car had shot out from a wood and blocked the road. Three men were pointing a machinegun at us from a turret.

My stomach dropped as the gun swung back and forth across the front of the bus. The talkative teacher next to me muttered '*Lufte, lufte, lufte*', War, war, war.

The tension was unbearable. One of the Serbs took out his side arm and pointed it straight at the driver. His eyes were visible only through the slits in a balaclava. The driver revved the engine defiantly. We were frozen in time and space.

Then the ice broke. The Serb laughed and stowed away his handgun, then they sped off towards the Kosova Liberation Army stronghold east of Prizren.

We hit Gjakovica ten minutes later. Gjakovica was infamous for its lawlessness in Ottoman times. The Sultan's troops virtually gave up here.

We had been travelling along one of Kosova's many murder miles, where the local Serbs and the Albanian middle class in Djakovica fear the KLA, and everyone is terrified of the Serb police. 'We have a lot of trouble with the police here,' the teacher said.

Unknown to us, a massacre of Albanian civilians was taking place the same day. But it could have happened in many places here. We were lucky.

I produced some other more or less routine war coverage on skirmishes between the KLA and the Serbs near the Peje road, and then there were one or two very quiet days when the war seemed to be marking time. The weather turned even worse, and neither side could do much, with Serb armour immobilised by solidifying diesel fuel, and a thick layer of freezing fog spreading across the plain so that nobody had any idea where anyone else was positioned. It would have been a good day to shoot film footage about the battle of the Somme, even to the extent that the KLA were learning to dig a decent trench. I thought I would go back to Sofia for a day or two, and try finishing the labyrinthine negotiations with my Sofia publisher. The bus ran happily down to Macedonia, and it was a nice day there, the warmer air from the Mediterranean was seeping up the Vardar river valley. Then my mobile phone rang in the bus, when I was just over the border at Gjusevo. It was Veton Surroi.

'James, where are you? There is a very big story breaking.'

'On a bus. In Bulgaria.'

I was missing a great scoop. He went on to explain the bare essence of what we now know as the Racak massacre. Forty-five Albanians had been found murdered and mutilated in a village near Shtime. That was the one big story of the Kosova war I never touched at all. In retrospect that was perhaps just as well, although it was maddening at the time, since it immediately became a target for Serb spin, aided by the French and Italian diplomats in Prishtina. This was not surprising. It was the first major atrocity story of the war. In media terms atrocity stories change the way a war is seen by the public, and are hard for governments to deal with. If you have disembowelled people and they have been photographed lying in a heap on the ground, there is not much even the most cunning spin doctor can do to wreck the story. People feel that wars come and go, but they are fought by soldiers who know the risks of joining an army. An atrocity story carries the war into the civilian realm and beyond the Geneva Conventions, and in modern political arithmetic this means a call for an intervention. This is nothing new; in the nineteenth century the Ottoman empire was shaken by reporters' revelations of the Batak massacre in Bulgaria. The Serbs, after their crimes in Bosnia, were peculiarly vulnerable to atrocity stories, and the dead at Racak did not sacrifice their lives in vain. After Racak I never had the slightest doubt that NATO would intervene to save Kosova from the fate of Bosnia. The only uncertainty was the timing, and finding a way to unite the fissiparous NATO countries around a common policy, and stop the Europeans and Russians sabotaging a principled policy. Why was Racak so important?

A little village under the lee of a 200-foot hill on the outskirts of the town of Shtime, Racak had been in obscurity for generations. It is a sheep village and its grazing lands fade into the hill with its deep earth gullies made by the water from winter storms draining off the encroaching green beech and oak scrub. As in many villages in this area, pasture has been hacked out of the scrub and the limited

amount of arable land shared out between families to grow maize to
sustain a single milking cow. It is not classic Drenice, but has a similar economy, with about fifty houses and courtyards crammed into a
space by a stream. In the autumn some tobacco and deep red peppers hang up to dry under the eaves. Old people grow vegetables or
keep chickens to raise a little cash on a stall in the street market.
Shtime town had been a strategic place from the earliest days of 1998,
with control of the town on the edge of the central plain opening
up opportunities for an Albanian advance on the main Prishtina-
Ferizaj road, something the Serbs could not countenance. Shtime
market had plenty of food, and Racak on the outskirts had been on
an important supply route for the soldiers in the forests to the south
and west. The Serbs probably knew this, and regarded the villagers
as active collaborators of the KLA.

The Shtime people were indeed mostly behind the KLA, unlike
Suva Reka to the south-west, a similar sized strategic small town that
was a Rugova stronghold. Shtime paid a heavy price for its militancy,
exacted by the Serbian police and army. Racak was a satellite village to Shtime, and a predictable place for an example to be made.
On 14 January several hundred heavily-armed Ministry of the Interior troops descended on the village, and the massacre took place.
The local KLA tried to defend the rebel families, and some were
shot too for their pains. The OSCE monitors arrived, led by William
Walker, for many years a senior CIA officer and a veteran of many
wars, mostly in Latin America. He is a friendly, unpretentious ano-
rak-loving man with big glasses and driving energy. He could have
been a professor of engineering at some Mid-West university, the
man who is clever on paper, but also knows how to get things done.
His enemies in the British diplomatic set-up later claimed that he
was high up in the CIA, and had armed the Contras in Nicaragua.
I do not know whether he did or not, but he was a great friend of
the Kosova Liberation Army.

In his first press conference William Walker said 'As a layman, it
looks to me like executions.'

French journalists objected, saying that the KLA may have fabri-
cated the evidence for the cameras, but that interested nobody. Even
the Serb cameramen had shot yards of footage showing the infantry
attacks on the houses. It was yet another example of how the French

media were more pro-Serb nationalist and more indifferent to human rights issues during much of the Kosova war than many Serbian journalists. We had all got used to some of the French hacks sitting out the war in the Grand Media Centre bar and filing from VJ military handouts, but the reaction to Racak of the official French media and diplomats in Kosova, with a few honourable exceptions, has fundamentally altered my view of France. The deputy head of the OSCE mission, an ex-French ambassador to Belgrade called Gabriel Keller, refused to call Racak a massacre, and said there had only been 'killings'. But he added that diplomats must have cool minds; he didn't think he was biased towards Serbs or Albanians, and his relations with people on both sides had always been excellent. In fact, as soon as William Walker left Kosova for consultations in the United States, the OSCE and KVM began issuing numerous statements accusing the KLA of violating the ceasefire and grumbling at the fact that Remi's soldiers had taken over abandoned Yugoslav army positions near Podujeve. It also made more concrete a feeling I had had for some time, that in the end democracy in the Balkans and elsewhere cannot be defended without the commitment and principles of the United States. But because this was Kosova it took time for these perceptions to become clear to me, and they did not do so in a simple way. In much of its Balkan policy in the last ten years, France has betrayed its democratic traditions by collaboration with Serbian nationalism.

Kurt Schork had the new US peace plan, and ran a long file on it for Reuters on 30 January. It set out how Serbian sovereignty over Kosova would all but disappear, and was headlined in *Koha Ditore* as 'Disappearance of Serbian-eroded rule'. That had already been eroded by the presence of over 1,000 'verifiers', and the document said that 'the international community envisions autonomy for Kosova, including a police force whose make-up would reflect the ethnic Albanian majority here. Serbian police would have to leave. Yugoslav army troops would be confined to barracks and border patrols, and there would probably be a force of at least 20,000 NATO troops to enforce the agreement. No international border would be changed. Nominally Belgrade would still call the shots, but real political power in Kosova would be vested in the ethnic Albanians, and military power would reside with NATO.'

The floating of the plan, with its mixture of the good, the bad and the recycled ideas of the past ten years, was clearly preparing the ground for an international conference. In Kosova the key question was still who would represent the KLA. Although the original leadership and founding fathers like Jakup Krasniqi were very much around, individual soldiers like Remi, Fatmir Limaj and Ramush Haradinaj had made their reputations by their achievements in the field, and their views would be important. The Prishtina papers started to run more pictures of the mysterious Hashim Thaci—usually but not always in military uniform. I knew that the editor Veton Surroi was much closer to Thaci than the internationals realised, but it was such an ultra-sensitive issue that we did not discuss it even privately among ourselves, let alone write a story about it. A central question would also be not only who would speak for the KLA, but whether the KLA would come at all. Adem Demaci and some of the KLA commanders close to him were said to favour fighting on regardless, and they felt after Racak that they would have more international support. Hashim Thaci was the key figure on the Albanian side. I knew what Thaci had achieved in the last ten years of his ceaseless underground activity, and was wondering again whether to write something about him, but given the sensitivity and confusion of the situation it still seemed premature. Tom Walker had picked up the Racak story again, and was giving a good deal of attention to the French debunking allegations. Nobody had any idea who was going to represent the now substantial number of KLA soldiers who had come from a Kosova Democratic League background. It was the type of story where, after I discussed it in the morning with the Foreign Desk and hopefully had an order for copy, a telephone call would come to the desk from the MI6 or Foreign Office media departments after they had seen the GCHQ intercept of my conversation with the Desk Editor, and there might be problems. The Foreign Office was hanging on to the fiction of Rugova's exclusive right to lead the Kosovar Albanians like a drowning man clings to a spar. As always in the Balkans, the problem is not finding the stories but learning how to break them in a way that avoids playing into the hands of the spin doctors and the technical snooping apparatus.

Another immediate question was what would happen to the Verification Mission if the fighting between the KLA and the Serbs intensified and the military situation began to get out of control.

The verifiers were unarmed and had no means of defending them-selves in even the most minor skirmish. NATO would have to act from Macedonia. I went down to Bitola, then returned to Skopje and interviewed whoever I could find. The train journey back to Skopje saw Macedonia with open snowfields, drifts as high as the bramble patches covering the vines, and the train doors frozen shut when we reached our destination. A railwayman attacked the ice with an axe to let us out out of the train on to the platform. As the political situation froze solid, so the weather followed. Militarily it was not a reassuring picture. NATO's Skopje operations were French-led and Italian-staffed, and seemed to see Kosova in a very different way from some of the British and nearly all the Americans. It was not difficult to see that there was only one real option for the Verification Mission if the war intensified, which was a rapid evacu-ation. Yet nobody in authority among the Euroid military leaders in Skopje seemed to be thinking about it. A senior Italian officer with whom I tried to discuss it said he was not able to think about it because he was about to return to Italy to attend to his vineyard.

I filed copy to *The Times* on 19 January:

MACEDONIAN FORCE ON ALERT AS EVACUATION FEARS GROW

The 2,300 members of the NATO Evacuation Force in Skopje remained on full alert yesterday as the possibility grew of a direct intervention to remove international monitors from Kosova.

NATO has considerable military resources here but, as always in the Bal-kans, things on the ground can look very different from the way they seem in military planners' offices in New York or Brussels.

It is not clear what the future of the United Nations Preventive Peace-keeping Force will be if the NATO force gets involved in Kosova. The blue-helmeted troops have been patrolling the borders of the Former Yugoslav Republic of Macedonia since 1993.

The NATO operation here is French-led and few of the French officers expect direct involvement.

'We are firefighters, yes, but only for a very big fire,' one said. But many believe they will be used if the Serbs take hostages from the monitoring force.

Most of the Italian soldiers billeted in the Hotel Tourist in Marshal Tito Street agree. 'We would be invading Yugoslavia,' one said.

NATO plans, as always, are prey to the traditional Balkan loyalties of the big powers. The French officers are strongly pro-Serb. 'It is the Muslim problem. We have it in France,' a Breton said.

Some feel that NATO helicopters would be vulnerable to Serb anti-aircraft fire and it would require a large assault to bring off a successful hostage rescue.

On the other side of the *Times* page, Tom Walker was reporting the messy aftermath of Racak from Prishtina:

The local authorities and Belgrade have been given heart by reports of what French newspapers are said to be publishing today. These reports would throw doubt on the Albanian accounts of what happened at Racak. Several French journalists have studied video footage of the police attack on the village on Friday, and have concluded that the women and children were not separated from their menfolk, as has been widely reported.

This was all quite fair comment, but in the end I doubt whether this sort of activity by the French benefited the Serbs; quite apart from the ethnic issues, the controversy kept Racak in the public eye for weeks after the event, and brought renewed interest in Kosova from parts of the media that had previously been bored with the story. The inept French spin doctors only gave the impression of a possible or probable cover-up. It was by no means the only killing that was going on in Kosova, and not the largest, but the French efforts and the subsequent report by Finnish pathologists kept the story alive at a critical time; if they had not questioned the Albanian view of events, it would have fallen off the news pages in a few days. But the French and other basically pro-Serb countries knew that General Wesley Clark and the German General Klaus Naumann had met Milošević in Belgrade on January 19 and told him that force would be used if he did not pull his troops out of Kosova, and that the military plans drawn up for air strikes in October 1998 were still very much on the table. If they were to have any chance of protecting Serbia from NATO, it was essential to try to discredit Racak as an 'atrocity story', just as German spin doctors, if they had existed then, would have tried to discredit stories current in the First World War of Belgian nuns being raped by men in spiked helmets. It is, of course, one of the great 'what if?' questions of the Kosova war: what if air strikes had been ordered earlier, before the Rambouillet conference? I think much would have undoubtedly depended on which targets had been chosen; hits on the main Serb army barracks would have been very useful to the KLA, but unlikely for that very reason. Attacks on isolated and well-hidden artillery and tanks would have achieved little. There was a narrow and small-minded constituency (mostly of Southerners) in the US military who were anti-KLA and did not, as they put it, wish to become 'the KLA's air force'. In general they had a rather antiquated mixture of Cold War and Republican isolationist views, and appeared to retain some residual influence in the US air command.

A media climate existed in which events were beginning to achieve an uncontrollable momentum. Diplomacy was trailing after events with little chance of controlling them. It was a very similar situation to the fall of Gjirokastra in the Albanian rebellion of 1997: a key event acts as a media trigger and that in turn encourages actors in the struggle on the ground to promote their particular practical agendas. It is perhaps a little like the old days of touring theatre companies in Britain, when a performance would take place wherever an audience could be assembled. British soldiers like to talk of the 'CNN effect' on events, and tend to regard the arrival of the cameras as ominous. This is understandable, but the CNN factor is not a mechanical certainty, and depends on events having an escalating pattern of development. If the story does not meet the networks' expectation, as in Kosova in June 1998, the cameras actually diminish the importance of the story, and this aids the 'establishment' political forces in the conflict. Milošević was quite intelligent in allowing the big TV networks in during June 1998, to report on the feeble nature of NATO's warnings and the reverses of the KLA. In the usual arguments about the media and whether the modern apparatus makes diplomacy and conflict resolution more or less difficult, it is sometimes forgotten that quite a proportion of modern diplomacy actually takes place in the media.

Rambouillet continued on its rambling course for another two weeks, with much playing to the gallery. The conference was meant to be the Kosova Dayton, to provide a negotiated solution, but it was really the prelude to NATO intervention.[1] Morale in Kosova was raised with the dramatic news that Hashim Thaci had been elevated to be the main political spokesman on the Albanian side—this at a stroke removed the possibility of a sell-out to the Serbs. March dragged on and the only question of significance was the time when the first bomb would drop. A long period in Kosova history was over,

---

[1] See Vickers/Pettifer, *The New Albanian Question*, op. cit.

and when that took place on 27 March a new time began, which is another story. A certain amount of iron enters the soul of someone covering a long and complex conflict. Some of the best and the worst of the human spirit had been manifested on the 'cursed plain' in the preceding ten years, and some of the best international help (mainly American and British) and the worst (mainly Euroid). Those of us who were there tried to understand and bear witness to it all as best we could.

I was back in London for a few days, and then returned to the Balkans in February. The Rambouillet negotiations had started to conclude and my next move would be to see what was happening on the ground in the way of preparation for peace enforcement, if there was going to be a peace to enforce. Rambouillet was a strange choice of location for a negotiation, a château outside the most civilised of cities where delegates could fraternise and talk to friends and colleagues and generally do as they wished. It was a long way from the remote airbase at Dayton, Ohio, where the Bosnian war was brought to an end. There was a set timetable at Dayton, and the various parties had little option but to sign the agreement; it was coercive diplomacy at its most successful. It felt as though Rambouillet would not produce a deal, from the first day when the Serbs did not bother to attend the opening session, and spent the evening drinking and singing nationalist songs round the piano.

I flew back via Thessaloniki, wanting to see what was happening in Macedonia, clearly the next focus for NATO's ground plans. The story was spreading out on to the main European stage, via Rambouillet, and throughout the region, and Kosova refugees were turning up in every city and country in the world. My son Alexander was studying in Thessaloniki and we stood in deep snow on the sea front looking out across the cold sea to Mount Olympus in the far distance. There had been a freak blizzard, with the heaviest snow for years. The British soldiers of the Port and Harbour Regiment based in Portsmouth were brewing up hot tea in the area of the port already controlled by NATO, and equipment was arriving. The regiment was very friendly, and a sergeant explained how they were still trained to drive trains and look after ports. It was reassuring to see the British forces in theatre, even if in a somewhat exploratory way so far. The PR people were saying it was all just part of an Exercise—

Alexander the Great 99, which was to last ten days. I did not believe a word of it, particularly when a young female officer told me about her Kosova crisis pre-briefing. These forces were coming for the duration. The plan was that they would police a deal that was to be signed at Rambouillet—Bosnia again, but a few hundred miles to the south. The best of the British army has a wonderful timeless quality; they have been there, seen it all, and done it all in hundreds of years of operations abroad. Every battle-honour from Agincourt to Waterloo and El Alamein to Kabul is theirs, and in a real sense exists in the collective subconscious. There may conceivably be an infantry situation they have never encountered, but it is hard to think what it might be.

Great armies depend on memory, as well as training, equipment and discipline. Behind the men smoking Lambert and Butler in the improvised sergeants' mess of the harbourmaster's office were the shadows of the British army of the First World War Macedonian campaign. An old man who had worked for my family in Worcestershire once told me of the unbelievably primitive conditions he had endured at the front thirty miles north of Thessaloniki in 1917, in the course of stopping the Bulgarians from seizing the city. Soldiers' feet rotted inside their sodden disintegrating boots, uniforms fell apart, genitals were covered in strange fungal infections and were scratched compulsively. They are a little-known army, with no Siegfried Sassoon or Wilfrid Owen to evoke their lives and deaths there. The Port and Harbour Regiment are far from prominent in the public knowledge of the British army, but are discreet, professional and efficient. You can learn to do more or less anything in the British army, but train-driving is unusual. The élitism and politicisation of some of the special forces have given the British army a questionable reputation in some parts of the Balkans, but the great majority of regiments have won enormous respect.

In Thessaloniki they operated behind high walls and fences, filling the old olive oil market sheds with vast piles of camouflage netting, tools, metal sheeting, tin huts and all the messy, heavy, awkward-to-shift paraphernalia of infantry operations. A happy Colonel Brook was in charge.

'We are only a few hours behind schedule', he said 'The soldiers have worked hard and I am very pleased with them.'

A secure shed held ammunition. In reality NATO had begun to move already, or at least the British army had. Odd people from other NATO countries were around, including careful German officers in fatigues and high boots, writing lists on their clipboards. The modern German army is admirably democratic and has hardly put a foot wrong in Macedonia or Kosova. The 2,000 Americans who were supposed to have arrived in northern Greece were nowhere to be seen in Thessaloniki. I filed a short piece for *The Times* on developments, and pointed out that Greek agreement to a Kosova campaign would be vital, since NATO depended on Thessaloniki for its supply routes. The piece ran in the next day's paper:

More than 2,000 US marines and other support units are assembling south of Thessaloniki to join the Greek-NATO force. The NATO exercise underlines the increasing commitment of the alliance to reinforce political stability in the key Vardar valley that dominates transport routes in the southern Balkans—the road and rail links between Yugoslavia, Macedonia and Greece. The railway north from Salonika is being increasingly dominated by military transport. Greeks are bemused and not a little disturbed by this dramatic reminder of their proximity to the Kosova crisis. Salonika is as much a Balkan as a European city these days, in the wake of the huge influx of Serbs, Russians and Albanians over the last five years.

Perhaps I should also have filed that Greek public opinion was, as usual, very pro-Serb. There were the usual grumbles in the usual quarters, particularly the British embassy in Athens. Of all the British missions in the region, the Athens embassy was and is notorious for its obscurantism and hostility to the media. In retrospect, it had reason to worry since it knew something that nobody else did. It appears that a secret deal had been reached between the Greek government and NATO whereby the Greeks would allow NATO to use the port and its associated transport routes north provided they did not have to take any refugees. This was a shabby affair, but apparently what the Greek Prime Minister Simitis felt Greek public opinion would allow him to get away with. Nobody knew about it at the time, and I only did three years later in 2001. The Greeks are now the most unpopular nation in liberated Kosova, and Albanian interest naturally focusses on the issue of Albanian property seized by Greece in the Second World War period.

In Tetovo there were general fears about what Rambouillet might bring. I had a short interview with Arben Xhaferi who said that he thought Veton Surroi was in danger of being manipulated by the foreign diplomats, and that the Albanians regarded no agreement as preferable to a bad one. Later that night I spoke with Veton on the phone and told him what Xhaferi had said. He was uncommitted, and sounded as it he was trying to get himself in a frame of mind to head the Rambouillet delegation. This was absurd. The Americans had seen the political capacity of Hashim Thaci long before and if Veton wished to stay at the top of Kosova politics, he needed to associate himself more openly with the new KLA forces. I spent some time in Skopje, working yet again on the long and labyrinthine *Sunday Times* 'Insight' team investigation linked to the MI6 defector Richard Tomlinson, which never made the paper. But it was interesting to see the looming crisis of Macedonia developing. Skopje was full of the sound of gold coins rattling as every Western government bought what politicians it could. I met Boris Trajkovski, later President of Macedonia, who seemed to have re-branded himself as a 'moderate' politician and was anxious to prevent the MI6 material out of Skopje from reaching the paper, while the political bars were full of rumours that Llupjo Georgievski had thrown in his hand with the Greeks. A contact claimed that he frequently went to Athos, allegedly on a Christian Orthodox mission. Whatever the details, the old Macedonian political élite was being broken up by the pressure of the Kosova conflict and all the foreign activity in the country. Arben Xhaferi was sitting in his mountain fastness and worrying about Kosova, as ever. But he could also have been assessing the political opportunities for Albanian advance that were opening up in his own country.

The roads were becomingly increasingly dominated by huge convoys of NATO military vehicles, and some of them strayed into Macedonian towns. My minibus was nearly hit by a heavy armoured vehicle in a narrow street in Bitola. If NATO was going to invade Kosova, it was invading Macedonia first, and it was impossible to avoid the feeling that elements of the national sovereignty of the fragile land-locked state were disappearing. It was hard to imagine the circumstances when NATO would leave, once it had arrived, and local Macedonian soldiers were having to abandon their barracks to be used by NATO. Many years before Rugova had said, perceptively, that the region was in a *status quo* of crises, but now there was a single multifaceted crisis stretching from Belgrade to Athens, little as the Greeks were inclined to admit it.

The refugee crisis and the NATO campaign

Most big wars have their 'phoney war' period, and the NATO phase of the Kosova war was no exception. As the first tentative air raids began, Richard Holbrooke moved to Hungary to be ready to move to Belgrade to talk to Milošević. The State Department and some people in NATO still hoped that a few airstrikes would bring Milošević to the negotiating table, on the Bosnian model. In the abstract this was not an unreasonable theory, but it ignored the nature of the real, non-virtual war in Kosova that had been taking place over the last eighteen months and the nature of support for the KLA. The political psychology and objectives varied widely on both sides. From Milošević's point of view Bosnia was a focus of some Serbian vital interests, but not an integral part of the Serbian state. By contrast he saw the NATO campaign in Kosova as an attack on Serbia itself, and many issues that had been open to negotiation in Bosnia were closed in Kosova. From the Albanian viewpoint, the Kosova Liberation Army had achieved what many other Balkan democratic movements over the years had not, that is open military support from external Great Powers, in this case the world's most powerful military alliance. It had every motive for pressing the conflict on to last as long as possible, so that NATO military action would destroy the communist-period state and military structures in Kosova and open the road to independence. This was not at all how NATO mainstream opinion saw it, in that the bombing campaign was intended as a limited military action to force Milošević to stop the ethnic cleansing and allow the refugees and displaced persons to return to their homes. No war was ever declared, although the media universally referred to it as NATO's first war. This dialectic was to determine the basic parameters of what was to take place in the next two months. Each side had its own agenda, and the Albanian hand would be strengthened by the humanitarian crisis caused when, after the onset of the bombing campaign, the ethnic cleansing and refugee crisis accelerated and brought the nature of the Serbs' crimes home to viewers on every television screen in the world.

In the first day or two of the war, Kosova was largely closed to the media. Murderous threats were soon passed along the grapevine with the result that Antony Loyd, whose fine reporting of Remi's war in the north-east had particularly offended the Serbs, had to leave the region. I had passed on the warning to him from my Serb sources as well. In fact, Antony had been planning to stay in a remote area of rural Kosova, in a hide-out with the late Kurt Schork of Reuters, but a bizarre incident with their vehicle ruined their plans. As often occurs with newspapers, Murphy's Law became the motor of events. In the confusion I am not sure what occurred at Wapping, but the whole episode was a setback to my position as a regular writer, along with the usual recurrent disputes about my billing in my regular interviews on CNN from a certain tendency in the Wapping management. In a later article in *The Times* the defence correspondent Mike Evans, not normally my ally in internal office matters, actually said that Antony was right in his fears, but by then the damage had been done. At the same time Jim Pringle was being taken out of China, and in a strange decision he was made the paper's 'Balkan correspondent' and given a flat in Athens, although as far as I knew he had no experience whatever of the region. I was told that Jim had 'powerful forces' behind him, but nobody seemed clear who or what they were. Somebody also said that the bosses believed I was anti-Israel, a baseless claim since I never wrote anything about Israel or the Middle East and have a profound respect for traditional Jewish scholarship. The Balkans had come to Virginia Street. Bronwen Maddox, the foreign editor, told me that the paper would love me to write as many analytical pieces as I liked, but the 'structure of Balkan reporting' was being changed. Again this seemed an odd viewpoint, because it seemed to me that good desks thrive on a certain amount of chaos and confusion, and reporting didn't need management structuring of people who were any good at it. It was also widely seen in Fleet Street that *The Times's* Balkan coverage had been very influential over the previous years, with people of very diverse backgrounds like Antony, Tom Walker, Richard Owen and myself making a good fist of it. It was puzzling. But there was plenty of work from the Sunday paper, and the foreign editor Sean Ryan was particularly supportive.

I had a good story from Skopje the following week about the Serbian political underground, so I gave it to *The Scotsman*. That did not seem to please Bronwen, either, and our relations deteriorated. She is a gifted analyst and writer but seemed to have an ideal of reporting as something more akin to a science than the messy art that it usually has to be. A peculiar aspect of her work was to grill you over the telephone about your sources for something you said. Leaving aside normal professional obligations to protect people, the method could have had unforeseeable consequences in a war situation.

At the beginning of the bombing campaign none of this mattered much. The coverage was very suitable for a major television-set-piece Gulf-war-type operation, with people like Kate Adie, in Italy covering the bombing campaign, in their flakjacketed element. Television completely set the agenda, with the screens full of jet fighters screaming up from tarmac runways into the air towards Serbia. The newspapers did the best they could but, as in the Gulf War, television is all that matters in the first few days of a conflict of this type, and on some evenings it was difficult to tell whether it was new footage being shown or ten-years-old material from the Gulf war as aircrew were interviewed on the flightdeck of aircraft-carriers hundreds of miles away from Kosova. This certainly was the stage of the 'Virtual War' described by Michael Ignatieff in his book of that name, which in his estimation was fought between about 1,000 Serbian air defence specialists and 1,500 NATO pilots, and he called it the first post modern war in history. On television it looked like a full-scale war, as it was meant to, and in no time the NATO press conferences became a regular feature of all television news, with NATO's spokesman Jamie Shea intoning endless claims of success for the first raids. In reality little was happening. As the USAF historian Ben Lambeth has shown in his study of the air war, many of the early raids missed their targets, the number of bombs dropped was limited, and there were endless and intractable problems of agreeing on targets within the NATO command structure.[2] None of the targets chosen was strategic. A French pilot was reported as having dropped all his bomb load into the Adriatic rather than drop them on Serbia. This seemed credible, but more worrying were the sense that the Serbs would not come to the negotiating table, and the opposition of some members of NATO, particularly Hungary, to the possibility of their territory being used for a ground war.

[2] See Michael Ignatieff, *Virtual War*, London, 2000, and B. S. Lambeth, *NATO's Air War for Kosovo*. Santa Montica, CA: RAND, 2001.

I did not try to get into Kosova—it was pointless since, like Antony Loyd, I would certainly have been arrested by the Serbs or worse within a couple of days, and from my experience of reporting over the last two years I knew as well as any the limitations of what can be done and seen in the obscurity of the Kosova forests, and the difficulty of living there for more than a few days without SAS-type training and backup. In the towns arrest and imprisonment would be certain. Alistair Campbell, Tony Blair's press spokesman, later complained that the media failed to give a good picture of the ethnic cleansing in Kosova, but those of us who had been there on the ground had no illusions about what was involved. It was also crystal-clear to everyone who had reported in the last year that the conflict would spread to Macedonia through the refugee issue, and there would be many good stories there in a country I knew intimately and where arguably the fate of Kosova would be decided.

The last time I had seen Arben Xhaferi—in March during the Rambouillet conference—we discussed the nature of the coming conflict and he was convinced by my argument that NATO would only really move on Kosova if the stability of Macedonia was threatened. This was a realistic analysis, and I knew that after their dreadful experiences in the forests in the summer of 1998 the village people would want to leave Kosova completely *en masse* rather than wait to be surrounded and cleansed in informal small settlement that could not be defended. Human survival instincts and Albanian political interests would coincide. A massive story was looming. A human flood into Macedonia was almost certain, and the Macedonian President Kiro Gligorov had already discussed with the international community refugee corridors to move the people into Albania. In response to this it was certain that the Kosovar Albanians would not cooperate, because as soon as Milošević had the refugees far from their homes, in Albania or anywhere else, he would have won. The direction of events followed this parameter; within a few days of the onset of war a massive refugee crisis built up at Blace, the road border-post between Kosova and Macedonia in the vast and dramatic Kačanik gorge. Tens of thousands of people were living in squalor in a no-man's-land between the border fences, often without food, water or sanitation, and the Skopje government would not allow them to enter Macedonia. It was a scene of appalling human misery.

The media focus, and the focus of the war itself, shifted from the air war to the refugee crisis. The Macedonians treated the refugees somewhat worse than many of the Serbian police, and the newspapers picked up the humanitarian crisis that was developing, and generated much sympathetic coverage on all sides.

The odd new regime on *The Times* Desk made me unsure of what the paper would want. I was deluged with requests to be a TV pundit—particularly by CNN, by far the most important channel in the world—and that seemed a good use of my time when I was in Britain. It was clearly going to be a long-drawn-out war; unless NATO seized the candle and took on major strategic targets like power stations and oil refineries around Belgrade and the big cities, Milošević would just sit out the bombing and wait for splits to appear in NATO. Since the Serbs had hidden their artillery successfully in the autumn of 1998 from experienced monitors on the ground, there was no reason to suppose they could not hide it with equal success from air surveillance. I did not know how much to say on the media because public support for the NATO campaign in Britain was being undermined by the BBC, most of whose reporting reflected profoundly pro-Yugoslav assumptions. The Serb air defences had made a sensational hit on a US stealth bomber which had then crashed, and Milošević was on a roll. The humanitarian crisis banished indecision. I filed a *Times* Op Ed piece, written on my fiftieth birthday on 6 April, and Michael Gove ran it the next day. My book *The New Macedonian Question* was about to be published by Macmillan, and the time seemed right to make readers more aware of some of the main historical issues. The copy, dated 7 April 1999, ran:

MACEDONIA DESERVES SHORT SHRIFT

The West has another Balkan mess to fix

Clare Short may not be everyone's idea of a natural cabinet minister. But she has a wonderful ability to disregard conventional wisdom, hit nails on the head and reflect basic British decency and common sense. On Monday, in the chaos of the Blace refugee camp, she touched a raw nerve. Her response to the humanitarian crisis was more than an alarm call to the West. It raised deep issues about the Former Yugoslav Republic of Macedonia, currently home to NATO's nascent ground force, and highlighted the need for a tough Western policy not just towards Serbia but also in our dealings with the Skopje government.

Macedonia has been oppressing minorities for most of its life. Ever since it became independent from Belgrade in 1991, it has been rampantly anti-Albanian and discriminated against the massive minority populations of Muslims, pro-Bulgarian Slav-speakers, ethnic Turks and Gypsies.

But the West has fêted Skopje's ruler Kiro Gligorov as a moderate. Its support for his attempts to achieve 'stability' has acted as a quiet way of helping Serbia. In an unstable region, the apparent civil peace in Macedonia has looked to be a rare Balkans success story.

But there has been a high price to pay in civil liberties and human rights. Massive economic support has been provided by the IMF, but there has been no payback in democratisation of the Titoist political system. Although the situation had improved by last autumn, the 1994 Macedonian election was one of the most corrupt foreign observers had ever seen. Real political power, in any event, rests with the pro-Serb, Communist-dominated Ministry of the Interior.

The original state and its borders were a child of Stalinism, the communist 'solution' to the Macedonian Question that bedevilled late Ottoman Europe. Under Tito the Socialist Republic of Macedonia was a garden Suburb of Serbia, used for cheap holidays, wine and food, the bottom of the Yugoslav heap in every way. A pro-Belgrade Skopje élite was built up, a motley collection of hardline communists who were really Serbs thinly disguised as 'Macedonians'. They justified this hegemony through a manufactured history which was closer to mythology. But as long as all was peace and quiet, it didn't seem to matter much.

Beneath the surface, however, there is a dark side to Macedonia—a side stained by Serb influence, and tainted by criminal money. The élite made millions by breaking United Nations sanctions against Serbia in 1994 I remember sitting at the border checkpoint at night—the same place where the refugees are now suffering—watching convoys of fuel waved through and speeding towards Belgrade.

War criminals such as Arkan had substantial property business interests in Skopje, and the town's casinos are a haven for Bosnian Serb and Montenegrin money-launderers and their cigarette smuggling money. Zoran Janaković, the Yugoslav ambassador and a close crony of President Milošević, wields huge influence in Skopje. His writ runs in places that Western diplomacy cannot reach.

It is the dark side of Macedonia that we have witnessed this week, in its contemptuous treatment of the refugees.

The piece produced a less antipathetic reaction in official London than I had expected. Few people there knew much about Macedonia, and the Serb lobby was unsure how to react. The activity of Arkan was undeniable; I had written a story about his Skopje retail investments that had run in *The Times* some months before, and the Foreign Office spin machine was on very weak ground since the FCO had neglected Macedonia for many years. Nobody who knew anything at all about Skopje could deny that the casinos were full of very dubious people, or that Gligorov and his entourage were very recent ex-communists, or that huge fortunes had been made out of smuggling diesel. The intelligence service people were quiet, because they knew that the pre-1997 Conservative governments had allowed Technometal Vardar, a company controlled by the Serbian secret intelligence service, to operate sanctions-busting operations in London, even down to allowing the use of their offices to site the first FYROM embassy in London in 1992. British-Skopje cooperation to quietly help Milošević was not a pretty picture, and within a week or two, by the middle of April, the Blair people had realised clearly the unreliable nature of the Foreign Office advice they were receiving and struck out on a new course. A hard line was adopted with the Skopje government, and the construction of tented camps began in Macedonia. In turn this affected the direction of Kosova policy, with a new determination finally to face up to Milošević. Top press experts were dispatched from 10 Downing Street to harden up the wobbling NATO press operation in Brussels.

The story gradually moved from its initial focus at Blace and spread throughout the region, just as the refugees moved along the roads on their tractors and carts, and long lines of people filed on foot through the mountains. Children clutched toys in the backs of trucks. Old people stared into the distance, not knowing if they would ever see their homes again. It was a vast movement of people from Kosova along the lines envisaged by the most extreme Serbian nationalists, the emptying of a territory, an oppressed nation on the move. Although it was clear that most would wish to stay as near to Kosova as possible, the NATO Allied Harbour humanitarian relief operation had a new headquarters at Durres, and was far from clear about its objectives. One of the first camps to be built was near the south-east Albanian town of Korca, within thirty miles of Greece and almost as far from Kosova as it is possible to be in Albania. Korca has a long and distinguished history, and for a time was coveted by Greece in the disputed lands left from the Ottoman Empire. The rundown town with its brewery, textile factory, mosques and churches stands on an open plain, with high mountains in the distance. In the winter the north wind sweeps over it, and in the summer ten years ago as communism collapsed, villagers were dividing the land into small family plots and planting beans.

Some in the international community wondered what the reaction of the southern Albanians to the Kosovars would be, believing that the old Gheg-Tosk, north-south dividing line in Albanian society would mean communal indifference or even hostility. In the event they need not have worried since there were few refugees to worry about. When they did come Korca was very welcoming and a school was turned over to them as an accommodation block. I visited it in April, and it was full of mothers and small children; many of the men had stayed behind to fight in Kosova. The flagstone floors were scattered with blankets and toys, the corridors echoed with unfamiliar Kosovar vowel sounds. The boys played with plastic water-pistols and shot invisible Serbs dead. Kosova teenage girls eyed their shorter, less attractive but better dressed Tosk sisters in the street outside. Gradually the war, and the Albanian national question underlying it, was spreading over all the Albanian lands with the exception of Greece where, in breach of international law, refugees were not admitted. The northern town of Kukes, just down the road from Kosova, swelled to a refugee metropolis of over 150,000 people in the next two months, while distant camps like Korca remained almost empty. Industrious German soldiers dug deep trenches in the damp earth for latrines in the sheep-cropped Korca plain grass, and erected lines of circular tents that stretched in good German order far into the distance. UNHCR officials sat in the spring sun in North Face anoraks and Timberland shirts, and set up refugee and IDP registration systems for people who never appeared. In the middle of it all a large white food van from Dakota Salvation Army looked strange in this place, and the young American volunteers who had nothing whatever to do were glad to find a writer to have a cup of tea with them. The few families who did eventually come were blanker and less animated than the first refugees in the Kosova forests a year before. The children rushed around enthusiastically as a German army helicopter landed on the plain near the camp, but the

older people knew the exodus was final this time—that if the outside world did not come to their help, they would not see their
homes again.

A camp was set up at Elbasan, on the Shkumbini river in central
Albania, and the sight of heavy Turkish army vehicles marked with
the star and crescent lumbering through the town with its ancient
Byzantine and Ottoman fortress at the centre seemed like an ironic
commentary on the vagaries of Balkan and Albanian history.
Although Elbasan is of very ancient origin it was an Ottoman centre
for hundreds of years, and its great fort was a vital part of the military
system for central Albania under Turkish rule. The name Elbasan
means 'strong place' in Turkish. Now the Turkish soldiers were back
in humanitarian mode, some fresh from the war in Kurdistan where
they were hated and in continual danger. They were amazed at the
welcome that greeted them in Albania. After the Balkan wars in
1912–13 the Ottoman army—the world's greatest military force in
the sixteenth century when rumours of its approach produced terror—had left Albania a pitiful disintegrating wreck, malaria-ridden,
unfed and unpaid. In Elbasan that summer their trucks were a happy
sight, and the conscripts worked hard and effectively in the humanitarian operation. My daughter Julia took a job in the camp as a volunteer worker, and soon found herself running a field kitchen to
feed hundreds of people. Great sacks of flour and potatoes had to be
unloaded from lorries, and soon the tough women of the Has hills
(one arrived resplendent in her traditional costume) were working
as hard in the camps as on their family farms. It was impossible not to
be moved in the camps by the sense of a people undertaking an epic
journey to fulfil its national destiny, but there was also a darker side.
Groups of villagers from the Labinot hills came and raided the camps,
and in Elbasan some wanted money to protect local stallholders
from 'the mafia'. There was a pervasive stench from the latrines. And
all kinds of groups appeared from the fringes of the NGO and
humanitarian world with weird agendas, such as the fundamentalists
trying to convert the overwhelmingly Muslim Kosovars into born-
again Christians.

The greatest camp of all was inevitably not in Albania but in Macedonia. Here the well-worn epithets 'epic' or 'biblical' were entirely
appropriate for the scale and drama of events. Although the town of
Kukes had more refugees and became a tent city, nowhere was more

awe-inspiring as a monument to humanitarian endeavour than the camp at Cegrane, with its 43,000 people living below a bare and eroded mountainside near the town of Gostivar, known appropriately as Snake Hill. The Macedonians had characteristically provided the local rubbish tip as a camp site and conditions were awful. OXFAM was in charge of drilling boreholes which were capable of providing a water supply for 12,000 people, the original planned capacity of the camp. The truly heroic CARE officials, as the camp management, worked twenty hours a day flat-out and slept for four, and lived in a continual logistical and food supply nightmare. When one set of rations arrived, another ran out. This was not through any fault of CARE, which with the Swiss-based sections of the Red Cross is the best organised of all the big INGOs, but as one huge influx of people was accommodated, another arrived.

The refugees wandered all over the surrounding countryside and into Gostivar itself, and reduced the Slav-Macedonian-dominated police to total hysteria. By the middle of April there was a continual rush of VIP visitors, from mainstream politicians and relief experts to celebrities such as Bianca Jagger, to the odder members of the humanitarian community, including one man from Yorkshire who was a water diviner and thought he could succeed where OXFAM engineers had failed. The owner of the heaving, crammed bar by the camp entrance, a respectable grey-haired Albanian who looked like a bank clerk, committed murder when for the umpteenth time some young ruffian demanded 'protection money'. He took his handgun out from below the bar and just blew him away with one bullet above the right eye; there was a very dead man on the bar floor. The bar-owner was arrested but most people felt sorry for him, a CARE official gave evidence in his defence at the trial, and he got seven years in gaol, a light sentence. I met him a year later, when he was out on parole, and was photographed with him holding one of my books; he liked to have pictures of allegedly well-known foreigners to put on his cell wall. I had never been photographed with a convicted murderer's arm round my shoulder before; nor had the Austrian ambasador to Macedonia, who was snapped next after me, at the same function there celebrating the return of the camp to agricultural use on a freezing January day in deep snow. The bar-owner's ambition was to photograph Madeleine Albright and Tony Blair for his cell wall.

The days of April 1999 were nothing compared to the hellish cauldron days of May and early June when the temperatures soared into the nineties, numbers continued to grow, and water was scarcer than ever. I worked at Cegrane camp one day and interviewed a young man from Ferizaj with a broken arm and a huge swelling on his shoulder from being beaten with an iron bar in a torture house under Ferizaj police station. A Prishtina friend who was working with me as an interpreter and fixer collapsed with the heat and lost consciousness in a CARE medical tent while we were interviewing him there.

As numbers grew, the character of the people and the life of the camp itself also changed. The first refugees were nearly all families from southern Kosova and areas fairly near the border with Macedonia. They had heard about the ethnic cleansing in northern towns like Gjakova in the first week of the bombing campaign and did not wait to be given the same treatment. They hit the road south, got through the now reopened Blace checkpoint, and were taken in at the reception camp at Stenkovac, six miles down the road, north of Skopje. Here they were registered, classified, had a medical check, and if they had lost family or friends tried to find them. It was not a pleasant place, and the Macedonian police and the British army vied for control of the area. People weeping stuck pathetic little notes on a huge message board, asking for news and location of those who might well, for all anybody knew, be raped, mutilated, burnt alive in their houses or blown apart by a shell. The Macedonian police controlled the road in and out (road control is always a vital symbol of Balkan state power and prestige) and the surrounding open grassland. The British army ran the camp itself, and tough Geordie privates and sergeants bustled and organised, and counted and shouted and swore and made queues straight and conditions tolerable for angry and bitter and humiliated people, so that they could feel more or less human again. Conditions were primitive, with the stinking earth latrines hidden by a thin plastic sheet from the Macedonian police who watched women using them at night by torchlight. If the British army had not been there, there would have been riots and deaths, as many refugees saw the Slav Macedonian police, rightly, as little different from the Serbs and relished the thought of revenge.

I was astonished to see the burden of responsibility given in the British army to very young men and girls only in their late teens who often came from the bottom of the British social heap with bad family backgrounds, and had had little chance educationally. They coped so well with people from a remote culture, yet many of them had never been anywhere abroad before arriving in Skopje, or ever experienced such heat. Few of their officers had any experience of managing large-scale refugee inflows in a difficult and charged political environment. As in combat, so in refugee work, improvisation in wartime is vital. It was a story an idiot could have reported, with numerous articulate refugees, superb colour and easy targets in the form of the blundering, obtuse Macedonians many of whom would have cheerfully machine-gunned a few ringleaders and driven the rest of the refugees back to Kosova if given the chance. At this stage there was no British press operation and it was easy to talk to all ranks, who were often outspoken about the vices of the Macedonian authorities and the violent, inhuman atmosphere they had created. The perimeter fence with its thuggish Macedonian police patrolling with Alsatians looked like something from a Nazi internment camp in the Second World War. The British army deservedly got an excellent press, largely because no control was put on journalists, and there were no spin doctors to try to point people in a particular direction or block access to the ordinary soldiers. Although the refugees often arrived in shock and traumatised, family units in the first group were usually intact and had some basic belongings with them, and not many people were physically injured. The second major group in the annexe camp, Stenkovac II, came from the cleansing of Prishtina: these people were town dwellers, more prosperous and in better physical condition than the villagers to start with, and had usually managed to hide some money from the Serbs. The Prishtinaites had not been refugees before, unlike many of the rural people, and this gave a novelty to their experience. The crisis had brought the reality of the war home to them at last, after most of them had been able to deny it for so long.

Another camp where I spent a good deal of time was Neprostino, just north of Tetovo and twenty miles south of the Kosova border in north-west Macedonia. This place, below the high Sar peaks, was small compared with other camps, with only about 3,000 refugees by the end of April. It was also very close to Tetovo itself, which was steadily filling up with refugees who had family connections in the town. Tetovo was a hive of KLA support and back-up activity, and most of the Prishtina media community had moved there. Veton Surroi had recommenced production of his newspaper *Koha Ditore* in Tetovo, with British government help, and a meagre tabloid was soon on the street.

The Neprostino refugee camp was run by the German army, which was acutely aware that given the strategic importance of the Tetovo-Prizren road the KLA was likely to take a close interest in developments there. The German officers had also been told from Bonn that because this was the first-ever foreign deployment of the Bundeswehr in a humanitarian crisis, the camp must be a showpiece and a good advertisement for German humanitarian military skills. As a result, money and talented people, both military and civilian, poured in and it duly became a model of organisation and humanity, with neat rows of dark green tents and, inevitably, not a speck of lit-ter to be seen in the walkways. As if by magic, an extraordinary array of leisure, medical and practical educational facilities was provided. An adventure playground was built around a large oak tree for the children, who swung from ropes and hid in wendy-houses. In no time volunteer workers from Germany were teaching adults how to paint, read books and generally pick up the threads of a normal life. Germany has had the great advantage in the southern Balkan crisis of having universities with a high standard of Albanian language teaching, and thus a supply of Albanian-speaking German experts in different disciplines. Unlike in some other camps the Albanian flag was flown, and from time to time you would see young men in KLA T-shirts either inside or on the perimeter. I interviewed an elderly man with a white lace skullcap from Tetovo who told me how it all brought back the 'good days' of his youth in the Second World War, when under the German occupation Albanian culture thrived. It was an awkward subject, I could not think of how to write about it in the right way, and a half-finished story still sits in my notebook for that month. The Macedonian police more or less gave up trying to keep order and spent their time organising a quiet bribe and extor-tion system from the camp suppliers. It was possible to see, in micro-cosm, how in the future a part of the Albanian world might emerge from Macedonian control. Inevitably it had its humorous side: nailed to the trees were lists of available activities for the day—the last time

Germans had run camps there were lists of what was forbidden. Here Germany was on the side of life and hope.

Yet the agony and the terror of Kosova were not far away. Every so often groups of people arrived for reception. One fine May morning I was sitting with a new acquaintance, a Catholic volunteer from Mainz, and regaling him with tales of my happy student times in Berlin, where there was a Wall, and wonderful beer seemed to be more or less free. Sue and I had walked by the sombre but beautiful Wannsee, and the political drama of the Cold War was ever present. I have never been to Mainz and he thought I should go and see the cathedral, but just as he was describing its Gothic magnificence a lorry drew up with as broken and pathetic a human cargo as I saw in the entire war. A man crying in agony from his shattered leg was lowered off a stretcher. The bone protruded from bloody flesh that should have been covered by skin. Behind him an old man was lowered by two helpers. He had been beaten to a pulp, his face was something that could have come from a butcher's slab. He was clearly aged well over eighty, pitifully thin, in a dirty brown suit that he had probably worn on Fridays for many years to go to the mosque. It had great bloody stains, and blood still ran down one leg making a little pool beside the truck. His wife was next, dead and wrapped in a sheet, with that very still final presence of all wrapped corpses. Her sister followed, her head bound in a scarf so she could hardly see, but at least she could walk and would live. We were at the end of a production line of evil, the ethnic cleansers were working away at the other end of it and Neprostino camp received the results. The Four Horsemen of the Apocaplypse were riding over Kosova villages, crushing all that stood in their path. A tall German soldier picked up the old man like a feather and carried him to the medical tent. He died an hour or so later, his dead wife in her shroud lying on the next stretcher. A doctor from Marburg photographed them before they were taken to the mortuary. The war seemed endless, but gradually the NATO campaign prevailed. That is another story. These bleeding and battered old villagers were the last people I saw die for Kosova. I wish I knew their names.

Epilogue

The dawn is a rectangle of cool autumn Prishtina morning light falling on the bedroom wall. Six months have passed and now the future is clearer. Many have taken the Kosova way over the fourteen years since Trepce, like the first missionaries from the Gjakova *tekke* spreading their faith over the Ottoman Balkans, a hard mountain way for some, the soft life of the towns for others. Some are alive and have prospered, others are dead. Some live in distant countries. Some have fallen by the wayside, victims of Serbian bullets, others have lost all their property and are rebuilding their lives. We mourn colleagues, relatives and friends, some dead, some disappeared. Some survived underground. Veton Surroi spent much of the bombing campaign in the cellar of the Second World War Partisan leader Fadil Hoxha's house. Hashim Thaci lived in the forest, and planned the first government. Ramush Haradinaj became a military leader, the defender of Kosare. Agim Ceku is building the first national army. Fehmi Agani is dead, one of many like Kurt Schork of Reuters, once in the old Grand Hotel Media Centre and who died in a cruel ambush in Sierra Leone. It seems only yesterday that we were eating pizza in Bath and discussing the possibility of war in Macedonia. He did not live to report the 2001 conflict.

The survivors now live in a new world. The opportunities for heroism are fewer now. Perhaps the correct understanding of war in Kosova is that it gave the ordinary person the opportunity for heroism, which peace does not.

I met Adem Demaci by the graves of the Jashari family at Prekaz, with Miranda Vickers and Sir Reginald Hibbert. Reg had met Fadil Hoxha, the Second World War Albanian Partisan leader, earlier in the day and the two old warriors had stood in the sun and been photographed. Fifty-four years had passed since the end of hostilities, but they talked of nothing but war. Three English visitors rested their shoes or boots on the short grass, cropped by sheep. In Prishtina the journalists' signature wall from the terrible summer of 1998 is still lovingly cared for in the *Koha Ditore* offices. Here the Jashari house was being rebuilt as a national monument, workers thumped hammers on wood on the roof, flowers covered the graves of the dead above us on the grassy hillside. Demaci was thinning in old age, with just a wisp of white hair. He too was a national monument, but still spry and bright. He had a party of Scandinavian visitors to show round the birthplace of the dead heroes. The incorruptible organiser of the illegal underground who spent twenty-eight years in prison was now only organising tourists. The Kosova Mandela wore a new lightweight suit. He told me my Albanian was improving. I was silent but wished I had the courage to tell him I thought I understood him better than most foreigners and it would be nice to see something friendlier than that intense look.

'Is Kosova free now?'

The look that his gaolers must have come to dread disappeared in a flash. He smiled and shrugged, his glasses glinting in the sunlight. It seemed right to talk to him here, he was enjoying freedom on an open sunny Kosova hillside after twenty-eight years in Tito's gaols. He replied: 'Part'

He twiddled his hands up and down, signalling that the man who opposed signing the Rambouillet deal was not completely happy with the present. Many of his friends had died in obscurity and defeat in the previous generation. Compromise was not a word they knew. But in the morning sunshine Adem Demaci was cheerful, eminent, as clear as ice-cold water from Dragas. He was standing on grass in the new Kosova which is awaiting its independence.[1]

---

[1] For a good picture of the world of the political underground under Tito see Ibish Neziri, *Ahmet Hashmi nje jete te tere ne levizjen ilegale*, Prishtina, 2001. For Demaci's own life see Hakif Bajrami, *Dosia Demaci*, Prishtina, 2003.

Index